GW01185690

To:

_____

From:

_____

Date:

_____

HE WHISPERS YOUR NAME

CHERIE HILL

CHRISTIAN ART
PUBLISHERS

Published by Christian Art Publishers
PO Box 1599, Vereeniging, 1930, RSA

© 2016

First edition 2016

© Three Streams Publishers
Bloomingdale, USA

Cover designed by Christian Art Publishers

Images used under license from Shutterstock.com

Set in 9 on 11 pt Century Gothic by Christian Art Publishers

Printed in China

ISBN 978-1-4321-2372-7

16 17 18 19 20 21 22 23 24 25 – 10 9 8 7 6 5 4 3 2 1

Preface

This book is more than a devotional—*it's an invitation to hear from God*. You may find yourself in the same place I did over ten years ago. I knew God, but I didn't know how to *talk* to Him, and I certainly didn't know how to *hear* Him.

As I pursued loftier heights of faith, I stumbled upon Sarah Young's classic, *Jesus Calling*. I marveled that she was able to hear God speak to her in the way that she did. I thought her gift must be so unique that I couldn't possibly hear from God in that same way. It wasn't until recently that I found out that she herself was inspired by writers who heard from God in the very same manner—two women in the 1930s, who wrote a book called *God Calling*. So, in an effort to hear God in the way that these women did, I began rising before dawn, meditating upon Scripture, and sitting in silence to hear God's voice. And something happened within my spirit that completely transformed my faith. I listened, and God spoke to my heart in ways I didn't think possible. The things I wrote during my devotion times are what you'll find within this book. The year is divided up into 52 topics that are listed in a handy index at the back of the book.

Here's the thing: God wants to speak to YOU. Although God can use others to speak to you, He also wants to speak *directly* to you and have you hear Him. He wants an intimate relationship with you so that you might stand firm in your faith. I challenge you to begin, just as I did, setting aside time to meditate on Scripture, asking God what He wants to say to you, and trusting what He has promised:

> "Call to Me and I will answer you and tell
> you great and unsearchable things
> you do not know."
>
> JEREMIAH 33:3 (NIV)

Anxiety

Heart Knowledge

You say you "know" the truth, but the worry within you says something entirely different. Your restless soul begs for stillness, a peace that gives you the confident hope you need to carry on. But the troubles of life trump your faith and you find yourself growing too weary to believe what you know to be true.

Listen to Me. I've never forsaken you, and I'm not about to now. Within My grasp is every detail of your life—past, present, and future. You know this—just be still for a moment and listen closely to My still, small voice. Until your last breath, until that moment when you enter into My presence, I AM with you at all times and in all ways. Trust in who I AM, and *nothing else*.

Your faith can't carry you unless you remain fixed on Me. I'm the God who created all things and keeps the universe in motion. Your universe, the problems within you and without, are not bigger than I AM. What exactly do you think is too big for Me? What miracle is it that I can't perform? Whatever it is, just be still, and know deep within that I AM God.

"Be still, and know that I am God."

PSALM 46:10 (NLT)

Trust Me in Everything

You tend to trust Me to work the small miracles in your life, but remain unsure of My abilities to perform the bigger ones. I am not a lesser God according to your circumstances or the current state of your faith. My power and presence in your life is unchanging, so depend upon Me as if your life depends on it ... because it does.

My will for your life may allow for troubles, but I will always give you grace in proportion to them. Trusting in Me means living with the unknowns, facing fear with faith, and believing in what you know is true. When you're consumed with anxiety, drowning in despair, and unable to walk in the faith you profess, fall to your knees in prayer and I will be there. I'll meet you where you are. In your weakness, I will be your strength.

Thank Me for all I've done and all I have yet to do. In everything, the good and the bad, the laughter and the tears, the strength and the fear, don't allow your heart to be moved. Stand firm in your faith and trust Me completely ... in *everything*.

Do not be anxious about anything, but in everything by prayer and supplication with thanksgiving let your requests be made known to God.

PHILIPPIANS 4:6 (ESV)

Let Go of Your Burdens

You are holding on to what you need to let go of. You're holding tight within your grasp what should only be gripped in Mine. All of your worries, every burden that weighs you down, aren't meant to be carried by you—I allow them to drive you into dependence upon Me. There is purpose in all I do and all I allow. There is no need to worry about tomorrow and what it holds, just know that *I hold* every tomorrow—and live in today.

Rest assured, I'm able to deal with what you cannot. But I can't take control of what you refuse to let go of. I will not force My love or My hand on you. I need you to *choose* surrender, to give Me the burdens you carry so that I can deal with them in My perfect way. As long as you remain in control, I can't be—I need you to give Me your joys and sorrows and everything in between. Come to My throne of grace in surrender and you'll find abundant peace to help you to just *let go*. There's nothing to fear, there's nothing I can't do, and I will always take care of you.

> Give your burdens to the LORD,
> and He will take care of you.
>
> PSALM 55:22 (NLT)

When You're Overwhelmed

Do not be surprised by the overwhelming circumstances in your life. Obstacles may appear insurmountable, but nothing is too difficult for Me. The magnitude of your troubles may be too much for you to handle, but My promises will trump your trials. Though you may not know what to do, I'm the One who leads you to quiet waters. Peace and hope is found in My presence. Fear has no place in the face of faith.

When you're fearful of the unknown and overwhelmed by what lies before you, know that I've promised that I AM aware of all you need. If you're striving to please Me, focusing your eyes upon Me, you can rest assured that I will take you through every challenge and enable you to rise victorious. It may not be the way you wanted, or at the time you desired, but you can have confidence in My perfect plan for your life. If you grow weary in the waiting, you can rest under the shadow of My wings.

I will comfort you and give you peace—so be anxious for nothing. I will never allow you to endure more than My grace can overcome. If life seems out of control, do not fear. Do not be overwhelmed. Allow Me to overwhelm what overwhelms you with My presence, power and peace.

When my anxious inner thoughts become
overwhelming, Your comfort encourages me.

PSALM 94:19 (ISV)

Trapped by Troubles

It happens unexpectedly; suddenly you find yourself weighed down and worn out, with no way of escape. It's easy to succumb to the worries of life and drown in despair—but there's no reason why you should. I AM here—a ready help in times of trouble. There's no reason to feel *trapped* within your *troubles*. My promises will give you the strength you need to rely on My grace.

I know it's not easy to rely on Me. You want to trust in what you see. But it's your faith in Me, the unseen God, that will guide you through the obstacles of life, assured of My presence and power at all times and in all ways.

It's easy to feel as though I'm not there and I simply don't care—you want visible proof that I am beside you. You want your faith to take sight. You need Me to show My face, and I will. Just seek it. Don't allow your pursuit and desire for My hand to get in the way of simply and continually seeking Me alone. My hand will move in due time, as your faith moves My heart.

> "Be careful, or your hearts will be weighed down with … the anxieties of life, and that day will close on you suddenly like a trap."
>
> LUKE 21:34 (NIV)

Content in Christ

Feelings tend to get in the way of your faith. Faith isn't easy, but it will make all things possible. You should never be in want because I AM all you need. I want you to trust Me with all your worries.

Your trust in Me tends to *waiver*, and that's why you're filled with *worry*. I want you to rest in My peace as I work out My plans and purposes for your life.

When you find yourself becoming anxious, come to Me in prayer. Allow Me to handle what you can't. Only I know what tomorrow will bring. So trust Me when I say that the plans I have for you are for your good, to give you a future and a hope. Just because things don't work out the way you planned doesn't mean they won't work out the way you'd hoped.

I AM always listening to your heart—all I ask is that you trust in Mine. I AM with you always. Find your joy and peace in Me. Let nothing move you, let nothing distract you from relying on My promises. Be still and know that I AM God.

Be happy with what you have
because God has said, "I will never
abandon you or leave you."

HEBREWS 13:5 (GW)

Under Control

Having control over your troubles begins with keeping your heart from being troubled. There are few things you can control in life, but you *can* control your heart. Though it's deceitful above all things, I give you My Word to saturate and transform your heart so that it will be unshakable in the midst of uncertainty. Keep yourself under control when everything in life is out of control. Know that everything is in My control, and you can trust Me.

Life is going to take you many directions, but I'll be there along the way to guide you into My will. It may not be the path you would have chosen, but if I'm with you, there is nothing to fear. What you can't do, I can.

Trust Me to deal with every detail of your life. No matter how simple the situation might be, turn to Me immediately when you are filled with anxiety. Let Me replace the panic with My peace. Stay in My presence and talk to Me continually, honestly, about all of your worries. And when you've turned them over to Me, when you've decided to trust Me completely, don't try to take your troubles back. Leave them all in My hands and trust My heart with yours.

> "Don't let your hearts be troubled.
> Trust in God, and trust also in Me."
>
> JOHN 14:1 (NLT)

Faith

Faith Fixed on Christ

When you feel like giving up, remember who I AM and what I've done. Focus upon nothing else; fix your eyes on Me and allow nothing to move you. You may be in the midst of a raging storm in life, but I AM in it with you. I AM all-knowing and all-powerful. NOTHING has authority over Me.

I'll ask you to walk through impossible situations so that you will fully experience My presence and My power. Through the unthinkable, you'll develop a deeper faith than you ever thought possible. But it won't be easy. You'll want to walk away from your faith. Your soul will declare that Jesus is not enough. It is in these times of doubt and despair that you need to remain fixed on Me. Your faith will find stability and security in My promises. You'll be tempted to believe that I may never answer your prayers, that I'm simply not listening, but I AM. My answers may be delayed, but I AM at work, using all things for good. Wait in faith. Trust in confident assurance. Walk in the midst of your troubles, knowing that I AM faithful to My promises. Hold on to hope. Take shelter under My wings. Find strength in Christ, and I will calm the storm.

When your trials linger and seem to have no end, you can be certain that you're in the place where miracles happen. In the desert of your life I will show you My provision, display My protection, and keep you from complete destruction. Your moment of deliverance is not passed. My Word assures you that My timing is perfect. If you'll fix your faith on Me, I'll fix everything else.

… Fixing our eyes on Jesus.

HEBREWS 12:2 (NIV)

Faith's Foundation

Your faith must be built upon the foundation of believing that I AM leading and guiding you in every area of your life. My ways are perfect, and I want to lead you in the path that may not be the one of least resistance; but is the way that is everlasting. When you are saved through the sacrifice of Christ, you are given all of the spiritual benefits as you submit to My ways.

Yet in your daily life, I see you going down paths I've never led you down and making decisions that are contrary to My Word. You received My guidance in the past, you witnessed My miracles, yet you forget them. And as time goes on, you tend to believe My miraculous workings were a stroke of luck or mere coincidence. Don't allow yourself to believe the lie that My guidance is nothing more than a series of unrelated blessings. Everything is sovereignly orchestrated when you trust in Me. Though you can't see the whole of My plan, you can trust in it. And you can have full confidence that My plan is a tapestry woven together with each and every thread of your life.

It is critical to your faith that you have full understanding that you are forgiven; but it is just as important for you to walk in the assurance that My hand is upon you, delivering you from trouble time after time. I want you to know not only My love for you, but My provision, protection, and present power in your life. Build your faith upon that truth.

Teach me Your way, Lord;
lead me in a straight path.

PSALM 27:11 (NIV)

Greater Faith

Each and every day you must decide in whom, or in what, to put your trust. You can choose to place your trust in the things that are unstable and uncertain, or you can choose to trust in Me. It is by trusting in Me that you find peace and joy, even when your world is falling apart. When you trust in Me, you will not be overwhelmed with confusion but will instead enter into My rest.

Greater faith calls for trusting in Me as God and trusting in My ways, even when you can't understand them. During times of despair and hopelessness you are able to see where you have placed your trust. The things of the world will always change, but I never do. When you put your trust in Me, you will never be disappointed because My purposes are for good. I am the same today, forever and yesterday—nothing can thwart My plans or pillage My purposes. My will is always done.

When you are overwhelmed, turn to Me and declare that you will trust Me with all of your heart and mind. Declare that you will not rely on your own insight or understanding, but that you will instead accept that My ways are higher and better. If you are to walk in victory, I need you to trust Me. With me, ALL things are possible.

Some trust in chariots and some in horses,
but we trust in the name of the Lord our God.

PSALM 20:7 (NIV)

Faith in Times of Darkness

Your times of testing, which mark and enrich your soul, are those times when hell seems to let loose in your life; when you're trapped, and you are certain that I've permitted you to suffer through the unthinkable. You were walking in My light and then darkness closed in with no warning.

Your faith struggles because it seems that moments of splendor, when your spirit is filled with Mine, are immediately followed by the deepest darkness. You are singing My praises, and then your heart falls silent amid the gloom that descends out of nowhere. Your spirit seems crushed beneath the weight of confusion, but I AM not a God of confusion (see 1 Corinthians 14:33). There is purpose, even in darkness.

In the darkness, My light shines brighter. The wilderness prepares you for the Promised Land. In those times, when you were wholly filled to overflowing with My Spirit and glory, and you are immediately cast into the desert, you can be assured that the preceding light has prepared you for the darkness. I fill you to the full with My light so that I can uphold you in the darkness.

Rest assured that the time in the wilderness and the descent of darkness is temporary. It's a time that always ends in triumph. If you will commit your soul to Me and trust in My divine favor, you will find the truth in My Word that promises I work all things for good, and there is a sixty-fold harvest that surely follows the faith that you sow.

> Immediately the Spirit drove
> Him into the wilderness.
>
> MARK 1:12 (NKJV)

All You Need

Before you rise in the morning, remember that Jesus has risen. I've redeemed your past, present and future. I stand with you; I AM all you need. I provide mercy for every moment and grace that is always sufficient. In your times of doubt, when faith loses out, remember My promises. I am faithful, even when you are not.

Though you sleep and slumber, I never do. You can rest in knowing that I AM always at work, overseeing your circumstances. There is nothing to fear, for I always provide enough grace and mercy for each new day.

I know that you are tempted to walk by faith, but your sight will deceive you. Trust Me in the dark. My Light appears more glorious there. When you're overcome with doubt, cling to My Word. I have promised you My provision and power. There is no need to toil and spin. Consider the lilies of the field. I will care for you. When all hope seems gone, there is faith, and faith will carry you through.

When you're in need of hope, seek My face. When you long for mercy, it's already waiting for you at My throne of grace. When you need comfort and strength, My arms are open wide. My love for you goes far beyond words. I AM all you will ever need. Draw near to Me and I will draw near to you.

Great is His faithfulness; His mercies begin
afresh each morning. I say to myself,
"The Lord is my inheritance; therefore,
I will hope in Him!"

LAMENTATIONS 3:23–24 (NLT)

Believing Is Seeing

I know that in the daily struggles of life, you tend to lose heart and hope. Trusting Me means looking far beyond what you see to what *I* see. I've promised you that your light affliction is producing an eternal weight of glory that is far beyond all comparison. What you see is temporary, but what you can't see is eternal. I'm asking you to endure, while keeping your eyes on Me. I want you to see your circumstances for more than they are on the surface. I'm taking your faith deeper than you imagined, and where we're going, you simply can't walk by sight. Faith doesn't demand a miracle—it believes it, then sees it.

I want you to learn to have faith in Me at all times. When life isn't going according to your plan, you can rest assured that it's still going according to Mine. Though the circumstances seem to contradict the faith you cling to, you can be certain that My ways are not only higher, but better. I see My plan from beginning to end, and everything in between is woven into My masterpiece. Though I can accomplish My plans all on My own, I invite you to join Me in faith, walking intimately with Me in bringing about My glory. I've created you for that purpose, to experience the joy of being a part of My plans.

When you're unsure of the path that lies ahead, listen for My voice; I will guide you along the way that you should go. You will find Me when you seek Me. Our relationship has gone to depths where no words are necessary. In that moment you can be certain that you are walking by faith.

We fix our eyes not on what is
seen, but on what is unseen.

2 CORINTHIANS 4:18 (NIV)

Without Faith

I need you to trust Me. It is your trust in Me that defines your faith. Your faith moves My heart *and* My hand. Your faith is the driving force that unleashes My presence and power. I know that you believe in Me, but do you fully trust in Me? Do you trust in what I've promised? A lack of faith is a lack of belief and trust.

When you're filled with fear, you're not trusting Me. You need to dive deep into My Word and cling to the promises I've made to you. They will assure your heart and mind, enabling you to walk forward in faith with calm surrender, trusting fully that I AM in control and will work all things together for good.

You can trust Me with your past, present and future. I will take care of your every need. I will help you through the insurmountable obstacles of life, comforting your heart and strengthening your spirit as we go. I AM with you always, and there is never anything to fear. Live in faith instead of fear. Choose to trust Me, no matter what.

It is impossible to please God without faith.
Anyone who wants to come to Him must
believe that God exists and that He
rewards those who sincerely seek Him.

HEBREWS 11:6 (NLT)

Simple Faith

Your prayers are always heard, but you wonder why they seldom seem to be answered. It's not the asking part, it's the believing part. I need you to believe that I hear you and that I will answer you. Dare to ask for your heart's desires specifically. That way, when the answer comes, you'll know for certain that I AM God and there is no other.

An unwavering faith is critical when it comes to prayer. When your faith is wavering, doubt is revealed within your heart. Life can be hard, but faith is simple. Just trust in what I've promised and drown yourself in My Word instead of your doubts.

Don't be discouraged by the trials of life. There may be obstacles, but they are also opportunities—opportunities to trust instead of doubt, to live in faith instead of fear, to seek My face and fully experience the power of My presence. When you come to Me, expect My presence, receive My peace, and have the confident assurance that I will answer your prayers. Be ready to receive the grace that I will pour out upon you. Be consumed with My love and trust My heart as I calm and comfort yours.

> "I tell you, you can pray for anything,
> and if you believe that you've
> received it, it will be yours."
>
> MARK 11:24 (NLT)

Prayer

Consistent Dependence

I haven't made you to live independently of Me. I created you to be in consistent dependence upon Me. But too often you rely on your own strength and resources and you grow weak and weary—ready to give up and give in. So I need you to look at your life and examine the areas of your life where you act independently of Me.

Look at the areas of your life where you are not praying. Reflect on the people, problems, attitudes and decisions you make, and examine whether or not you've been bringing all of it to Me in prayer. What is it—everything and anything that you *haven't* talked to Me about—that you need to bring to My throne of grace?

In order for you to walk in My will and for your life to bear fruit, you must *remain* in Me. Allow Me to address everything in your life as I remain in you. All of your efforts can never compare to what I can do through My sovereign hand.

Examine your prayer life and make it your utmost priority to depend on Me for all things. I want you to submit everything you do, think, feel and say to Me. When you don't know what to do, look to Me. Call to Me and I will answer you (see Jeremiah 33:3). I will lead, guide and direct you. You must continually take each step of faith … on your knees.

Pray continually.

1 THESSALONIANS 5:17 (NIV)

Ask Me for Guidance

It amazes Me how often I see you seeking advice from other sources, rather than Me. Over and over again I have watched you ask the opinion of others, yet you forget to ask for Mine. You so easily forget that I AM the source of all wisdom and knowledge. Only I hold the answers that you are looking for; only I can give you the right advice every time. I AM the source of strength, hope, joy and peace, and I AM the source of wisdom you need in order to walk according to My good and perfect will.

If you have questions in your life, regarding anything, ask Me. I AM the One who holds the answers. I may not be able to give you the answers that you are looking for, but you will find comfort and peace in knowing that I know them. You must find your strength in Me by relying on My wisdom and My love.

When you call out to Me, do not doubt that I will answer you. I want you to expect to hear from Me. Do not shut out My voice when I don't tell you what you want to hear. I tell you what you *need* to hear, so that you might experience victory. Although you may not understand My ways, you must trust in them. You must trust Me in the darkness; I will be your light. Do not walk by sight; walk by faith. I will lead and guide you each step of the way. There is no good thing that I will withhold from you as you surrender your life fully to Me. Whatever you need, just ask.

If you need wisdom, ask our generous God,
and He will give it to you. He will not
rebuke you for asking.

JAMES 1:5 (NLT)

God Is Fully Aware

You often think I'm unaware of the details of your life. You feel as though I'm simply too busy with more important things, like managing the universe and keeping it all in motion. But if I'm able to fine-tune the planets and stars, their rotations and temperatures, and the gravity that keeps it all together, why is it that you find it hard to trust Me with the finite factors of your life?

I'm fully aware of each tear that falls, the fears that keep you awake at night, the faults that leave you overwhelmed with guilt and shame, and everything in between. I know. And I AM with you in it all. I want you to keep coming to Me with every detail of your life. There is nothing too big or too small for Me. I delight in *every* detail of your life.

Life may not always turn out exactly as your prayers have petitioned. You will more than likely not understand My ways, and you'll often find yourself questioning them. It is okay to doubt. I can use it to strengthen your faith as I draw you nearer to Me. But never doubt My love. My love for you trumps *all* things.

Whatever it is in the past, present and future that concerns you, I've already addressed it to bring about good in your life and glory to My name for eternity. Come to Me with everything. Pour out your heart and spend time with Me. Speak every detail of your joys, pains and sorrows, even though I already know.

"Your heavenly Father already knows."

MATTHEW 6:32 (NLT)

Love beyond Words

In your crushing sorrow, your bitter disappointments and your unexpected sufferings, I know you are longing to hear My voice. I know You need Me to answer, but your beckoning only seems to bring My silence ... and continued misery meets you once again. Know this: I love you beyond words (see Zephaniah 3:17).

My mercy is not measurable. I need you to know My heart that is abundantly gracious. It aches as I witness your impatient heart. I want you to know that I do not answer your prayers according to your nearsightedness. Your tears blind you to My love, which sees far into your future. You see, I know your story from beginning to end. I know *when* to answer prayers and *how* to answer them in ways that will be for your ultimate good and enable Me to reveal My glory.

My silence is as powerful as My words. Do not see the silence as My disapproval, but as evidence that we have an intimate relationship that goes far beyond words. I need you to trust Me through the unseen and the unheard. Praise Me, even in My silence.

If you are crying out to Me and there is no response, know that it is not because I'm not here, not listening, or don't care, but that I am working in you with eternity in mind. Our relationship has come to a place where it is independent of words, where you walk by faith and not by sight. My power in your life during times of silence means that I am working miracles that go far beyond what words can express.

Jesus did not answer a word.

MATTHEW 15:23 (NIV)

Continually Seeking the Lord

The troubles of life can keep you overwhelmed and searching for answers instead of searching for Me. You must find your strength from Me because your worries will leave you weak. But in your weakness, I will be your strength. Continually seek Me and you will find all you need to walk firmly in your faith.

Let our time together not be momentary, but continuous. Let your desperation drive you into My presence. I need you to search for Me not because I'm hiding, but because your constant desire to be in My presence draws you closer to Me.

I AM always with you, a ready help in times of trouble, but part of the answer is in the asking. When you come to Me in prayer, your faith is displayed in ways that My grace responds to. Your voice beckons Mine and your heart draws in My own.

I have always meant for you to walk through every moment of your life with Me. My desire is that you would continually be filled with My love and assured of My presence. When you seek Me, you will find Me, and I will strengthen your heart and increase your faith as you trust in Me.

Search for the LORD and for His strength;
continually seek Him.

1 CHRONICLES 16:11 (NLT)

Help from Above

Listen to Me. I hear your cries for help. I'm paying attention to your prayers and I am working all things together for good. As you await My power, rest in My presence. Trust that I hear every word and every thought. At My throne of grace, I prepare answers to your prayers that you can't contemplate. I'm full of surprises.

There will be some answers to your cries for help that you're expecting, but more often than not, I'm going to pave paths that are unpredictable. I'm teaching you to trust Me, to walk step by step. Your reliance upon Me will yield more miracles than you can fathom. Don't miss out on what faith does. When you pray, trust that I can do what needs to be done, and leave My presence *knowing* that it will be done. Your confident expectation in prayer drives open the gates of heaven.

There is no good thing that I will withhold from you, so don't think for a moment that I will not bless you abundantly in My wisdom and knowledge of what's best. And though we may not see eye to eye, you don't need to have it all figured out. Let Me do My job and trust that I can and will do what is best. My love for you is boundless; My answers to your prayers and My ability to help you in times of trouble will come at times when you're least expecting it. So wait confidently and patiently. Help is on the way.

Listen to my cry for help.
Pay attention to my prayer.

PSALM 17:1 (NLT)

Spiritual Battle

Defending Yourself against Satan's Lies

Don't let the circumstances of your life shake you. Do not fear the unknown when you know Me, the all-knowing. Through your daily battles, you tend to turn to inward and declare yourself unworthy. You're consumed by the evil that wages war against your soul, and you start to believe the enemy's lies that you stand alone, unchanged, unsaved, and unable to win the war. Don't give in to the lies. The enemy wants you to worry over your circumstances, doubt your faith, and believe that you aren't saved or sanctified. He wants you to see the race as impossible so that you'll give up and give in. Trust in My truth.

I am the One who arms you with strength and makes your way perfect. I will make your footing firm and will train you, strengthen you and equip you for the battle. I will enable you to overcome the obstacles of your faith— doubt, unforgiveness and fear. When you trust in Me, you will conquer every obstacle because I AM with you and My right hand will support you. As you struggle to take one more step of faith, I will make a wide path for you to walk, so that you don't stumble (see Psalm 18:30-39).

Do not fret over your failures. Repent and rise again for the battle. Be assured of My power AND My presence. It is not by your might that the battle is won, but by your faith in My victory that is already given.

For every child of God defeats this evil world,
and we achieve this victory through our faith.

1 JOHN 5:4 (NLT)

The Unseen Battle

You have an enemy, and he is not of this world. There may be times when you feel that the world is against you. The broken world testifies to the reality of the devil's existence. And no one needs to tell you of the reality of his existence in your own life.

Satan will craft specific attacks, customized just for you, relentlessly striking everything you hold near and dear, especially your faith in Me. Though he cannot steal your spirit, he can and does harass you physically, mentally, emotionally and spiritually. Every attack is meant to injure your faith and defeat your witness so that you will be kept from living a victorious, Christ-centered life. He is not omniscient, but he is knowledgeable and crafty. He observes your life and determines which area to attack—which will have the most devastating effect. He sets a trap and patiently waits for you to take the bait. He'll use friends, family and familiar faces to work out his schemes. He stops at nothing except at My command.

Yes, there is an unseen battle that rages, but I AM with you. Victory is sure for eternity. The enemy aims to drive you into defeat in this life. It is his revenge. But all the forces of hell cannot compare to the supernatural power that is available to you in Christ Jesus. The same Christ who was triumphant over death at the Cross and claimed the final victory over Satan is the One who lives in you today. Claim the victory over your spiritual battles in His name. The victory is sure.

The one who is in you is greater than
the one who is in the world.

1 JOHN 4:4 (NIV)

Taking Control of Your Thoughts

The ongoing desire to be in control captivates you to the point of standing between you and My blessings for your life. The most important challenge of your faith is to surrender to the fact that I AM God and you are not.

Living in a fallen world will taint your thoughts and try your trust. But whatever battles you're losing, are lost in your mind. It is there that wars are fought. Yet I have given you the weapon of My Word. It is sharper than any double-edged sword. It penetrates even to dividing soul and spirit, joints and marrow; it judges the thoughts and attitudes of the heart—so use it to win the battle within. Victory is yours as you trust in Jesus.

Don't let your actions be controlled by your feelings and emotions. The heart is deceitful above all things. Set your mind on My promises and stand firm in the battle against the lies of the world. If you will learn to think My thoughts, your emotions will begin to line up with truth. As you take control of your thinking, you will find yourself experiencing peace in the most treacherous storms of life, and My grace pouring down when all hope seems gone. If you desire victory in life, take control of your thoughts and know that in Christ, the battle is already won.

We demolish arguments and every pretension
that sets itself up against the knowledge
of God, and we take captive every
thought to make it obedient to Christ.

2 CORINTHIANS 10:5 (NIV)

Armor for Life's Battles

I've promised that in this world you will have trouble. Your life is a testing ground. You'll find yourself in despair, and at moments, you'll find it difficult to carry on. But that's when I carry you. There's nothing you must do but stand firm in your faith and wait for Me to embrace you with My grace.

You cannot stand without the armor I've given you to protect you against the spiritual battles before you. You must stand your ground, firmly, with the belt of truth—the assurance of My promises through My Word—fastened around your waist. You'll need the breastplate of righteousness to protect your mind and emotions against the enemy's attacks through lies and deceit. Wrap yourself in righteousness, protecting yourself from the temptation to sin by keeping your life pure. Wear the shoes of peace that remind you that you are at peace with Me, reconciled and walking in faith because of My Son. You are saved, set apart, protected by Me at all times.

Use the shield of faith to extinguish the flaming arrows of hatred, immorality, pride, doubt, fear, despair, anger, and temptation. Rely on the helmet of salvation to protect you from discouragement and doubt. Believe what you know, resting secure in Christ. And before all these things, use your sword: My Word is your first defense. Use it to thwart every lie of the enemy and be assured of My promises of victory in every battle you face.

Put on every piece of God's armor so you will be able to resist the enemy in the time of evil. Then after the battle you will still be standing firm.

EPHESIANS 6:13 (NLT)

Running Scared

There is nothing for you to fear. Whatever you are facing in life—the crushing daily responsibilities that you can't seem to get away from, the pain and sorrow of regret and loss, or the failing health of a body that is supposed to last you a lifetime—there is no need to give in to despair. I AM here, and I will help you through it all.

I realize you may not want to go through it. Your prayers call for a way around, and mostly a way out, but My ways are higher and better. If you will trust Me, I will work out your life in ways you can't imagine. Pain will be turned to joy, and in weakness you'll find strength.

Don't try to understand faith, just trust Me and your faith will take flight in My perfect timing. All you need to do is surrender, or submit, to Me continually. You'll be tempted to give in to doubt and demand a way out. Your enemy is continually encroaching upon your faith. Don't run; stand firm in your faith in Me and I promise that you'll send the enemy running scared. Face every fear with faith and you won't be disappointed.

Submit yourselves, then, to God.
Resist the devil, and he will flee from you.

JAMES 4:7 (NIV)

Faith Match

It's easy to believe that the battle is between you and whatever or whomever stands before you. Sight is easier than faith. But your battle is something far different from what you think it is. You need to understand the battlefield before you'll ever win the battle.

You exist in the physical world, but the spiritual one is even more real and is working within your physical world. There is good and there is evil, and a battle rages between those two spiritual forces.

It is vital that you recognize each and every obstacle you face, every attack against you, for what it is. You are either living for Me or against Me, and that decision changes everything in your daily battles.

I AM with you to deliver you. Never will I leave you or forsake you. The spiritual forces that come against you are no match for My Word, which stands eternally. Trust in what you know. Walk firmly in your faith, relying on the promises I've given you. Don't wrestle with what you shouldn't be, for the battle belongs to Me.

This is not a wrestling match against a human opponent. We are wrestling with rulers, authorities, the powers who govern this world of darkness, and spiritual forces that control evil in the heavenly world.

EPHESIANS 6:12 (GW)

The Battle Cry

You pray it, and I hear it—the cry for deliverance from all that is evil. It's a battle cry that awakens every angel in heaven for the war that must be waged for your soul. When you don't know what to do, when evil surrounds you and the darkness closes in, remember to look up when you're down.

At times, I'll want you to walk into the battle. You will be surrounded by an army of angels that will guide you and protect you. But at other times, I will simply deliver you. I will rescue you and pull you out from the war that rages.

Your faith is critical in giving you patience to receive My battle plan. You'll often have to wait for guidance, and often longer than you'd like. With each and every spiritual battle you face, there is a purpose in it and victory that I will bring from it. But your trust in Me is key. I will deliver you through your faith. Cry out to Me and I will answer you. There is nothing to fear; I AM with you always. Wait expectantly, be on watch, on guard, and know that you can rest under the shadow of My wings.

"Deliver us from evil."

MATTHEW 6:13 (ESV)

Peace

Choosing Peace

There is no gift that I have given you, other than salvation, that is greater than My peace. You will never fully understand the power of My peace. When you find your life consumed with fear and despair, it is My peace that will lead you beside still waters.

You want to know Me, you want to hear from Me, and I desire to show Myself strong on your behalf, but I need you to be obedient in all that I ask you to do. And I ask you to choose peace. In a fallen world, following a path of righteousness will cause you to continually face resistance. But because I AM with you, there is no need to fear. I have given you My peace (see John 14:27), but you must choose Me and My ways.

Know that the enemy is out to destroy your faith and steal your peace. I have put before you life and death, and I tell you to *choose* life. I put before you strife and peace, and I tell you to *choose* peace—My will and My ways.

In order to walk with Me, you must choose to walk in My ways. I give you the choice to walk your way or Mine. Rest assured, My ways are always best. Obedience to Me brings about a greater reward than you can ever imagine. With all the decisions you must make on any given day, the greatest daily decision is whether you will walk in My will or live out your own. That one decision will determine whether or not you have peace. Listen to Me and obey My Word so that all may go well with you. Choose peace.

Make every effort to live in peace …
and to be holy; without holiness
no one will see the Lord.

HEBREWS 12:14 (NIV)

Divine Peace

I know there are countless, critical decisions that you must make each and every day. I know you feel restless about what to do and which direction to take. I know that the circumstances can be overwhelming, to the point that you instinctively give in to your emotions. You forget that I AM here to counsel you, advise you, to give you wisdom. Come to Me and wait upon My voice.

Don't make a decision in your life, even a small one, without accessing the infinite wisdom that I possess. When you consult Me and seek My guidance, you will find yourself being led into My will for your life. I will make your path straight when you lean on My understanding and not your own. Any advice you need should come from Me. I see the entire scope of the situations in your life, from beginning to end, and I take into account the consequences for decisions that you cannot possibly foresee. When it is hard to hear My voice, sit quietly and wait. Do not move ahead of Me, for My delays are with reason.

While you wait, meditate on My Word continually. It is My Word that will lead you into My will. Listen for My voice and focus upon Me at all times. Expect My voice to calm the storm and bring about divine peace. Keep your eyes upon Me and know that there is nothing to fear. Even when you can't understand them, trust My ways … they are perfect.

And let the peace (soul harmony which comes)
from Christ rule (act as umpire continually)
in your hearts [deciding and settling with finality
all questions that arise in your minds …].

COLOSSIANS 3:15 (AMP)

Strength and Peace

In the restlessness of life, when all your strength is gone, it's My peace that will bring your soul into a place of rest. In the midst of the chaos, I am giving you what you desperately need—the comfort of knowing that I AM with you, listening to your prayers and orchestrating their answers.

It is when the troubles of life cause your vision to become blurred that your faith demands sight. I want you to learn to rest in Me and rely on Me through all the uncertainties that consume you. I have chosen to simply bless you with peace, amid any and all circumstances that try to steal it.

My peace is not a feeling, but a place of being. In My presence, within My grace, is the peace that surpasses all understanding. It is in your weakness that I will be your strength. Every trial that tears about your soul is the opportunity to draw near to Me and embrace the unconditional love I have for you. Receive the blessing of peace I give to you and you will find the supernatural strength you need to trust Me as you take one more step of faith.

The LORD gives strength to His people;
the LORD blesses His people with peace.

PSALM 29:11 (NIV)

Stayed

Life changes, but I do not. I know it's easy to find yourself on a path of life you never meant to travel. You may have been driven down roads that led to dead ends or experienced tragedies that left you helpless in a ditch of pain and suffering. Your heart might be breaking, and anxiety may be great within you, but in the midst of it all, you can search Me and find Me in your time of need.

When you can't change your circumstances and you are helpless against them, you need My peace to help you remain in a place of peace. If you'll stay focused upon Me, if you'll rely on Me and trust in Me completely, you can confidently place your hope in Me.

It is your hope and faith in Me that changes everything. When you're all alone, facing the unknowns, know that I'm guarding your life and overseeing every detail of it. There is nothing that is beyond My grasp, and My grace will be sufficient in all things and at all times. Trust, wait and hope confidently in My perfect and constant peace.

You will guard him and keep him in perfect and constant peace whose mind [both its inclination and its character] is stayed on You, because he commits himself to You, leans on You, and hopes confidently in You.

ISAIAH 26:3 (AMP)

Perfected Peace

I want you living in My continual joy and victory because of what I've done for you. My hand is in every detail of your life. The sacrifice of My Son has made a way for My love and grace to pour out to you unconditionally.

If you're living in My peace, My joy and My victory, it doesn't mean life will be without challenges. If you lived free of troubles, you would never have the opportunity to experience the power of My presence. You'd never be assured that your faith was real. You'll find the grace and strength you need in My presence.

I am using your circumstances, good and bad, to deepen your relationship with Me. No matter what you face, even the worst adversities are within My control. And I've promised to deliver you in My way and time. Trust that I know what I'm doing. Whether or not you rest in My peace depends on how deeply you trust My character and how surrendered you are to My will for your life.

Let go and let me do what only I can do. In the midst of your trials, worship while you wait, and know that I'll make a way. My joy and victory aren't far behind; just keep looking up. Be confident and at peace.

I have told you these things, so that in Me
you may have [perfect] peace and confidence.
In the world you have tribulation and trials
and distress and frustration; but be of good
cheer [take courage; be confident, certain,
undaunted]! For I have overcome the world.
[I have deprived it of power to harm
you and have conquered it for you.]

JOHN 16:33 (AMP)

Peace in Believing

Life gets overwhelming in a hurry, and decisions and achievements are difficult at best when your soul is consumed with anxious thoughts. You may not know how you'll get through the day, but with Me you can do *all* things. Listen to My still, small voice that is assuring you that I AM all you need, I AM your strength when you are weak. I will lead you and guide you, I will work out all that concerns you. There is no need to worry. I AM here to help you.

It is through the Holy Spirit that you are given all you need to walk forward in faith. I came to enable, equip, energize, and empower you for every challenge you face, no matter how difficult. I will guide you and give you strength to take one more step of faith, even when you can't see the very next step in front of you. Look for Me in your life, listen to My Word, obey My voice, and trust Me to lead you in the right direction. I will give you peace. Just believe, and I will be your source of hope, I will fill you with joy, and your Spirit will overflow in faith.

> I pray that God, the source of hope, will fill you completely with joy and peace because you trust in Him. Then you will overflow with confident hope through the power of the Holy Spirit.
>
> ROMANS 15:13 (NLT)

In Pursuit of Peace

You need peace with Me in order to have peace with others. And in order to have peace, you need to pursue it. I know it's difficult to be peaceful in all situations at all times. People are dynamic and difficult. But understand that I'm not asking you to compromise your beliefs. I'm simply asking you to act in love, communicate in a godly manner, and operate under an attitude of forgiveness.

You can live in peace with other people by trying to understand, through prayer, the position of others, seeking to grasp why it is that the situation upsets you and why the words and actions of individuals in the situation cause you distress. We must always, in an attitude of love, give others the benefit of the doubt. There are always motivations to behaviors, and sometimes you can lose sight of the root of the issues at hand.

Pursuing My peace is not easy, but it's the only way to live according to My will in order to receive My blessings. In the same way that I have mercy on you, you should show mercy to others. Do not allow yourself to operate out of hate or anger, but rather choose the path of peace through love.

Search for peace, and work to maintain it.

PSALM 34:14 (NLT)

Life and Peace

You can rest assured that as you seek My will for your life, I will always guide you into the things of the Spirit. I will guide you into what is best for your future, and knowing that can give you peace. I want you to fully enjoy life, but I also want you to live according to My will, which yields to you every good and perfect thing. You must be careful to walk by the Spirit, not by the flesh.

Living according to your flesh will cause you to lose your peace, because living for the flesh separates you from My Spirit, and you can't have peace when you're separated from Me. Know that your old, fleshly nature is constantly at war against the Spirit within you. You must constantly bring your flesh under control of the Spirit by living according to My Word.

Set your mind to abide in Me. Listen carefully to My voice and yield your will to My own. Pray continually that you will obey Me. Ask me to reveal your shortcomings, so that you may repent and live life to the full, with joy and in peace.

The mind governed by the flesh is death, but the mind governed by the Spirit is life and peace.

ROMANS 8:6 (NIV)

Trials & Troubles

Help in Trouble

Troubles will come; they're inevitable in a fallen world. Struggles may be fierce, and you'll face fears that will threaten to overcome you. You'll find yourself wrestling within and unable to defeat the debilitating doubts. Know this: When you face obstacles of any kind, I will either take you around them, or give you the strength to endure. I AM with you always. Never do I leave your side, not for a moment.

You will continually question My ways, I know that. Come to Me with your questions, and trust Me even when I cannot give you all the answers. I have purposes for all that I permit within your life. I use your troubles to teach you powerful lessons and to strengthen your faith. At times, I'll lead you deeper into the darkness, where nothing but My light shines on the next step you must take. I'm teaching you to trust Me completely. I want you to see obstacles as opportunities, not as difficulties. When I test you through the troubles of life, put My promises to the proof. Claim as many of My promises as your situation renders. These times of doubt are where faith is grown.

I know you want out—a quick escape. And there are two things you can do: You can try to get rid of your troubles, or recognize that your trials are challenges that will bring about blessings in your life. I'm offering you a larger measure of My divine grace. When you're tempted to give up, remember that you're a conqueror through My Son who loves you.

God is our refuge and strength,
always ready to help in times of trouble.

PSALM 46:1 (NLT)

Eyes of Faith

Through the trials of life, I know you sometimes believe that I AM allowing more difficulties than you can endure. You feel as though the walls are closing in and your spirit is crushed beyond the point of words being able to describe the anguish. I AM with you. Do not forget what I've assured you, "In this world you will have trouble" (John 16:33, NIV). But I never abandon you. I give you My peace through the most treacherous storms of life.

If you profess your faith in Me, you can be sure that you will meet resistance to that faith. You are moving against the ways of the world, and that creates friction. It will seem as though all of your pain and suffering is in vain, but it is not. I have promised to repay you for your suffering in My name. I'm not asking you to trust by blind faith, but to walk with eyes of faith that see what I see. It is through the Red Sea moments that you are given the opportunity to experience My rescuing power. It's in the fiery furnace where you come to know what it's like to not be consumed by the flames and have no smell of smoke about you. Don't resent or pray away those moments that bring about miracles. It is in the midst of your troubles that you find My presence and delivering power. In the ease of life, you fail to experience My provision; you become a stranger to My help, healing and amazing grace. Through eyes of faith, you can know that your troubles will turn to triumph.

We are hard pressed on every side, but not crushed; perplexed, but not in despair; persecuted, but not abandoned; struck down, but not destroyed.

2 CORINTHIANS 4:8-9 (NIV)

No More

There comes a time when enough is enough. I am aware of every struggle and sorrow in your life. And yes, there are times when I allow them to linger in order to grow your faith in Me and to bring about answers to prayer. I've heard your cry, "O Lord, how long will You look on?" And I want you to know that there is a limit to your affliction. Whether or not I send it, I can remove it. I give and I can take away. But I'm asking you to patiently endure your troubles until I declare, "No more." In My love for you, know that I will not remove the afflictions until they reach the fullness of their purpose. It's My refining by fire.

If I have sent the affliction to test you, then it is so that My grace can be displayed and My glory revealed. I want your praise to override your problems. Know that in the blink of an eye, I can bring about the very same intensity of happiness that you currently experience in sorrow. It's not difficult for Me to turn night into day. If I'm allowing it to continue, it is with good reason. Keep walking in faith; it's a journey, not a destination.

Trials and sorrows are only for a season. The storms will pass. Your light affliction is but for a moment. If I am overseeing every part of your life and I've promised to never leave you, then I am exerting an extraordinary amount of patience in allowing your trial to linger. I am doing it because I know that it will bring about a far more exceeding and eternal weight of glory. Nothing happens in your life that has not been appointed by My love and careful foresight. Trust Me in your trials.

"I will afflict you no more."

NAHUM 1:12 (NIV)

Tested and Tried

When you face trials of many kinds, you tend to ask Me what you've done to deserve such troubles. You forget what you know: "In this world you will have trouble" (John 16:33, NIV). I've called you to follow Jesus, and that will mean walking righteously in a world that is unrighteous. When you walk in faith, light will meet the darkness and there will be resistance. But you walk with My power, protection, and presence, so you have nothing to fear.

I want you to be ready for whatever comes your way, and so there will be tests that try your faith and prove what is in your heart. The tests are not for Me; I already know what is in your heart. The tests are for you, so you can take note of the areas of your faith that need to be strengthened. The test will alert you to rely on My promises more heavily than before. I am growing your faith through the trials that threaten to destroy it. Trials will reveal what is lacking in your faith walk with Me, and My grace will give you the strength you need to accept any faults and failures, repent, and move forward in faith.

Through the testing, I'm preparing you to be lacking in nothing, ready for anything, and confident in victory. Do not grow weary in the testing process. Hold firm to My promises and trust that I AM with you through it all. You can know through My faithfulness that if you are not delivered *out* of your trial, you'll be delivered *through* it. And when I have tested you, you will come forth as gold.

I know also, my God,
that You test the heart.

1 CHRONICLES 29:17 (NKJV)

Pain for Gain

Though it seems I have left you in darkness, I AM in the shadow, leading you to discover the treasure of My presence. Know that faith is not developed from being certain, but from walking through doubts, fears, and overwhelming uncertainty. I AM not far off, I AM not indifferent to your pain and suffering. I AM with you in it. Though you come to the end of yourself, it's in your emptiness that you will discover the treasure of immeasurable gains through your trials. Dare to believe that I have purpose in your pain and that the gain is far greater than anything you can imagine.

Though you cannot see Me, I AM with you always. Don't rely on your feelings, but on your faith. My Word will guide you either around the obstacle to your faith, or through it. My provision and protection will be all you need to walk forward in confident faith. Though you must endure for a time, there are blessings beyond the brokenness. Whatever is lost in the fight of faith, I will repay and restore. I AM a God of redemption; there is nothing in your life that I cannot redeem and use for your good and My glory. When you are faced with circumstances that threaten to overcome you, I AM closer to you than I've ever been. When fear tempts you to doubt My faithfulness, stand firm in and expect My hand to move powerfully in your life—in unexpected ways and on uneventful days. Always trust that My power trumps every trial, and every tribulation is a trial turned into triumph.

Why, Lord, do You stand far off?
Why do You hide Yourself in times of trouble?

PSALM 10:1 (NIV)

Oppressed but Blessed

Events in your life may leave you feeling helpless and hopeless, isolated and insignificant. You may be failed by those you love, feeling as though no one understands and no one cares. The pressure weighing down on you can leave you in a state of unbearable weakness, and the obstacles that arise can seem insurmountable. But these hard places in life are where you must trust Me in your troubles. Don't allow the everyday struggles to steal your joy and leave you defeated and full of doubt.

I have not abandoned you. You are never, ever alone. Your faith is not in vain. I am drawing you in so that you will seek Me and so that I can reveal Myself to you in more profound ways.

Don't ever underestimate what I can do through the most difficult circumstances of your life. I am intricately involved in not only the significant things in your life, but also the seemingly insignificant matters. Seek Me and I will show you My glory. Allow Me to lead you and teach you more about Myself and your faith in your troubles and trials. You may be oppressed, but you can have confident hope that you will ultimately be blessed.

Though the Lord gave you adversity for food and suffering for drink, He will still be with you to teach you. You will see your teacher with your own eyes.

ISAIAH 30:20 (NLT)

In Trouble

Don't face your troubles with fear, for it leads to instant defeat of the soul. See the outcome through My eyes, through My Word, with confidence in the promises I've made you. Don't allow the world to convince you that your troubles are bigger than they really are. I AM always bigger.

I have never lost control over My creation for even a fraction of a second since the beginning of time. Likewise, your life is always within My control—every detail of it. Recognize and accept My sovereignty. If you'll come to believe that nothing that is related to you is beyond My control, you'll find the inner peace you need to have faith in times of trouble.

I AM your protector, the One who meets your every need and cares for you in every way. No matter what happens, I have a plan to bless you and reward you in eternity. It's not all about this life. This is your testing ground, preparing you for eternal life. If you'll trust Me, I will turn all of your troubles to triumph. Know that My desire is to give you the very best in life, withholding no good thing. So call on Me, trust that I will answer, know that I AM with you, and be assured that I will help you.

"When they call on Me, I will answer;
I will be with them in trouble. I will
rescue and honor them."

PSALM 91:15 (NLT)

The Good and the Bad

Life is filled with disappointment. In intense times of suffering, I know you can be tempted to blame Me. I haven't let you down; My promises will prevail in every problem you face.

When doubt overcomes your faith, stirring up despair and bitterness, call upon Me and seek My presence. Come to Me with a humble, submissive attitude and honor Me in the midst of adversity. The way you respond to disappointment has an enormous impact on the outcome of your troubles.

Don't listen to the enemy. Don't believe the lies. I AM with you to deliver you. I am merciful, full of love, and eager to pour out My grace into your life. Don't always take your troubles at face value; I have ways of working within them that go beyond your comprehension. I have a plan for you that goes far beyond all you can hope for or imagine, so don't be surprised by setbacks. In this world you will have trouble, but My victory is always assured when you're trusting in Me completely, accepting the good and the bad, living in hope through faith.

"We accept the good that God gives us. Shouldn't we also accept the bad?"

JOB 2:10 (GW)

Brokenness

Brokenhearted

You tend to believe that My ways are so "spiritual" that they have no earthly good, yet My power has no bounds. I am a very present help in times of trouble. I know every tear you've cried and I bottle each one. One day I will wipe every tear and you will remember them no more. My healing comes through the hope found in My Word. Though the storm rages within your soul, the healing rain that falls will soften the soil in which I will grow your faith. As you cling to My promises, know that those seeds will grow a harvest of hope in your heart that will enable you to trust Me, even through the pain. I AM with you, where you are … in your brokenness.

I know there are places in your heart that are so wounded that you believe no prayer can adequately express the pain. But no words are necessary. You need only remain in My presence. Through your tears, I can give you an eternal perspective that will bind up your wounds and heal them.

I know that as you endure, you grow and that the joys to come will last forever. If it feels as though your heart is being ripped out, you can know that I'm at work. I've promised to take the heart you have and give you a new one. The pain is part of the process. My promises can cast out the despair, depression and doubt, flooding your spirit with light in your darkest hour. When you're brokenhearted, allow My heart to bind up yours. Healing is in My hands.

He heals the brokenhearted and bandages their wounds.

PSALM 147:3 (NLT)

Beyond Broken

You may experience the same trials over and over, wondering why it is that I've forsaken you and allowed you to continually go through pain and suffering. Sometimes it is part of growing your faith. At other times it is because I'm trying to bring the issues in your life that need attention to the surface. If I AM to set you free, I will have to point out the destructive attitudes and behaviors that keep you from experiencing My very best for your life. My desire is that everything in your life would honor Me.

Take heart. Know that the pain and sorrows you are experiencing at the moment will be transformed into unthinkable joy. I am freeing you from your self-sufficiency, so that I can demonstrate My sovereign power and wisdom in and through you. Though you might think there must be another way, it is often only through brokenness that you'll surrender your will to Mine.

I want you to stop depending on your limited knowledge and resources and start relying only upon Me. I want to remove anything from your life that keeps you from fully trusting Me. I AM all-wise, loving, and always working every situation in your life for good. Beyond your brokenness there are blessings, so wait expectantly, with confident hope.

When He tests me, I will come out as pure as gold.

JOB 23:10 (NLT)

It's Not the End

Though you may be tempted to believe it, this is not the end. Your heartache and hard times are not without purpose. Everything I allow is for your good. I know it's hard to trust Me on that. Though you find yourself in a pit of destruction, I've promised to bring you out.

Know that I will do whatever is necessary to set you free from the bondage of despair that consumes you. Though you might be tempted to act within your own resources, your best course of action is to run to Me, turn completely to Me, and rely on Me for your every need. I always have your best interests in mind. I only ask that you turn your worry into worship and beckon Me through praise and prayer.

Trust that I will do exactly what is necessary to fully heal your broken heart and bring joy out of your pain. There is no tear wasted or unnoticed; I collect each one. And in due time, I will bring beauty from the ashes of your failed expectations of life. Though you're weary and losing hope now, I AM working all things together for good. And when I have, you'll be firm in faith, lacking nothing.

He brought me up out of the pit of destruction,
out of the miry clay, and He set my feet upon
a rock making my footsteps firm.

PSALM 40:2 (NASB)

Disheartened

I know that you are desperate and in need of direction. I know that your brokenness challenges your faith in more ways than you could ever have imagined. I know that My silence disheartens you. But know that I have not abandoned you, I have not forgotten you, and I care for you more than you will ever know.

I know you grow more desperate in the times of waiting, but be assured that I will answer your every prayer in My perfect timing. This is the opportunity to trust Me, even as your soul cries out for mercy. Going through difficulties is never easy, but it builds your faith in greater ways than a way out of your troubles. My delays should not disappoint you. I will arrive, exactly on time.

My desire is to bring you into a new intimacy with Myself. I only ask that you keep seeking Me, assured that I will answer you. I will reward your faith beyond all you can dare to hope for or imagine. When I AM silent, trust Me more than you want to, and your faith will bring about My most revealing presence and unlimited power in your life.

> "If you believe, you will
> see the glory of God."
>
> JOHN 11:40 (NIV)

Held Close

Know this: I love you—unconditionally, without end. You may be surrounded by people who cause you deep distress, making you feel alone and unloved, but I AM here. The painful feelings of worthlessness are not the truth about you. I determine your value, and you are wonderfully made, created to bring Me glory.

You don't have to be perfect, you don't need to please the world, you need only please Me by seeking Me with all of your heart. Don't believe the lies that others say. Don't allow wounds that have no place or validity in your life.

You belong to Me, and I hold you within My everlasting arms. I love you and accept you. I enable you to do all that I've created you to do. I dwell within you, and I AM always a ready help in times of trouble, especially when your heart is breaking.

You can overcome the feelings that are causing you to sink into despair by believing the truth that I've told you. I have assured you through My promises that I will make you worthy, accepted, and able to do ALL things through Me. I AM the One who gives your life purpose, and in My eyes you are more than worthy. I will be your comfort; I will hold you. When you are empty, yet filled with sorrow, know that you are held.

The Lord will hold me close.

PSALM 27:10 (NLT)

Counting Loss

At times your thoughts are only consumed with what you've lost instead of what you've gained. I know that in the difficulties of life, it's easy to lose sight of your blessings. But they are countless. The frustration and discouragement you face are often caused by focusing on the wrong things, and the end result is a lack of faith. When you focus on what you don't have, you rob yourself of peace, energy and joy. But when I am the primary focus and priority in your life, the blessings that will pour in are far beyond your greatest hopes and desires.

Instead of spending time counting your losses, refocus your time in My presence to be reminded of your countless blessings. View your life through My eyes, My promises, not your own. Seek Me at all times; fully grasp the sacrifice that has been made to free you of your sins and enable you to experience My peace that surpasses all understanding.

Pursue Me with greater passion in your brokenness. I AM worthy of your trust, I can heal every part of your heart that has been torn apart. If you will place Me first in your life, you will never be disappointed. Nothing in all the earth can satisfy your soul like I can. Follow Me faithfully and count everything as loss in comparison to what you and I have into eternity.

I count all things to be loss in view of
the surpassing value of knowing
Christ Jesus my Lord.

PHILIPPIANS 3:8 (NASB)

Thirsty

When you're empty, I can fill you. In the desert of your life, I AM the living water that will quench your thirst. You may be going through a season of defeat, feeling drained spiritually, but it's in this moment that I will show you that I AM all you need when you're in need.

I AM always looking to mature your faith, to draw you closer to Me. In your thirst, you will be tempted to be filled with the things of the world. But if you will turn to Me, entering into My presence, you'll find all you need in Me. You will thirst no more. Simply cast off all things that hinder you from seeking Me, from continually desiring My presence in your life. If you don't feel My presence, that is a sign that you're focusing on something other than Me.

When I see you off-track, not traveling along the path I've purposed for you, I will create a thirst for Me that cannot be quenched without drinking of the Living Water that I provide. I love you that much. If you are thirsty, return to Me, rebuild the relationship we are intended to have and seek Me continually. I have promised that if you seek Me, you will be satisfied.

**My soul thirsts for God,
for the living God.**

PSALM 42:2 (NIV)

Overcoming Obstacles

Overcoming Unbelief

When you trust in Me and your faith stands firm in My promises, you can find peace in knowing that nothing is impossible for Me. Though your sight is limited and it appears that I may never show up to help you, rest assured that My help is on the way. You are not able to see how I'm working at all times, so I know it's easy to see the challenges of life as obstacles, instead of opportunities to trust Me. I'm only asking you to believe that if I've promised you something, it's as good as done.

Do not become disheartened and overcome with doubt. I need you to continue to trust Me even when at times it is hard to believe. I'm going to allow obstacles in your life so that you have the opportunity to increase your faith, and to challenge you to trust Me, looking beyond the natural world. Don't lean on your own understanding, simply praise Me for My provision and trust in My plans. Every promise I've made to you will be fulfilled—consider it done.

No unbelief made Abraham waver concerning the promise of God, but he grew strong in his faith as he gave glory to God.

ROMANS 4:20 (ESV)

Blessed in Believing

When you're overwhelmed by the obstacles of life, I know it's easy to feel all alone and helpless. But you're never alone; I AM with you always. Though it may seem like hope is gone, it is not. I AM hope, and I am the same yesterday, today and forever. My promises are given to assure you that I will never leave you nor forsake you, and there is nothing to fear because I AM always victorious.

Through every doubt, I AM able to display My presence and My power in your life; not only to restore your faith, but to increase it. In times of distress, I simply want you to cling to My promises. Sometimes you will be fully aware of My presence, sometimes you will not. In My silence, as I'm working on your behalf, I need you to simply trust in what I've promised you. Sometimes I will comfort you and provide immediate answers. At other times I will not, and I'm giving you the opportunity to increase your faith.

Do not give in to the doubt that comes with darkness, but instead be overcome by the light that My Word provides. It is a lamp unto your feet, a light unto your path. There is nothing for you to fear; I will bless you because you believe.

"You believe because you have seen Me.
Blessed are those who believe without seeing Me."

JOHN 20:29 (NLT)

Profound Power

I know you face situations that ultimately leave you powerless, and that is by design. I need you to learn to continually depend on Me to give you strength in your weakness. I need to be your all in all.

No matter what your challenges are—physical, relational, financial or some other—I am well aware of them, and you can trust Me with every detail. If I've allowed an overwhelming obstacle in your life, you can rest assured that I will bring good from it.

I will never abandon you, and your times of weakness are moments when I can display My profound power. You don't have to be afraid or feel helpless or hopeless when you're trusting in Me. I have allowed trying circumstances in your life so that you can deepen your faith, learning that you can count on Me at all times and in all ways.

Do not allow yourself to be overwhelmed by anything other than My love for you. I will make a way for you to experience My glory. Just trust and rest.

*Do not be afraid. Stand firm and you will see the deliverance the L*ORD *will bring you today.*

EXODUS 14:13 (NIV)

More Than a Conqueror

I know that sometimes you need an assurance of some kind that everything is going to be okay. I know your soul longs to know that you'll make it through and that I AM with you, always working in and through your circumstances to make you a conqueror. Although you must endure trials, I always promise triumph.

It is through the difficulties of life, the moments that cast you into a pit of despair, that I will take you to new heights in your faith. The challenges of life are the training grounds that I use to develop your character, preparing you for anything.

I want you to focus on Me, rising above your circumstances. I want you to have the joy and confidence through My promises, knowing beyond all doubt that I have assured you of victory over all your obstacles. Despite all that you must go through, know that I waste nothing. Your pain will be for gain, and every sorrow replaced with joy. Trust in Me because of My heart.

In all these things we are more than conquerors through Him who loved us.

ROMANS 8:37 (NIV)

Rising above the Obstacles

The "mountains" in your life cause you to face a choice: to be overwhelmed or enthusiastic. And that choice will either keep you from moving forward in faith or take you to the top of the mountain you face. I know it seems easier to just give up and give in, but you can't. And don't be deceived: You can be completely centered in My will and still face enormous obstacles.

Oftentimes, as you're moving in the right direction in your faith, challenges seem endless. This is because you have an enemy, and he opposes you when he sees Me at work in and through your life. So don't become disillusioned just because you encounter mountains of opposition. Simply look up and be assured of My presence and power that overcomes all obstacles to My will for you. Respond in faith, remembering that I can move mountains, but the mountain I really want to move is the one within you—the mountain of doubt that keeps you from moving forward in faith. You alone can move that mountain, by simply believing that I will move all the others in your life.

"Every valley shall be raised up, every mountain
and hill made low; the rough ground shall
become level, the rugged places a plain.
And the glory of the LORD will be revealed,
and all people will see it together.
For the mouth of the LORD has spoken."

ISAIAH 40:4–5 (NIV)

The Answer

I see you exactly where you are, through the trials and struggles that create turmoil in your soul. I have not forgotten you; I AM with you. I'm always walking with you, by your side, a ready help in times of trouble. I want you to be aware of My presence and My great love for you, and then I want your heart to understand what your mind knows. It is faith that will dispel the gripping fear that keeps you from the peace that comes through trusting in My promises.

You do not need to be afraid when you walk through the valleys of life. They are part of the journey, not the destination. I AM for you and with you in the midst of all your uncertainty and despair. I ask you to do only one thing: Look to Me. I AM the answer to every situation. I AM your Rock, your Strong Tower, and the Author of your salvation. I AM your only true hope. Therefore, find your hope in Me. All else will fail, but I never will.

As you're facing the trying situations in your life, know that I AM able to do ALL things. Everything is possible with Me. Your hope should not rest in anything but the Cross. At the Cross there is redemption and resurrection. The sacrifice of Jesus has removed all sin, sickness and sorrow. Jesus bore it all for you, so that you would have a life of victory and hope. The Cross is for you, right now, in the situation you are in, so that you might find My love and power in your life. For every situation you face in life, no matter how impossible things might seem, I AM your answer.

"Everything is possible with God."

MARK 10:27 (NLT)

Against the Odds

Whatever stands in your way today, whatever impossibilities you face, now or in the future, the odds are not against you because I AM on your side. I stand with you and will not be moved, so you shouldn't either. Your sources and security may be crumbling down around you, but My resources, strength and power know no bounds. I do the impossible, so be assured that I will strengthen your hope.

Rest assured that I will provide for you in ways that you cannot imagine when you face the many challenges of life. In the midst of all the uncertainty and the seemingly insurmountable circumstances you face, simply remain in a place of praise. Worship through your worry. Soon you will realize that I have given you the victory; I've been working all along. Even though you couldn't see My hand, you'll learn that you can trust My heart.

Your triumph through your troubles is already prearranged, your faith just needs to believe that it is. Doubt never brings about deliverance, but defeat. Trusting completely in Me at all times in all ways, no matter what, will always overcome any obstacle. Have faith, get up, and walk into the victory I've given you.

"Get up! For the LORD has given you victory!"

JUDGES 7:15 (NLT)

Hope

Holding on to Hope

You find yourself helpless and hopeless and your soul is cast down to the point that faith no longer seems to matter. I hear your cries for help and I AM here. I search your heart and see that doubt and despair have consumed the hope that once dwelled there. But trust Me, hope is not gone—it may be hidden in the pain and suffering, but it is there. And although you may lose your grasp on your faith, I will never let go of you.

You can hold on to hope because I've made promises to you that you can cling to, even as you struggle to believe them. I want you to trust Me through the uncertainty and keep walking in faith, regardless of what you see. In your doubts, pour out your heart to Me. I hear every word, know every thought, and see every tear.

When you're tempted to give up, that's the time to hold on. Nothing is too difficult for Me, and I hold time in My hands. I AM able to see the full scope of your situation and work out every detail to My perfection. Trust that I know what I'm doing, even when it seems as though I don't. When your soul is downcast, receive My love and trust My heart. I AM not a lesser God according to your circumstances. I AM constant. I AM sovereign. And I will never forsake you. Put your hope in Me and hold on. We're about to take a journey to joy.

Why, my soul, are you downcast?
Why so disturbed within me?
Put your hope in God, for I will yet
praise Him, my Savior and my God.

PSALM 43:5 (NIV)

Hope-Filled

Your circumstances may leave you in a pit of despair, but My mighty hand can pull you out. It's your hope in Me alone that can conquer whatever is overwhelming you. You may not see how you will get through, but be assured that I will make a way. Listen to My still, small voice that will assure you that I AM able to do the impossible.

Though you may be tempted to place your hope in yourself, others or something else, you must resist the desire to walk by sight. I have given you My Spirit to teach, prepare, enable and equip you for all that challenges your faith.

Know that I will energize and empower you to be more than a conqueror. If you will listen to Me and obey Me, you will see hope become a reality in your life. I AM the God of hope. Let Me fill you to the full so that you might have peace and joy in the midst of pain and sorrow and trials and tribulations—hope in Me is all you need.

I pray that God, the source of hope, will fill you completely with joy and peace because you trust in Him. Then you will overflow with confident hope through the power of the Holy Spirit.

ROMANS 15:13 (NLT)

The Anchor

Though there are days where you feel that I am distant and it's difficult to sense that I AM with you always, I AM. Life brings about circumstances that change rapidly and without notice, but I AM in control of them all. Though your life moves in different directions, I always remain the same yesterday, today and forever—nothing moves Me.

My love and provision for you is unshakable, eternal. It is the anchor in which your hope should reside. If you are filled with fear, uncertain of the future and overcome with anxiety, examine your heart and your mind. Reset your focus upon Me instead of the circumstances of your life. Realize that you may not be able to control the details of your life, but I can.

I want you to draw close to Me as the raging seas of life threaten to take you under. Turbulent waters may cause you to drift, so you must be anchored in hope through My promises. I want you to be strong and steadfast, trusting in Me at all times. It is My Word that will assure you that there is victory ahead. The storms of life will come, but I AM your shelter—I will protect you and provide for you. When you place your hope in Me, I will anchor your soul so that you can have faith to make it through.

God has given both His promise and His oath.
These two things are unchangeable because
it is impossible for God to lie. Therefore, we
who have fled to Him for refuge can have
great confidence as we hold to the hope that
lies before us. This hope is a strong and
trustworthy anchor for our souls.

HEBREWS 6:18–19 (NLT)

Above All Else

I realize that you are in need, hoping against hope, uncertain if I hear your prayers, unable to hear My voice and questioning My presence, but I'm asking you to maintain a confident faith that keeps you looking to Me. I know that faith is not easy, but when your faith is failing, it is My Word that will give you the strength to keep believing.

I know it's the waiting that compounds the difficulty of faith, but it is in My delays that you will discover I AM drawing you near, preparing your heart for answered prayer, teaching you to trust Me to a greater degree. It isn't easy when I don't answer you in the ways you hoped I would. Remember that My ways are not your ways because I see into eternity. My ways are better; you're just going to have to trust Me on that.

When you are questioning Me, you must examine your heart, and ask if there is anything that is separating you from Me. Let nothing stand between us, for I AM everything you need. I AM never off My throne, I AM always in control, and hope in Me is what will give you immeasurably above all that you could dare hope for or imagine.

Put your hope in the LORD.

PSALM 37:34 (NLT)

Heart of Hope

Your hope is not in vain when your hope is in Me. Though you may be in the midst of despair and life seems to be crumbling down around you, I AM the rock that is the foundation of your faith. Do not be moved. No matter what your current circumstances are, rely on the Savior whom I sent to save you. Regardless of your situation, no matter how hopeless things may seem, there is hope in the victory of Jesus. It is My Spirit that will help you to continue to fight the good fight of faith. My joy should be your strength. Your hope in Me should provide you with all you need to remain at peace as you wait upon My hand to move.

I want you to live above your circumstances, focused upon Me and relying on My promises. If you will trust Me, you will find yourself in a state of peace that surpasses all understanding. You can rest in My unwavering and unfailing love.

Do not despair. Though you may experience defeat for a moment, your hope can never be taken from you, and hope drives My heart and hand into bringing about miracles. I want you to expect Me to do great things. I will never fail you. Cling to Me through the doubt and set your heart on hope.

This is why we work hard and continue
to struggle, for our hope is in the living
God, who is the Savior of all people and
particularly of all believers.

1 TIMOTHY 4:10 (NLT)

Faithful at All Times

You are not alone. I AM in your struggles, with you at every moment, aware of all that concerns you. I have promised that I will never leave you nor forsake you, and I won't. So place your hope in My truth, and rest as you wait.

Your faith will be tried; faith isn't faith unless it is proven by testing. Receive My promises and rely on them for every situation in your life. Whatever your struggle is, I AM able to deliver you. There is no obstacle too great for Me and there is nothing that I can't do. If you believe in Me, trusting Me at every turn, you will have all the strength you need to take just one more step of faith. And that's all I'm asking you to do. I give you grace for the moment.

I want you to be assured that you are not alone in the trials you face; My mighty power is with you through your hope. I will never disappoint you if you place your hope in Me and trust Me to deliver you. Trust completely that I will help you, find peace in My promises, and wait eagerly for your faith to bear fruit.

Such things were written in the Scriptures long ago to teach us. And the Scriptures give us hope and encouragement as we wait patiently for God's promises to be fulfilled.

ROMANS 15:4 (NLT)

Choosing Hope

I know it's difficult to pray for My will when you're truly hoping that your own will be done. I know it is difficult to trust Me when your faith is walking by sight. But I need you to cast yourself into My care, trusting in My love for you. I need you to truly believe that whatever I have planned for you is better for you than anything you could bring about yourself. I am always seeking opportunities to draw you near to Me, to grow your faith and to show you My power in your life. Know that I'm at work, and keep your hope in Me.

Hope is not a feeling; don't be deceived. Hope is the assurance that I AM with you—and for you—and that you can rely on every single promise I've made to you. Each and every day I am presenting you with a choice to hope. Look at your trials and tribulations as just that, and choose to believe. I want you to learn to trust Me, no matter the outcome, assured that I have your very best interests at heart.

I want you to surrender, abandon yourself to My will, rely on My provision and protection, and find assurance that I will provide the path that will take you to victory through even the worst of adversities. I will lead you faithfully into victory.

> "And he who believes in Him
> will not be disappointed."
>
> 1 PETER 2:6 (NASB)

Praise

The Shout of Faith

Though the walls of doubt stand before you, it is your shout of faith that will bring them crumbling to the ground. Though your moans of wavering faith pierce My heart, it is the shout of faith that moves My hand. I have told you that I have *given* you the victory, not that I "will give." Declare what you know and walk firm in your faith.

Do not be shaken; let nothing move you. I AM with you always, and there is never anything to fear when you're trusting in Me. The secret to your victory lies within your shout of faith, on the authority of My Word to claim the promised victory. You are to shout in faith when there are no signs of victory to be seen, when your circumstances contradict the faith you profess.

If I have declared My promises to you, then it is your faith that will reckon them to be true. In the moments when My ways fail to make sense and reason gets the best of you, call out to Me in faith and listen to the confident assurance of My voice.

Your shout of faith will cause the walls of doubt to fall, and My victory will be eminent. As you face obstacles that appear insurmountable, trust what I've told you: "Take heart! I have overcome the world" (John 16:33, NIV).

When you hear them sound a long blast on the trumpets, have the whole army give a loud shout; then the wall of the city will collapse and the army will go up, everyone straight in.

JOSHUA 6:5 (NIV)

The Power of Praise

In your darkest hour, all power is in praise. Regardless of the chains that bind you, I can break them. In the deepest pit of despair, focus upon Me, your ever-present help in times of trouble. There is nothing that will set you free faster than praising Me, expressing your trust in My presence, power and unfailing love for you.

Your circumstances may be unjust, you may be imprisoned by your own wrong choices, but I can still set you free. There is nothing that moves heaven more than the shout of praise in the midst of circumstances that appear less than praiseworthy. Your praise demonstrates your belief in My sovereignty and My boundless love for you. I will prepare the way and make provision in your life through your praise.

Sometimes you won't feel like praising Me and you'll be more tempted toward anger and doubt; but you must refuse to walk by sight, and allow your faith to praise Me even when you don't want to. Though your circumstances seem insurmountable, I'm asking you to rejoice anyway. Praise Me for your past, rejoice in the present moment, and I will bring about joy in your future. Choose faith—exalt Me above your circumstances as being worthy of all honor, glory, power and praise.

Around midnight Paul and Silas were praying
and singing hymns to God, and the other prisoners
were listening. Suddenly, there was a massive
earthquake, and the prison was shaken to its
foundations. All the doors immediately flew open,
and the chains of every prisoner fell off!

ACTS 16:25-26 (NLT)

Prayers of Praise

Pray to Me with praises. Even though there may not be anything in your life's circumstances that makes you feel like praising, lift up praises anyway. Always approach My throne of grace in praise, for it opens My heart and moves My hand. Your praise brings you into My presence more readily than anything else.

When you praise Me, you are laying aside your worries and exalting Me, summoning Me to move on your behalf. Your heart of faith pierces Mine. I AM in control over all that concerns you. I hold every detail of your life in My hands. As you praise Me, you will have an unshakable assurance that I AM with you, working in and through your circumstances even when you can't see My hand at work. Your faith in Me will strengthen you to hope in My power to resolve all of your problems. Your faith trusts that I have the wisdom and power to bring about My very best in your life.

When you are faced with fears and filled with despair, there is nothing more powerful than to offer up praises to My name. I AM your deliverer, and I never change. You can trust in Me no matter how impossible your situation might be. When you're down on your knees, with nowhere to look but up, simply pray through praise and rest in My presence as I unleash My power to bring about your peace.

It is good to give thanks to the LORD,
to sing praises to the Most High.

PSALM 92:1 (NLT)

Resting in Christ's Work

You don't have to strive to be perfect. You don't have to work so hard trying to meet standards that you simply can't meet. Don't appraise yourself by wrong standards. Jesus makes you adequate. I gave Him to you, knowing that He could do what you can't. You are to do all things through Him.

I don't expect you to be perfect; no one can do what is right all the time and live a sin-free life. You can't escape every temptation. You will need the Spirit to strengthen you each and every moment of your life. You can have great joy not because of anything you've done, but because of everything I've done. I have made a way for you to live in joy even in a fallen world filled with temptations and struggles and pain and sorrow. I bring beauty from ashes. Lift up your praises with the anticipation of victory.

Release your fears, let go of your striving, and rest in the finished work of Christ that makes you triumphant and keeps you from stumbling, slipping or falling. You are forever secure in Me.

Now to Him Who is able to keep you without
stumbling or slipping or falling, and to present
[you] unblemished (blameless and faultless)
before the presence of His glory in triumphant
joy and exultation [with unspeakable, ecstatic delight].

JUDE 1:24 (AMP)

Lifted Up

You'll constantly face seemingly impossible situations. Let them be what drives you into My presence. I've made you promises, and you can rely on them. You'll find yourself at your wits' end, unable to see a way through your situation and desperate for a way out. But remember that I've never failed you. There have been times in the past when you were certain you couldn't go on, fearful that you'd never make it through, yet you find yourself at this moment, before My throne. I will never forsake you.

I can do anything in your life. Lift Me above your circumstances. I AM always faithful to fulfill My promises, so stand firm in your faith upon each of the promises I've made you. You'll need to dive into My Word, listening for My still, small voice. I'll guide you in My Word, leading you to those promises that You must claim for each and every detail of your life. There is nothing in My Word that I have not addressed; I've left nothing undone.

I AM with you to lead you through life with assured hope. I'm asking you to trust Me regardless of how difficult and challenging the circumstances of your life may be. Nothing is too hard for Me. Let Me do what you cannot.

O Sovereign LORD! You made the heavens and earth by Your strong hand and powerful arm. Nothing is too hard for You!

JEREMIAH 32:17 (NLT)

At His Feet

Worship is the greatest evidence of your faith. If you fully trust in My sovereignty, you'll find yourself continually at My feet, before My throne of grace. And when you're there, I'm asking you to praise Me instead of focusing on your problems. It's a time of surrender, letting go of your pride and acknowledging that I AM your God, and there is no other.

The circumstances of your life may leave you feeling weak, depressed and forsaken, but your feelings do not determine your future; I do. It is when you worship in humility, focusing upon Me, that I pour down My grace. It's when you exalt Me that everything in your life becomes smaller, including the insurmountable obstacles that stand between you and your faith.

It is when you are down on your knees in prayer that you'll find the comfort you need to bring peace to your soul as you wrestle with the frustrations of daily life. Don't miss out on your time with Me: time to simply sit in My presence, to allow Me to assure you of My promises, to simply increase your faith by realizing that I have everything under control. I don't want you to be anxious; I want you to have peace at all times. The peace that surpasses all understanding is found under the shadow of My wings. Come, sit at my feet, rest and trust.

Exalt the LORD our God! Bow low
before His feet, for He is holy!

PSALM 99:5 (NLT)

Time for Worship

I want you to connect with Me. In worship and prayer, you immediately enter into My presence. In true worship, you are entering into the spiritual world, declaring your faith in My sovereignty. I want you to sense My nearness, but when you don't, I want you to simply be assured that I AM with you. I want you to have a deeply personal experience of My presence, love and power.

Too often, you go through the motions of worship, but don't try to engage with Me. I need you to spend time in My presence, attentive, quietly listening for My voice in My Word. Genuine praise is going to come from a heart that is completely surrendered and willing to embrace My will.

I want you to trust Me and worship Me through making a melody with your heart. When you are filled with My Spirit, praise will naturally flow out. If your heart is not filled with praise, draw near to Me, allow Me to take control of all that is burdening you. Let go of what is drowning you in despair and grab hold of the promises I've made you. Call out to Me, ask Me to show you My glory, and I will.

"The time is coming—indeed it's here now—when true worshipers will worship the Father in spirit and in truth. The Father is looking for those who will worship Him that way."

JOHN 4:23 (NLT)

Guidance

Trust in Uncertain Times

I will give you opportunities to step into the unknown, calling your faith to cease demanding to walk by sight. You will continually face situations and decisions that must be made and will be unsure about what you should do. The uncertainties are not in your life to cause you to doubt, but to teach you to rely upon Me for each step you take and to strengthen your faith. I will use these situations to try your faith in new ways. I'm in the process of making your faith tried and true. So do not fear the overwhelming unknowns.

Realize that if you could handle every situation in your own wisdom and with your own resources, you would not be taking steps of faith. You'd miss the opportunities for Me to display My presence, power and peace in your journey through life. When I challenge you to take a step of faith, I'll make sure that I provide you with all you need to walk in confident hope. If I've asked you to step out in faith, you can be sure that I will lead and guide you into victory. I simply ask that you seek, trust and obey Me as I direct you, fully assured that I will never leave you.

"I will lead the blind by a way they do not know, in paths they do not know I will guide them. I will make darkness into light before them and rugged places into plains. These are the things I will do, and I will not leave them undone."

ISAIAH 42:16 (NASB)

Guided into Glory

You may not know where you're going, but I do. And when you're weary, feeling all alone and unable to take another step of faith, I need you to know that I AM with you always, guiding you into glory.

I know far more about the situations you face than you could ever know. I see your life from beginning to end, and every detail in between. Therefore, you can trust Me with your future. I have brought you to this point, and I will not forsake you. If I've led you in, I will lead you out. Know that My wisdom and direction are all you will ever need for the journey of faith. And when I call you to walk upon the water, it's My power that will enable you to do so. Every situation you face is all about trusting Me.

So don't fall into despair over your overwhelming circumstances. Do not be tempted to let go of your faith and walk by sight. Come into My Presence, rely on My still, small voice to lead and guide you, trust in My wisdom and power, and rest in faith. Hold on to My hand.

"Yet, I am always with You. You hold on to my right hand. With Your advice You guide me, and in the end You will take me to glory."

PSALM 73:23–24 (GW)

A Planned Path

Life can lead you down paths you never expected and never wanted to take. When you've wandered down a path that was not in My will, you'll continually find yourself frustrated and living without peace. If I'm leading and guiding you, all of your obstacles will be overcome.

Every struggle is an opportunity to turn to Me so that I can bring you to a place in your faith where you fully grasp that your life is completely in My hands. I want to always direct your path so that you will have victory with each step of faith you take.

I know you make plans, but I have bigger plans for you—plans to give you a future and a hope, plans to prosper you. I don't want you trying to figure life out on your own. I want you leaning not on your own understanding but on Me, so that I can direct your paths and make them straight. I need you to let me lead you step by step, allowing Me to do what you cannot. Accept the challenges that come, trust Me completely in and through them, and I will position you to walk in victory every time. Surrender your will to Mine, for Mine is always better.

We can make our plans,
but the Lord determines our steps.

PROVERBS 16:9 (NLT)

Paths of Uprightness

I want to continually speak to your heart and lead you into a place of constant peace. There is so much more to having a relationship with Me than simply knowing that I've saved your soul and sealed it for eternity.

You also have the great blessing of walking with Me through life. I AM with you always, to guide and direct you into My righteousness. The situations in life that stretch your faith beckon you into My presence so that we might have the intimacy that I desire to have with you.

You can always rest assured that if I allow a situation in your life, either "good" or "bad," I do so with great purpose and with the desire to increase your faith by drawing you near to Me. It's when you're facing circumstances that require wisdom and strength beyond your own that you are forced to look to Me. My desire is that you would learn to rely on the Holy Spirit at all times, not just when you're facing trials and tribulation.

I want to lead you into the abundant life you're supposed to have, but sometimes the path of uprightness comes by way of difficulties—situations that cause you to trust in Me like never before. Simply trust Me at all times and everything will work out in the end.

I have taught you in the way of skillful and
godly Wisdom [which is comprehensive insight
into the ways and purposes of God]; I
have led you in paths of uprightness.

PROVERBS 4:11 (AMP)

Each and Every Step

I may not always light the path before you in such a way that you feel certain and sure about the future. Know that when I choose to keep you taking one step at a time amid the darkness, I'm doing so with great purpose. Often, I want to lead you carefully in each step, building your trust and reliance upon Me.

In order to move forward into My purposes for your life, you can't expect to have all the answers. I want you to learn to trust Me. The pressure of some of the challenging paths you must take will be what pushes you into My presence. I don't want you to be dismayed or full of fear. Know that I have you right where I want you and that I AM with you to rescue you.

The path I plan for you always leads to victory—maybe not in the way you want or in the timing you desire, but My will is perfect and you must trust in it. I don't want your faith to rest in anything or anyone other than Myself. So surrender to Me fully. Know that I will give you the strength you need as you obey each step of faith I reveal to you. Everything I'm doing, the ways in which I'm leading you, are for your good and My glory.

He renews my strength. He guides
me along right paths, bringing
honor to His name.

PSALM 23:3 (NLT)

The Plan

When your day doesn't seem to go as planned, try not to lose focus on Me. My plans prevail, and nothing can thwart them. I know you get frustrated when life takes you on detours and even dead ends, but there is nothing to fear. When life seems out of control, it's still within My control.

Though you'll be tempted to believe otherwise, My plans for your life will bring about true peace and contentment. Although you may not be able to see the scope of My plans at this very moment, I can assure you that I *always* have your best interests at heart. My delays and detours are not denials of your hopes and desires; I just have a better way. It may not be the easiest route, but it will ultimately bring about greater good.

Know that through the valleys, in conditions that seem hazardous and impassable, it is I who part Red Seas and provide a way in the desert of your life. I never abandon you. There may be times when you feel alone, but the truth is you are never alone. So whenever you struggle for direction in your life and need guidance and protection through all of the uncertainties, come to Me, and I will show you the way. In the end it will all work out; if it's not working out, *it's not the end.*

"I know the plans I have for you …"

JEREMIAH 29:11 (NLT)

Walking God's Chosen Path

I want you to come to a place where you no longer fear the unknowns of life. I want you merely trusting and resting in My will. If you will draw near to Me at all times, you can be confident that I will not allow you stray from the path I've chosen for you. I have amazing plans for you, but I need you to learn to trust Me completely with each step of faith you take.

I want you to let go of trying to control your life, and surrender to My plans and My power to bring them about. I simply want you to surrender and allow Me to work in and through you. I don't want you to struggle to understand My ways; I simply want you to trust in them. My ways are perfect.

Accept what you cannot change and trust Me to do what seems impossible, for there is nothing too difficult for Me. And know that everything will not fall apart if you simply let it go into My hands. When your life is falling to pieces, it's really just falling into place. I promise to strengthen you, to uphold you. I only ask that you seek My will, let go of your fears, and walk the path I've chosen for you by faith.

> The Lord directs our steps, so why try to
> understand everything along the way?
>
> PROVERBS 20:24 (NLT)

Fear

Fear Only God

Each and every day is filled with opportunities to be overcome with fear. The world is filled with uncertainty. I see your circumstances, and I know that that they threaten to overwhelm you. I AM your shelter from the storm and your Shepherd through the valley of the shadow of death. I AM with you always; there is nothing to fear. Lean on Me, trust in Me, and set your hopes in Me alone.

Do not be deceived by your senses. Don't take directions from the devil, and don't rely on your own strength to get you through. It is through Christ that you can do all things, not yourself. Don't believe the enemy's lies that there is no way out, no way through, and nothing can save you. If I AM with you, who or what dare be against you? Trust in My truth, which always leads you into triumph.

When you go through deep waters, I will be with you; when you pass through rivers of difficulty, they will not sweep over you. And when you must walk through fire, you will not be burned. I AM in control of all things. I alone can deliver you. Through the trials of life, I will protect you and keep you safe. Have faith in Me. It is your faith that will *always* defeat your fear. Fear Me and nothing else.

Make the Lord of Heaven's Armies holy in
your life. He is the one you should fear.
He is the one who should make you tremble.

ISAIAH 8:13 (NLT)

Faith That Drives Away Fear

Yᴏu will face situations where you are overwhelmed and thrown into despair. Despair can take you within its grip at any moment, leaving you hopeless and helpless. But regardless of the circumstances or how it originates, fear should always be conquered with faith.

Come to Me when you are full of fear, facing overwhelming unknowns, or in the midst of trouble. I AM here to release your fears and fill you with My peace. You don't need to live in fear. It will keep you from walking in faith and hold you back from My greatest blessings in your life.

Trust in My promises to you. Face your fears with the faith that is grounded in My Word. The promises that I've made you can conquer whatever battle you're facing. Trusting in My Word will take down every stronghold that challenges your faith.

When fear consumes you, come to My throne of grace and allow Me to embrace you with My love and calm you with My peace. Trust Me to help you, protect you and provide for you at all times and in all ways. There is nothing to fear, I AM here.

Don't be afraid. Just stand still and
watch the Lᴏʀᴅ rescue you today.

EXODUS 14:13 (ɴʟᴛ)

The Fear of the Lord

My desire is for you to fear Me in a way that is nothing less than an awesome awareness and understanding of My sovereignty. Your reverence of Me will produce the humility you need to walk confidently in faith, obedient to My will for your life.

I've never intended for you to be afraid of Me, unable to trust and approach Me because you're afraid you've sinned too much or frightened that you can't be forgiven. The truth will set you free from false fear and allow you to fear Me in a way that will transform your heart and soul. I will always do what is best for you; there is nothing to fear if you trust in Me completely.

Don't pay attention to the fears that keep you from experiencing My peace. Those fears will prevent you from being obedient to Me, and disobedience always brings about unhealthy fear. If you fear Me, there is no need to fear anything else.

I AM above all, sovereign. If you believe that, what is there to fear? Whatever you are going through, whatever is consuming you with anxiety, make the choice to believe instead of doubt. Choose to have faith and conquer your fear. Fear Me above all else, and I will give you peace that surpasses all understanding.

The fear of the LORD is the beginning of knowledge, but fools despise wisdom and instruction.

PROVERBS 1:7 (NIV)

A Time to Trust

Don't be surprised by the emotion of fear. You will experience fear; it's not a matter of if, but when. There are countless ways that anxiety can grab hold of you unexpectedly. Life is hard, but faith in Me will make all things possible. I use the overwhelming circumstances of your life to bring you to the end of yourself so that you will choose to trust Me. Instead of surrendering to your fears, surrender to Me. I'll rescue you and bring your heart into a place of peace and rest. Whatever it is you can't handle, I can.

When fears threaten your faith, rely on My Word. Trust in what I've promised you. I have promised you provision and protection wrapped in My grace and love. I have never abandoned you, and I never will. You can trust Me in all things. Look at your fears and then look to Me. Let nothing move you.

Stand firm in your faith and trust that in the face of impossibilities, I can do the impossible. Allow your faith to drown out your doubt. You know My love for you. You know that I AM all-powerful, above all things. Trust in what you know.

When I am afraid, I put my trust in You.

PSALM 56:3 (NIV)

Casting out Fear

Don't ever doubt that I love you. My love is not the love that judges and punishes, but rather draws you in by My grace. If you are filled with fear, you aren't receiving My love. Don't try to hide yourself from Me; I know you completely. I want you to feel safe and secure in My presence, without fear. Even when you've turned your own way into sin, don't close yourself off from Me, for that will keep you from experiencing the joy that comes from My grace.

I want you to set aside all the uncertainties and rest in My unconditional love. I have promised that nothing can separate you from My love, so don't believe otherwise. There is nothing you can do that will weaken My love or lessen My grace. There's nothing you've done to earn My love and nothing you can do to lose it. So stop doubting and simply believe what I've promised you.

When you're struggling to make sense of it all, cease reasoning and simply trust Me. My ways are far higher than yours, and My love is far greater. Nothing compares to My love, which goes beyond your understanding, so simply receive what I'm offering you—perfect love.

Such love has no fear, because perfect love expels all fear. If we are afraid, it is for fear of punishment, and this shows that we have not fully experienced His perfect love.

1 JOHN 4:18 (NLT)

First Things First

You want to know the answers to life's problems, to know exactly which step to take and which ones not to. But common sense won't give you the answers. Don't be tempted to draw conclusions about your circumstances without consulting Me. Seek Me first. Your reverent fear of Me will enable you to enter into My presence, where you can see your life through My eyes instead of your own. Without viewing your troubles from My point of view, you can never take the proper steps of faith. You need Me to guide you step by step. There is no other way to victory.

There are things you simply cannot know or understand. There is a spiritual world in which the battle rages over your life. I have secured your soul for eternity, but the battles of life will not end until you enter it. Don't rely on yourself, your own wisdom and understanding, for it will be faulty at best. Seek Me first, in a humble fear of who I AM, and I will unleash My power over anything in your life that is outside of My will. Victory will come, but you must come to Me. First things first.

The fear of the Lord is the beginning of wisdom,
and knowledge of the Holy One is understanding.

PROVERBS 9:10 (NIV)

The Battle Is the Lord's

I know it often seems like you are in a constant battle for your faith. Doubt attacks unexpectedly, and in your weakness you fail to seek My strength. As circumstances compound and there seems to be no way out, I'll make a way through. Life will get overwhelming, but there is nothing to fear—the battle is not yours—it belongs to Me.

I see you struggling when you should simply be trusting. Many of the battles you face are spiritual in nature, and you're waging war in a physical world, relying on material resources that can never win a spiritual battle. It is My supernatural power that can unleash an army against your troubles, but you must come to Me and completely rely upon Me.

You need to trust that I AM able. There is no reason to be afraid or discouraged. Everything is always under My control; it's just a matter of whether or not you truly believe that. More often than not, the battle is in your mind and you must cling to My Word as the weapon that will disarm any doubt. So don't be disillusioned by the battlefield or the army that stands before you. Whatever it is that is threatening to conquer you has no victory over Me. And if I AM for you, who or what can dare to be against you?

This is what the LORD says: "Do not be afraid!
Don't be discouraged by this mighty army,
for the battle is not yours, but God's."

2 CHRONICLES 20:15 (NLT)

Grace

It's All Free

Out of My love for you, I have given you a gift that can never be earned or repaid. My grace has set you free from the sin debt that hindered your relationship with Me and kept you from experiencing eternity with Me. Don't doubt My love for you; do not allow the enemy to cause you to question your salvation. Don't get discouraged and question what I've done, the sacrifice I've made on your behalf.

When life gets hard and you can't seem to find Me, when you are fearful that I've left you all alone, you should know that the enemy is at work in the battlefield of your mind. Don't believe the lies. Don't think that you have to prove yourself to Me or struggle to keep My grace. My grace is freely given, not based upon your feelings, but upon My love. Your salvation is safe and sure, freely given through the sacrifice of Christ. When He hung upon the Cross, He thought of you. He knew all that you have done, and made the choice to die so that you could live. It was all about you.

So stand firm in your faith when you feel like you're disappointing Me and are afraid that you might lose your place with Me for eternity. Know that I've promised that you are Mine from the moment you believed. Nothing can separate you from My love.

By grace you have been saved through faith. And this is not your own doing; it is the gift of God.

EPHESIANS 2:8 (ESV)

In Your Weakness

My grace is meant to lift you from under burdens, to assure you that I AM here to help you when you're too weak to carry on. When you remain in Me, I remain in you and you have all the strength you need to walk in faith through every unknown. Your relationship with Me is what allows you to continue to grow in your faith, learning to fully trust in Me for every detail of your life, knowing that you don't have to struggle or strive, but just stand in your faith.

I continually work in and through you to accomplish My purposes, which are always for your good and My glory. Just because you fall short of My glory doesn't mean I can't bring you into My glory. No one is perfect, not even one person. Sometimes it's your failings and shortcomings that allow Me to more powerfully work within you. When you're weak, you're in the perfect position for Me to make you strong; you're in the perfect place for Me to show you My power like never before. When you're weary, take heart. If I've overcome the world, I can overcome all the troubles in your life. I will help you. My grace is all you need.

He said, "My grace is all you need. My power works best in weakness." So now I am glad to boast about my weaknesses, so that the power of Christ can work through me.

2 CORINTHIANS 12:9 (NLT)

Just Enough Grace

My grace will be just enough for the moment you need it, nothing more and nothing less. I give you grace for each and every day of your life, but tomorrow's grace will be there tomorrow, not today. This is why I tell you not to worry about tomorrow. I want you focusing on today, this moment, where My grace is sufficient. I'm teaching you to live one day at a time, trusting in Me completely and learning to live in the peace I provide to carry you through each and every situation.

Often I see you frustrated and consumed with worry about what the day will bring, or overwhelmed with fear about all your tomorrows. Stay right here with Me, right now, and let Me carry your burdens. Be anxious for nothing. I want you to enjoy every moment of life.

I know it's a challenge to live in the moment, being confident in your faith and trusting that I will take care of every detail of your life, but I AM faithful at all times and in all ways. If you aren't living in My momentary grace, you'll miss the life I've intended for you to live. Live in My grace right now, and experience the peace that will allow you to rest in your faith and trust that I AM with you always.

"Give us this day our daily bread."

MATTHEW 6:11 (NKJV)

More and More Grace

I've given you My grace, now fully receive it. When you receive the grace I give you, I provide you more and more. So don't receive My grace in vain. I want you to clearly understand that it's no longer you that lives, but Christ in you. You now live by faith, relying on and trusting in Me completely. I've offered the sacrifice so that Christ might live in and through you—allowing you to experience the joy that is only found in Him.

It is My Spirit that helps you live in the peace of giving up the struggle and allowing Me to fight your battles so that you don't have to. Don't try to save yourself. Stop trying to do everything on your own. That's why I'm here, full of provision and power.

Come to Me. Come to My throne of grace and realize that you need Me each and every moment of your life. Trust in My promised love to you and rest in the knowledge that I have numbered every hair on your head. Every detail of your life is within My grasp. Be with Me, talk with Me, and watch Me pour down My grace more and more.

Working together with Him, then, we appeal to you not to receive the grace of God in vain.

2 CORINTHIANS 6:1 (ESV)

Lacking No Good Thing

I never want you to worry. Although life brings about challenges that awaken anxiety within you, there is no need to give in to your fears. I want you to be not only assured that I AM able to supply all your needs, but confident that I will do so. I don't want you lacking peace; I want you to be consumed by it.

There is nothing too difficult for Me. There's no mountain in your life that I can't move, lead you around, or strengthen you to scale. Regardless of My plan for the obstacles in your life, I AM with you, and that's all that matters. I want you to believe in your heart what you know in your head. I AM truly with you to care for you in every way. And nothing can separate you from My love.

My love for you is unchanging. All I ever ask is that you come to Me, that you trust in Me, and that you rest in the peace that I provide as you stand firm in your faith. You can completely rely on Me to meet every need, to care for you in every way so that you are never lacking any good thing.

Those who trust in the LORD will lack no good thing.

PSALM 34:10 (NLT)

Complete Reliance

Don't worry when you fail or fall short; it will happen more often than you'd like. I use the overwhelming circumstances of your life to help you understand that you need to completely rely on Me. I've given you special talents and abilities, but none of them can be adequately and fully utilized without My strength and power. You need Me. I want you to realize that you can't accomplish My purposes in your own strength. I never meant for you to travel through life on your own. You were always meant to walk with Me.

My goal is to use your life to accomplish impossibilities, pointing others to Me through the unbelievable works that I do through you. My desire is to have others stand in awe of your life, realizing that only I could perform the miracles they witness in your life. I want you as well as others who look upon your life to realize that they need a Savior. I want your life to be a trophy of My grace.

However, to fully receive My grace, you need to seek Me at all times and joyfully receive what I'm giving you. You need to surrender your will to Mine and allow Me to accomplish what only I can. All that you must do is walk in faith and receive My grace, completely relying on Me each and every moment of your life.

It is not that we think we are qualified to do anything on our own. Our qualification comes from God.

2 CORINTHIANS 3:5 (NLT)

Having It All

I want you to know that you can fully trust Me—that I will supply all your needs and there is no need to worry or be anxious about anything. I AM all-wise, all-powerful, and all-loving. I AM your heavenly Father, the One who watches over you each and every moment of your life.

Keep focused upon Me, not on what you're lacking. And don't try to supply your own needs. I can do far more than you can hope for or imagine. My provision for your life is perfect, while yours never will be. So rely on Me for the blessings you long for, but long for Me more than those blessings.

I want you to fully trust in Me to be the source of everything. When you're feeling as though your life is falling apart, know that it's falling into place, in My hands. The key is trusting Me in every detail of your life. It is your faith in Me that will allow you to live in a state of peace amid all the chaos. Whatever you require, I can and will provide. Seek Me first, and I'll make sure that you have all you need.

Do not be anxious about anything.

PHILIPPIANS 4:6 (NIV)

God's Love

No Greater Love

You will never fully understand love until you receive My love. I know at times you struggle to believe that I truly love you. Your circumstances make you wonder if I do. You are fearful that you've sinned and I've turned My back on you, but I could never do that. I've promised I will never forsake you, so believe it.

When you doubt My love and care for you, come back to the Cross, where I saved you and set you free from sin. My suffering was sacrificial in ways that you can never comprehend. But it was necessary to give you the life I intend for you to live.

I want you to always be certain of My unconditional, divine love for you. It's an unfailing love, even when you fail and fall short. Out of My great love for you, I have graciously made the choice to pay the price for you so that you don't have to. You didn't do anything to earn My love, and you can't do anything to lose it. Remember that I loved you completely when you were sitting in the worst of sin, in the pit of destruction, in the darkness that consumed you. My love has saved you, and I will continue to work in your life to make you more like Me.

God showed His great love for us by sending Christ to die for us while we were still sinners.

ROMANS 5:8 (NLT)

Made Alive

Whether you realize it or not, you were once dead. You lived a daily life, but the spirit within you wasn't living. It's because of My profound love for you that you now live, alive in Christ who died for you. It is because of My sacrifice, the slaying of sin in your life, that you are able to experience a glimpse of heaven through My peace and joy.

At times you may feel unworthy and unlovable, but feelings do not determine reality. You must live in the truth I've provided you, assured of your salvation and all of the promises I've made you.

The difficult situations you face in life will mislead you to believe that I'm not there and I don't care, but that's not truth. If I laid down my life to save you, why would I abandon you in your time of need?

I will never withhold any blessing in your life that is good for you. Trust that I know what I'm doing and that what I do is out of My love for you. So stand in praise, live in My presence, receive My love and rest assured in My grace.

Because of His great love for us, God, who is rich in mercy, made us alive with Christ even when we were dead in transgressions— it is by grace you have been saved.

EPHESIANS 2:4-5 (NIV)

Set Your Heart

You are so precious to Me, more than you will ever know. You were created to know Me, to walk with Me through this life and to enjoy the abundant life I desire for you to have. I don't just want you to know about Me, I want you to fully know Me, intimately. I want you to truly experience Me, and that will require you seeking Me with all your heart and soul.

You will never be able to fully grasp how deeply I love you and the amazing plans I have for your life if you do not fellowship with Me continually. Without Me, you will experience an emptiness that is inexplicable and a void that you will be unable to fill. I AM all you need to experience the peace and joy you're intended to have. You must constantly pursue Me and diligently desire a closer relationship with Me.

If you will draw near to Me, I will draw near to you. Seek My face instead of continually seeking My hand. I can and will do all things to bring about good in your life, but your focus must be on your desire to surrender yourself to Me, with complete trust. I want you to fully experience My presence and learn to rest in the shadow of My wings. Set your heart on Me and you will find comfort in My all-sufficient love that will fill you to the full.

Seek the LORD your God with all your heart and soul.

1 CHRONICLES 22:19 (NLT)

Riches of Glory

My light can flood your darkness and illuminate the confident hope I've given you. Your inheritance is My immeasurable riches, an abundant life beyond all you could dare hope for or imagine. I want to fully supply everything you need in life, but you must receive My grace without hesitation. Don't second-guess what I'm giving you. Just rejoice in praise and be sure of My great love for you.

If you need strength, I will give you strength in your weakness. If you need help in understanding, I AM all-wise. Come to Me and I will listen to you and tell you great and mighty things which you do not know. I can give you discernment and wisdom that will lead you through the toughest of trials. I AM with you always to help you through your faith, step-by-step. But I offer you so much more: peace amid the chaos, joy within the pain.

I can give you contentment in the confusion and enable you to take one more step of faith with the help of My grace. What I offer you is unchanging and cannot be exhausted. My glory is eternal. I AM all you need, and I rejoice in offering you the inheritance of My glory unconditionally, eternally.

I pray that your hearts will be flooded with light so that you can understand the confident hope He has given to those He called—His holy people who are His rich and glorious inheritance.

EPHESIANS 1:18 (NLT)

Abandoned to Love

Don't be distressed by the lack of love you receive from others that makes you feel unwanted and unworthy. My love conquers all; My love is all you need. You're always good enough in My eyes, always loved and always worthy to receive the fullness of My grace. Don't believe the lies of the enemy and others. They are not your keeper, I AM. You belong to Me, and I love you fully and unconditionally. So give up the struggle in trying to be better, and simply rest in knowing that you are loved just the way you are. But I won't leave you that way—I'll work within and through you to perfect you for eternity.

My Holy Spirit dwells within you, and you have My power living on the inside of you. There is always victory when you're trusting in Me. I make you worthy, I enable you to walk through the valley of the shadow of death because I AM with you. Whatever resources you need to accomplish the purposes I have for you, I will provide. Don't worry about the details, just walk in faith and be assured of My unchanging love for you. Though everyone else may abandon you, I never will. I will hold you close, love and comfort you, and pour My grace down upon you.

Even if my father and mother abandon me,
the LORD will hold me close.

PSALM 27:10 (NLT)

A Different Kind of Love

My love isn't anything like your own. My love challenges every emotion within you when it comes to those who are your enemies, those who cause distress and pain in your life. You will be hurt by people. The question is how you'll react to it. What will your response be in the face of an enemy? I AM asking you to respond in love, just the way I have responded to you.

I've commanded you to love your enemies, even though I know that goes against every emotion within you. See your enemies through My eyes and not your own. Know that they are souls trapped by their sins and in desperate need of deliverance. They need Jesus, just as you do. Never doubt that I can use your life to save these lost souls.

I need you to reveal Jesus to others, and though you can't change them, I can. If you respond in love, it opens the door for Me to work powerfully in the situation and move their heart. It is all about your response. And I need you to respond by letting everything you do and say be representative of Christ so that His power might work in and through you to bring about My glory. Give love and grace in the face of every situation, just as I do with you.

"To you who are willing to listen, I say, love your enemies! Do good to those who hate you."

LUKE 6:27 (NLT)

Brought to Completion

My love, the love that is unconditional and unwavering, is within you. It fills you to the full even when you feel empty. I always pour into you an extra measure of My love, so I'm asking you to freely give what I've given to you. Receive My love and then give it away. The more love you give, the more you'll receive from Me. Allow My love to flow through you into others, blessing countless lives and bringing about unthinkable glory.

You can't give away what you don't have, so you must first fully receive My grace and love. I want My love to affirm you and give you confidence that you are fully loved, but I also want you to have a heart that gives to others what they need to receive.

Those who don't know Me can experience My love through you. I know that that responsibility can sometimes be an overwhelming burden, but it will ultimately result in countless blessings in your life and in the lives of others. My goal for your faith walk is for you to walk in love. For without love you have nothing, and you were meant to live life in abundance.

No man has at any time [yet] seen God. But if we love one another, God abides (lives and remains) in us and His love (that love which is essentially His) is brought to completion (to its full maturity, runs its full course, is perfected) in us!

1 JOHN 4:12 (AMP)

Overflowing with Love

I don't want you to just survive life, but to thrive in it. You are made for My love and will be filled continually with it when you ask for it. Love does more than you think. If you'll respond to each and every situation with love, it will change everything.

I know it's difficult when you are facing challenges that tempt you to react in fear and anger, but if you deal with them in love, you will find that the outcome is always in My hands.

I haven't just asked you to love, I've commanded it. Seldom will you "feel" like responding to pain, sorrow or betrayal with love, but you must. You will have to make the choice to love just as I made the choice to give My life on your behalf. There is no greater display of My love, and that love must be shared with all those who will receive it.

I want you to be a vessel of My love, so it's vital that you receive My love each and every day. Come to Me in prayer so that you will hear My voice and know for certain that I love you. I want to fill you so that you might overflow with love into the lives of others.

Love means doing what God has commanded us,
and He has commanded us to love one another,
just as you heard from the beginning.

2 JOHN 1:6 (NLT)

Seek the Lord

Simply Wait

I know it's difficult when you pray and nothing seems to be happening. When what you desire is unattainable, I do the impossible, so all you must do is simply wait in faith. Nothing can prevent My promises from being performed. I AM all-powerful. Though My promises may be delayed, they are never denied.

No matter how long it takes, no matter how things might seem, be assured that I AM faithful to fulfill every one of My promises to you. I have never and will never forget you, leaving you in the midst of peril. Every moment that your prayer is not answered is an opportunity for you to draw closer to Me and to learn to trust Me in greater ways than you have before.

The work of My Spirit within you will create a strong, courageous soul that endures until the end. Simply pray for patience and strength as you wait upon My hand to move in your life. I AM a ready help in times of trouble. Call to Me and I will answer you, lean on Me and I will give you all the strength and patience you need to obtain the blessings you seek.

> Wait for the Lord; be strong and
> take heart and wait for the Lord.
>
> PSALM 27:14 (NIV)

Waiting Quietly

Your worry comes from your lack of trust in My timing for the blessings I have in store for you. Each one is precisely orchestrated, and it's necessary at times that you wait, quietly and assured that My answers to your prayers will happen at the precise moment I see best. While you wait, I want you to embrace the blessing of My presence. Just be with Me.

Don't give in to the temptation to move ahead without Me. Rest in your faith and trust that I will show you the next step whenever the timing is right. I will provide guidance for you just as I do your "daily bread." I will always give you just enough grace for the moment, and you will need to depend upon Me for the next moment's grace. This is by design. I want you to learn to rest in Me, trusting Me for your every need.

I don't want you to be anxious or concerned about the past, present or future. I just want you to be content in the moment you're in, knowing that I have everything under control and I AM ALWAYS sovereign. There is never a moment when I have let you go, and I never will. Just stop, look and listen for My guidance as I lead you into My very best for your life.

I wait quietly before God, for my victory comes from Him.

PSALM 62:1 (NLT)

Seek My Wisdom

Each and every day you have countless decisions to make that could ultimately change your life's course. I never want you to rush into decisions and move ahead of discerning My wisdom. I know at times you feel an urgent need for quick guidance, but don't move forward blindly without seeking My advice.

You'll notice that the enemy wants you to be impatient, to move ahead quickly and he encourages you to act instantly, but his desire is to rush you into a destructive path. If you'll wait on Me, seeking My Word and diligently listening for My voice, you will make better choices and avoid the pit of destruction. I will always lead you down the path that is best for your life.

I need you to be willing to listen to Me persistently and patiently. When you continually come into My presence and wait patiently upon Me, you are stretching your faith, strengthening it in more ways than you can imagine. I have promised that when you call upon Me I will answer, and I will. I may not answer you right away, or give you all the details at that moment, but I will lead you step by step. So trust Me, wait upon Me, and allow My joy to be your strength.

"The seeds that fell on the good soil represent honest, good-hearted people who hear God's word, cling to it, and patiently produce a huge harvest."

LUKE 8:15 (NLT)

Looking for Help in the Right Place

I know sometimes it seems as though the world is against you, as if you are helpless and powerless in the face of the war waged against you. But I am a ready help. Instead of struggling to survive, offer up praise through prayer. I will always move My hand for the heart that is loyal to Mine. Know that you need Me and Me alone, because you'll never survive the battle on your own.

It may seem like defeat is inevitable, but I do the impossible and the victory is always Mine. Don't allow the enemy to dishearten you. The only thing you need to do is to stay focused upon Me, assured that I AM your help. I will provide all you need as you walk through the battles of life in faith.

Realize that you are not able to handle the situations of your life without Me, and rest in the knowledge that as you rely upon Me through each and every moment, I AM working all things together for good. Even when you can't see that I'm at work, I AM. Regardless of your circumstances, I can and will help you. Trust Me to do the impossible, and wait patiently while staying focused upon My faithfulness.

We are powerless against this mighty army that is about to attack us. We do not know what to do, but we are looking to You for help.

2 CHRONICLES 20:12 (NLT)

Trust My Timing

I don't ever want you to forget that My ways are not your own, and neither is My timing for the blessings in your life. The answers to your prayers may be delayed, but they are not denied. I may not work out your life the way you hope, but I will work all things together for good. In the end you will clearly see, but in this present moment you have limited, finite understanding. Trust that I know what I AM doing.

You tend to think in temporal terms, but My plans are eternal. You want immediate results that can sometimes "feel" like the best way, but often your emotions get in the way of discerning that My ways are always best. And typically that means you'll have to wait longer than you'd like.

Because I love you, I must be patient and deliberate in all that I do. I hear your prayers, and I know you'd rather Me work immediately, answering your supplications, but that is not always what is best. I love you too much to give in to your pleadings if they are not ultimately what is best for you. I need you to trust Me and My timing, for without doing so, you'll never experience the satisfaction and enjoyment of life that I intend for you.

My times are in Your hands; deliver
me from the hands of my enemies,
from those who pursue me.

PSALM 31:15 (NIV)

Confident Hope

Here's the key to experiencing the fullness of My joy: put your hope in Me and My unfailing love. Don't forget how to hope, and never allow doubt to deter you from fully trusting in Me. Others may fail you, but I never will. Put your hope in Me alone.

No matter what situations you face, what obstacles threaten to keep you from moving forward in faith, you can know that I've prepared a way that will lead you into victory. There may be difficulties to deal with and losses to endure, but ultimately I will lead you into great blessings that will transform your heart and soul.

I want you to have a heavenly hope, assured that I will meet your every need, fulfill every desire that is within My will for you, and satisfy you with My joy. Rely on Me completely, be content and confident even though the darkness closes in and it's hard to find the light of day. I AM with you in your darkest, most desperate moments to be your help, to protect you, to offer you mercy and to fill you with My loving-kindness. Simply rest in faith and confidently wait upon Me.

Our inner selves wait [earnestly] for the Lord;
He is our Help and our Shield. For in Him does
our heart rejoice, because we have trusted
(relied on and been confident) in His holy name.
Let Your mercy and loving-kindness,
O Lord, be upon us, in proportion to our
waiting and hoping for You.

PSALM 33:20-22 (AMP)

Strength

Quiet Confidence

You need Me. You become frustrated and restless in your heart because you have a yearning for Me to help you. You need to rely on My presence and provision instead of relying on yourself. Don't allow your faith to fail when the details of your life don't play out exactly as you expected. Life will go according to My plan if you'll trust Me to lead you step by step in your walk of faith.

I don't expect you to handle the situations in your life by yourself, relying on your own resources; they are grossly limited at best. You please Me when you fully rely on Me, not looking to what you can do, but what I can do. I need you to refuse to worry and let go of the struggle. Rest in Me. My devotion and love for you is perfect and unconditional, so you can always come to Me, no matter what situations you face.

Return to Me each day, approaching My throne of mercy and grace. I have all that you need. My power can overcome all the impossibilities you'll ever face. I need you to simply come to Me and allow your faith to destroy the doubt so that you can live moment by moment in quiet confidence.

> "Only in returning to Me and resting in Me will you be saved. In quietness and confidence is your strength."
>
> ISAIAH 30:15 (NLT)

Searching for Strength

You may have had strength yesterday, but today you find yourself weak and unable to hope in anything. You struggle to find Me when you need Me and can't understand why I'm not answering when you call upon Me. But there is no reason for you to question My presence or My provision. I AM with you always, through My Word, which holds every promise you'll need to overcome any obstacle. My promises should be your inspiration and reassurance as you wait for mountains to move and miracles to happen.

Simply seek Me when you're not sure of what to do or which direction to go. When you need strength, I will supply you with all you need. Walking in My strength and not your own will enable you to overcome the weariness that the struggles of life brings. It is through My Word that you will find strength and the direction you need for every situation you face. You will need to carefully obey My Word, following My instructions for your life without hesitation. Whatever it is I lead you to do through My Word, know that I will be with you every step of the way, giving you all the strength you need while encouraging you and providing you with the peace you need to rest in My care.

Search for the LORD and for His strength; continually seek Him.

PSALM 105:4 (NLT)

Waiting with Hope

You need to continually keep focused on Me so you can follow the guidance and direction I provide. There will be countless distractions that blur your vision and distort the truth, so you will need to constantly remain in Me so that I can direct you specifically into My will.

Sometimes it seems like there must be another way. You perceive your weakness and struggles as an indication that you're moving in the wrong direction. I know you want instant answers and immediate relief, but you must always remember that My ways are not your own—My ways are better. There will be times when I will make you wait. I'm building your faith, drawing you near, preparing you for a greater revelation of My presence, power and provision than you can imagine. It is during these times that I am perfecting your faith so you will come to depend upon Me more.

You will stretch your trust in Me further than you ever imagined you could or would, and you'll see that I bring good out of everything you endure. Don't allow your past to taint the promises I've given you for your future. I've promised to give you a future and a hope. Wait on Me, rely on Me for strength when you are weak, and your faith will soar.

Yet, the strength of those who wait with hope in the LORD will be renewed. They will soar on wings like eagles. They will run and won't become weary. They will walk and won't grow tired.

ISAIAH 40:31 (GW)

Strengthened and Blessed

In this world you will have trouble, and I know that even the knowledge of that truth doesn't help to endure all that you must. You have nothing to fear, for I will surely help you. I AM greater than any obstacle you will ever face and I AM able to do the impossible in any and every situation. Hold tight to Me during the tough times of your life and walk confidently forward in your faith. Don't give in to the doubt.

I may ask you to endure great hardship, but I will enable you to do so. I will give you strength through the hard times and increase your strength for the future by them. Don't doubt My presence when your pain becomes too much to bear, but rather surrender it all to Me and I will bless you with My peace.

You must continually pray, entering into My presence and receiving the grace that I will give you for the moment you need it. It is My promises to you that will enable you to have hope when all hope seems gone, and strengthen you to trust when you're suddenly consumed with doubt. Know that I walk with you. I will revive you, stretching forth My hand to save you. When you seek Me, I will quiet you with My love as you stand firm in your faith.

The Lord gives His people strength.
The Lord blesses them with peace.

PSALM 29:11 (NLT)

Strong and Not Discouraged

I have commanded you to be strong, and I would never ask you to do something that you are not capable of. But sometimes you will not feel like being strong. You will struggle as the battle intensifies and your resources may seem to be running out. You must choose to be strong, setting your gaze upon Me, and resting upon My promises.

Your choice to be strong in your faith will rest on your assurance that I AM with you and I AM for you. Your eyes of faith will help you to see the hopeful path I set before you and will enable you to take a step of faith when the darkness closes in. If you will continually look to Me and rely on Me, you will constantly find increased strength.

As you choose to be strong, you will need to refuse to worry and be discouraged. You'll need to remind yourself that I AM full of surprises. I AM never limited, for I AM all-powerful. Each and every prayer you pray is one step closer to your breakthrough. As you wait upon Me, you'll come to have a fuller understanding of My love for you. You'll gain a greater awareness of My presence and come to better understand My unconditional and boundless love for you. Quietly wait, be strong, and you will experience unexpected blessings.

"This is My command—be strong and courageous!
Do not be afraid or discouraged. For the LORD
your God is with you wherever you go."

JOSHUA 1:9 (NLT)

Trusting in the Face of Loss

I love to bless you both unexpectedly and in ways that are direct answers to your prayers. Know that I give and I take away; but when I take away it is for reasons that may be beyond your ability to comprehend. You must trust Me.

I know that when life is difficult and you're struggling to carry on, it's difficult to trust Me. It is easy to doubt My love for you when you experience loss. It is possible to be sorrowful, yet always rejoicing. So rejoice in the midst of uncertainty and doubt. Rejoice that I AM with you. Know that it is through your hardships that you will find the secret of being joyful in all situations. I will empower you to find joy in the midst of adversity; I will give you strength in your weakness.

No matter how difficult life's situations, I AM able to give you peace in the midst of it all. There is no reason to be afraid, for I AM with you. Nothing is too difficult for Me, and nothing you're facing poses a threat to My good purposes for your life. I need you to let go of whatever it is I'm asking you to. I need you to believe that loss is but for gain when you're trusting in Me. Know with all confidence that I'm taking you into glory.

"Be strong and courageous. Do not be afraid or terrified because of them, for the Lord your God goes with you; He will never leave you nor forsake you."

DEUTERONOMY 31:6 (NIV)

Strong in Spirit

Your spirit may grow weak, but I will remain the strength of your heart; I AM yours forever. I don't want you to be weighed down by yesterday or feel despair about tomorrow, because My grace is sufficient for today. In this moment, I AM with you. I want you to begin each day by seeking to please Me and walking in My ways. Focus on this moment, in My presence, and rest in knowing that you are safe and secure in My care.

Focusing upon the now, trusting in Me in this very moment, will transform your spirit and strengthen you in countless ways. I want you to understand that this life will be filled with problems and pain, but by completely relying on Me and believing in My promises to you, you are able to take this journey with joy and peace.

My Word will renew you, My Spirit is alive within you, and My grace is sufficient. Take courage in the midst of fear and know for certain that I AM with you, so there is no need to be discouraged. It may feel like your life is falling apart, but it's simply falling into place—into My plans. Don't lose heart; draw near to Me in your fear and allow Me to renew you day by day.

For this reason we never become discouraged. Even though our physical being is gradually decaying, yet our spiritual being is renewed day after day.

2 CORINTHIANS 4:16 (GNT)

Joy

Joy-Filled

My desire is to fill you with joy and peace. In receiving My grace, I fill you with My Spirit, who will enable My joy and peace to freely flow through you. Simply come into My presence and rest in Me. I will supply you with everything you need and strengthen you with My joy.

Search for Me at all times and in all circumstances. I will be your peace as you trust in Me. I will never fail you. It may seem like it, but I see your life from beginning to end, not just the moment that is consuming you with fear. As your faith presses through your fear, you will find a joy that is unspeakable.

I AM the God of hope. Hope in that truth and be certain of what I've promised you. My hope is the foundation of your joy. Life will be filled with trials and troubles, but I prepare a way through it all that leads to victory. I want you to live each moment of your life filled with faith and joy, resting in My promises. I want you to take comfort in knowing that I AM with you to rescue you and to give you a future and a hope. When you are weak, simply allow Me to fill you with My joy and you will have all the strength you need to take the next step of faith.

"Don't be dejected and sad, for the joy of the LORD is your strength!"

NEHEMIAH 8:10 (NLT)

Joyful in Hope

I will give you My Spirit of wisdom and revelation. As I open the eyes of your heart, you will be enlightened, so that you will know the hope that I give you. I want you to be joyful in hope. Not hope in a particular outcome to your circumstances, but a simple, resting hope in Me. True joy will come from hoping in Me, so don't place your hope elsewhere.

You have an inheritance that should fill you with unspeakable joy—the inheritance of My glorious riches. You are a co-heir with Me through your acceptance of Christ as your Savior. The blessing of the sacrifice was for you to live in joy, now, even in the midst of uncertainty. There is nothing to fear. I know that sometimes your life's circumstances make it difficult for you to be joyful, but you can choose joy as you trust in the hope you have in Me.

When your life seems to be falling apart around you, know that I AM holding the pieces together, so you can live each moment in peace, without doubt and despair. You must simply accept My grace. Know that your hope will not be cut off; I will give you a future and a hope. There is nothing you can do to earn that blessing of My grace and nothing you can do to lose it. Just be joyful in hope, patient in affliction, and faithful in prayer.

Rejoice in our confident hope.
Be patient in trouble, and keep on praying.

ROMANS 12:12 (NLT)

Choosing Joy

Even in a broken world, filled with pain and sorrow, you can expect to experience joy if you remain in Me and I remain in you. Don't allow anxiety to steal your joy. Your despair comes from not completely trusting in Me, but in yourself. I want you to cease your striving and simply be still and know that I AM God.

Right now you can choose to have joy; not necessarily rejoicing in your circumstances, but simply in knowing that I have a perfect plan for your life. You can choose joy here and now, even as life is unraveling and as fear threatens your faith. I am your refuge and your strength, and no matter what lies ahead, I have gone before you, preparing the way for your faith to take sight.

When doubts about My love for you consume you with fear, cling to My Word, the promises I've made you, and I will fill you with joy and peace that surpasses all understanding. Life won't always go according to your plan, but it will always, ultimately go according to Mine. I AM sovereign; nothing is out of My control and you are never beyond My boundless grace.

Blessed are the people to whom such blessings fall! Blessed are the people whose God is the LORD!

PSALM 144:15 (ESV)

An Opportunity for Joy

Life can be compounded with problems that leave you with little joy and even less faith. Come to Me immediately when you're seeking solutions. Too often you seek resources other than Me, things that can never help you through the obstacles you face. If you focus too much on seeking solutions, instead of seeking Me, you'll fall beneath the weight of your problems and darkness will come closing in. Don't let your difficulties get the better of you. Remember that I AM with you in the midst of all you must face, and I will work all things for good.

The adversities you're facing right now are an opportunity for you to fully know My presence and power, and for Me to show you specifically how I bring good out of evil. When you're filled with doubt and fear, pray to Me. Let go of your feelings and emotions and simply rest in Me.

As you rest in My presence, I will give you a greater perspective of your situation and fill you with peace to trust Me completely. If you'll stay focused upon Me, every trouble you face will become an opportunity for great joy and you'll find your faith growing in ways you never imagined. Faith is never faith until it's tested, so seize the opportunity for joy, even in your doubt.

Dear brothers and sisters, when troubles of any kind come your way, consider it an opportunity for great joy. For you know that when your faith is tested, your endurance has a chance to grow.

JAMES 1:2-3 (NLT)

Always Joyful

I know that it's not easy to be joyful when life gets hard and is continually leaving you empty. But these circumstances in your life are precisely designed to remind you that you are to have complete and constant dependence upon Me. You were never meant to be self-sufficient. Your joy depends on your dependence upon Me.

I want you to be joyful always and pray continually. There is always joy in My presence. Calling out to Me and sitting at My throne of grace will remind you that I will never leave you or forsake you. You can rest in My peace and count on My grace to find you right where you are. When you are continually praying to Me, you show a deliberate dependence upon Me, which moves My heart and My hand.

While you pray and study My Word, seek out the promises I've made to you so that your mind can be transformed. It is through My promises that you can live each moment assured that I AM with you and for you. My joy, which is your strength, will keep you from living in fear and being dismayed. I want you to simply delight yourself in Me and know that your faith glorifies Me, bringing about every good blessing in your life.

Always be joyful.

1 THESSALONIANS 5:16 (NLT)

Finding Joy

There's a time to rejoice … always. Each and every moment, I want you to choose joy. Life can become increasingly dark and painful, but the light of My presence illuminates the joy in pain and healing in the hurt. My light shines brightest in the darkness and My strength is best shown in your weakness. So find joy as your faith collides with your fears; trust Me for the miracles in your life.

No matter how difficult life becomes, you can still have joy. That in itself is a miracle. I will not always powerfully intervene in the timing you want and in the way you seek. I'm asking you to trust Me so that you might have a greater revelation of who I AM, enabling you to have greater faith.

Through your prayers and your praise I AM able to open your heart and allow you to see your circumstances outside of your limited vision. Things seem to be going wrong instead of right and you find it difficult to look up when everything is dragging you down. But in the midst of troubles, choose to be joyful. Drown out your doubts by digging deep into My Word. Allow My promises to transform your mind, to give you peace in the midst of the chaos, and joy in Me alone.

Blessed are the people who know how
to praise You. They walk in the light
of Your presence, O LORD. They find
joy in Your name all day long. They
are joyful in Your righteousness.

PSALM 89:15-16 (GW)

Overwhelmed by Great Things

You'll need to focus on My unfailing love for you as you face troubles in your life that tempt you to doubt. I AM your God yesterday, today and forever. I will care for you until the very end, until you see Me face to face. I AM with you. Rejoice in that alone.

There is no need to worry about the future if I'm the One leading and guiding you. Every obstacle you face is driving you to Me and making you more aware of your need to be dependent on Me for your hopes and desires. Don't allow your difficulties to cause you to doubt; just rest in your dependence upon Me. I will provide you with all you need. All you need is Me.

Don't be anxious, just pray and talk to Me about your deepest desires and the hurts of your heart. As you trust Me to heal your wounds and answer your prayers, stand firm in your faith and hold on to the hope I give you. Allow My peace to comfort you as you wait upon Me to overwhelm you with great things. And be continually filled with joy.

The Lord has done great things for us,
and we are filled with joy.

PSALM 126:3 (NIV)

Obedience

Active Listening

My desire is that you would constantly draw near to Me, continually growing stronger in your faith and depending upon Me more and more. If I AM going to lead and guide you, I need you to completely rely on My Word so that I can direct you down the path that is straight and narrow. I'm not asking you to be obedient for any other reason than that I love you, and your obedience shows Me that you love Me, too.

Your spiritual growth will occur when you apply what I've told you to your everyday life, when you're actively listening to My Word. I'm the One who has saved you, and I want to continue to save you. I know exactly what you need and how to develop your faith in a way that is long-lasting. Trust Me to teach you My ways through My Word, so that you might experience the great blessings I have planned for you.

I want you to be constantly listening for My voice. There will be times when I will use various resources to draw you into a particular place in My Word that I want to use to speak to you. So be alert and on watch for Me to show you a particular Scripture to specifically guide you. And when you hear My voice, be obedient and walk in faith.

Do what God's word says.
Don't merely listen to it.

JAMES 1:22 (GW)

Obeying the Voice

It is right now, in your doubt and disbelief, that I need you to trust in Me. You need My help to take each step of faith you must make—you were never meant to walk through this life alone. I have a way I've made for you, and it's vital that you obey My every command.

There will be times when you cannot see what lies ahead. Even in the very next moments, you'll need to have the assurance that I AM with you and that I've gone before you. You are to find hope in Me because I am caring for you constantly. I want you to simply enjoy our walk together, focusing upon My voice and listening to all that I will tell you.

If you focus on Me instead of your problems, you'll find that I will fix them in ways that can only be attributed to My power. Through the desperate situations where you must rely on Me, you'll find your faith establishing a firmer foundation.

This life is to affirm your trust in Me. I've eternally saved you, but I want to save you day by day. I want you to have a marvelous revelation of My presence and My boundless love for you. So do not despair, don't be disturbed. Simply hope in Me, listen to Me, and walk in the way I will show you. Rely on Me and My blessings are sure to follow you all the days of your life.

Who is among you that fears the LORD, that
obeys the voice of His servant, that walks
in darkness and has no light? Let him trust
in the name of the LORD and rely on his God.

ISAIAH 50:10 (NASB)

Closer and Closer

Whenever you start to feel stressed and overwhelmed by the troubles of life, draw closer to Me. Allow the times of despair to drive you deeper into your faith and closer to Me. Your prayers need not be spectacular. A simple "help me" is all I need to hear, so that I might strengthen you and fill you with peace. Your requests speak volumes to Me as I prepare My answers to your pleading heart.

Your troubles should be reminders to draw near to Me and listen carefully to My voice. This is why you can rejoice in trials, because you are able to fully experience My presence and My provision in ways you might otherwise never have been able to.

Turn your problems into prayers and the Holy Spirit will guide you into the path I've prepared for you to take. Stand upon My Word and your battle is won. Know that if you'll completely rely upon Me, I will teach you My ways and lead you on a path that leads to victory. So when you encounter trials, know that they have no power over My own. My Word should assure you of My unfailing love; it should remind you to trust in Me completely. I've never failed you and I never will.

So place yourselves under God's authority.
Resist the devil, and he will run away from you.
Come close to God, and He will come close
to you. Clean up your lives, you sinners,
and clear your minds, you doubters.

JAMES 4:7-8 (GW)

Remembering Your First Love

In all you do, put Me first. It may sound simple, but I know how easily life can get overwhelming and how quickly you can get distracted from focusing on Me. In a moment's notice your priorities shift and you forget your "first love". I AM all you need when you're in need.

Don't justify the error of your ways, simply seek Me and allow Me to guide you back onto the path I intended for you to be on. I want you to live purposefully, allowing Me to direct your steps, leading you from glory to glory. Make your relationship with Me your top priority at all times and everything in your life will fall into its proper place.

I want you to delight yourself in Me so that I might give you the desires of your heart. You must walk in the light as I AM in the light so that we might fellowship with one another. Don't allow the troubles of life to take away your trust in Me. Don't allow yourself to worry about tomorrow, for today has enough troubles of its own. Just prioritize our relationship, listen to My still, small voice and obey My every word. If you will, you'll live the abundant life you were intended to live—full of hope, joy and peace.

> Seek His will in all you do, and He
> will show you which path to take.
>
> PROVERBS 3:6 (NLT)

Finding the Way

I AM the One who will lead and guide you along the paths you're to take. Each and every step will be directed by Me, full of My love and wisdom, with My very best in mind for your life. Don't look back. Look up right where you are, and I will help you find the way for your future.

I see you hopeful at some times and hopeless at others, struggling to hear My voice and fearful of what lies ahead. The paths you take on your own will always lead to disappointment. It's vital that you rely on Me to give you direction. I know how hard the journey is, which is why I walk with you, step by step. The wisest thing you can do is trust Me, no matter what. The distractions of life can lead you astray and you can so easily give in to fear instead of standing firm in your faith.

If you'll trust Me, I will lead you along the right path. Your limited perspective can cloud your vision and keep you from walking forward in faith and trusting in Me. You become paralyzed by trying to understand everything I do, when you seldom will. Just rest, trust in My guidance and walk in the way I will show you.

The LORD directs our steps, so why try to understand everything along the way?

PROVERBS 20:24 (NLT)

Letting Go of the Struggle

I know it seems effortless to trust Me when life seems to be going well. The challenge comes when life isn't going so well and you're struggling to have any faith at all—a mustard-seed size seems even too big to muster. Yet faith calls you to trust in Me at all times, regardless of the circumstances of your life. I need you to trust in Me unconditionally.

I AM absolutely unchanging, My faithfulness does not change with your circumstances, so don't allow your faith to waver with them. You were never meant to bear the weight of your problems; I will carry them for you. Your worries can so easily weigh you down, and you desperately need to let go of the struggle. Don't allow your troubles to throw you into a pit of despair. Look for My light in the darkness.

My ways are higher than your own, and they are far beyond understanding. So don't try to make sense of what I do, simply trust in My Word and know that everything is under My control. If you'll lean on Me, trusting in the promises I've made you, I assure you there are great blessings ahead.

Trust the LORD with all your heart, and
do not rely on your own understanding.

PROVERBS 3:5 (GW)

Taking Thoughts Captive

My hope is an anchor for your soul. Your hope in Me will keep your faith firm and secure. Though the storms of your life rage, your spirit can be at peace, confident and calm that I AM with you and there is nothing to fear.

But your thoughts can stir up a storm and create a tidal wave of doubt within you as you struggle with the daily issues of life. You'll be tempted, amid the tempest, to doubt what I've promised you, to question what I've said. But My Word is truth, and you must rely on it at all times so that your emotions do not determine your course.

Any thought that causes doubt, despair or fear must be made obedient to My Word. Overcome the feelings that are draining you in defeat by replacing them with My promises. Doubt and faith cannot co-exist, so fuel your faith with the fire of My Word and allow it to transform your thoughts, making them obedient to Me.

Let nothing move you and tempt you to venture off course. Your faith will overcome your feelings if you're believing what I've promised you. Simply trust in Me, rest under the shadow of My wings, and I'll lead you safely through the journey, protecting you, providing for you, and giving you all the grace you'll need along the way.

We demolish arguments and every
pretension that sets itself up against the
knowledge of God, and we take captive
every thought to make it obedient to Christ.

2 CORINTHIANS 10:5 (NIV)

Patience

Receiving the Promise

Don't ever give up. Don't allow the feeling of hopelessness to dictate your faith. Doubt will come, but faith does not walk by sight. I know that it is hard to endure, even momentarily, the troubles of this world, but your struggle will yield greater faith if you continue to trust in Me.

There will be times when you'll want to quit, to cease struggling and give in to despair, but you cannot. You must make the choice to turn to Me in utter dependence, surrendering all that you are. I hear your prayers, I know exactly what you need, and I know that you get weary in the waiting. But I can intervene at any given moment. Your miracle has not passed you by. I AM full of surprises, able to do the impossible. Don't forget that truth.

I have not left you. I AM always with you and I will show Myself mightily on your behalf if you will simply endure patiently. Wait for Me, and allow Me to be your strength. You will receive My promises to you, you will experience great rewards if you will faithfully endure. Though you grow weary, trust in Me, obey Me, and I will move heaven and earth to fulfill the desires of your heart.

Don't lose your confidence. It will bring you a great reward. You need endurance so that after you have done what God wants you to do, you can receive what He has promised.

HEBREWS 10:35-36 (GW)

Watching in Hope

You may feel helpless, but hope is not gone. No matter how things appear, I AM your Savior and your God. I AM the God who saves, so you must put your hope confidently in Me.

My plans and purposes may not always be clear to you. You may not be able to see the work I AM doing in your circumstances, behind the scenes of your life. So you must trust Me, walking in faith. Don't grow weary in the waiting. Simply watch, expectantly, and your faith will be rewarded in My perfect timing and in My perfect way.

Trust that I hear you, that I AM with you and will intercede to answer every one of your prayers. Slowly but surely, you will begin to see evidence of My work in the situations of your life. I need you to believe that I AM with you in the midst of your doubt and disbelief. Find your hope in Who I AM.

I want you to have peace and rest in My calming presence, knowing that as you trust in Me, I will sustain you. Watch for Me and wait for Me. I will always help you in your weakness, and when you're too weary to even pray, My Spirit will intercede for you, expressing your heart to Me in ways that you cannot. I have made you and I will carry you. My grace is all you need.

As for me, I look to the LORD for help.
I wait confidently for God to save me,
and my God will certainly hear me.

MICAH 7:7 (NLT)

Waiting Expectantly

I know that it's hard to wait when your life's circumstances are consuming you with despair and you've lost all hope. But just as the darkness of the night yields, in due time, to the dawn, all of your desperation will soon give way to overwhelming joy. You can count on Me to bring light into the darkness.

You will need to learn to expectantly wait, to count on Me. I know it seems as though there is no light at the end of the tunnel, as if your problems will never be resolved, but My promises give you a reason to hope. My Word will light your way. You must watch and wait, confident that at any moment My grace will break through and your situation will change in an instant.

My miracles happen suddenly, without warning. I can immediately bring joy from pain and release you from the despair that binds you. So you must wait on Me, putting your hope in My Word. More than watchmen wait for the morning, you must wait on Me, and you will see My righteousness. Trust that I can and will do exceedingly abundantly above all you can ask or think. I will be your everlasting light and I will be your glory.

I am counting on the Lord; yes, I am counting on Him. I have put my hope in His word. I long for the Lord more than sentries long for the dawn, yes, more than sentries long for the dawn.

PSALM 130:5-6 (NLT)

Persevering Faith

I know that fear tempts you to doubt when problems linger longer than you ever expected them to and I'm not answering quickly enough to secure your hope. But don't judge your day by your circumstances or your expectations about them. Simply rejoice in Me continually so that you might have persevering faith.

Keep focused on Me instead of your problems or your faith will easily fail. Your hope must be consistent, grounded in My Word that provides you with the peace and strength you need as you take steps of faith into the unknown. And you'll need to praise through your problems and worship through your worry. Thank Me in everything, expressing gratitude even when you don't feel thankful.

If you are joyful in hope, patient in affliction and faithful in prayer, the blessings to follow are countless. Even in the midst of your despair, you can focus upon Me, rejoicing and being glad at heart continually. You can always be thankful for My steadfast love. Lift up your soul to Me and know that I will lead, guide and protect you at all times and all ways.

Let me hear of Your unfailing love each morning, for I am trusting You. Show me where to walk, for I give myself to You.

PSALM 143:8 (NLT)

Never Give Up

I see your faith in My promises, and I know the doubt that arises as you must wait for their fulfillment longer than you feel is necessary. You struggle with your faith because you're afraid that you're falsely hoping and time seems to be running out—but it is not. I am always perfectly on time and My miracles are never late.

My delays are not denials, so don't give up, though there seems to be no hope in sight. You won't see My miracles coming. I act suddenly, without warning. So keep praying and keep hoping in faith, no matter how long it takes. Every delay in the answers to your prayers is an opportunity for you to trust Me to a greater degree, to strengthen your faith and gain a greater revelation of My faithfulness.

Know that I will use these challenging times of waiting to work within your faith and create a firmer foundation to carry you through the difficult roads that lie ahead. I will never forget you or forsake you, so you are not waiting in vain. Allow My grace to consume you, My love to comfort you, My help to strengthen you, and My peace to enable you to rest and wait—help is on the way.

Let us not grow weary of doing good, for in
due season we will reap, if we do not give up.

GALATIANS 6:9 (ESV)

Patient and Established

I know it's hard to understand why My timing rarely matches your own. The hurried world demands instant answers and gratification. But I have eternity in mind. My plans aren't temporary, but long-term. I know that it's difficult not to live by your feelings. I know you are constantly tempted to walk by sight and not by faith. But immediate answers aren't always what is best for you, and I want this in every area of your life.

I can't allow My blessings for you to be born prematurely. I want My miracles in your life to be properly prepared, carefully orchestrated so that the fullness of them will take effect. Trust that I see and understand what you cannot always see and understand.

I want you to put aside your tendencies to try and figure out your situations—a practice that easily frustrates you. Trying to grasp what is only within My power will only lead to despair. If you'll trust Me to work all things together for good, and if you'll cease striving, you can rest, knowing that I am preparing you for My plans, to give you a future and a hope. Just be patient, and establish your heart to wait expectantly for Me.

You also, be patient. Establish your hearts,
for the coming of the Lord is at hand.

JAMES 5:8 (ESV)

Strengthened with All Power

Your worries seem to drown out your worship, and I see your soul needing to be refreshed. You must come to Me, allowing Me to give you rest from being heavy laden and overburdened. I can carry what you cannot. I don't want you to be anxious, struggling with your faith. I want you to have rest for your soul no matter how difficult life becomes.

You will never be able to be patient or at rest in your faith if you are not completely trusting in Me. You tend to trust Me *for* things, but not *in* things. I need you to let Me be God. Realize, as you wait upon Me to answer your prayers, that you're going to have to trust Me in the waiting times. It is impossible to find rest for your soul unless you trust Me completely, no matter what. If you're trusting Me to be at work in your circumstances, then you'll have a peace that surpasses all understanding.

Realize that you lack the resources and vision to solve every problem in your life. You'll need to continually surrender the big things and small things to Me. Realize that your dependence upon Me is not making you vulnerable to anything other than My profound miracles in your life. Wait patiently, and let My joy be your strength as you do.

May you be strengthened with all power,
according to His glorious might, for
all endurance and patience with joy.

COLOSSIANS 1:11 (ESV)

Worry

Watching Your Worries

Y ou need to know that I care for you affectionately and care about you watchfully ... and that includes all your worries. Worrying can be a stronghold that will cause your faith to fail. Worrying is a habit that's not easily broken, but all things are possible with Me, and through My help and strength you can do ALL things—even stop worrying.

You need to be willing to give up your worries, trusting that there is nothing to worry about when I'm in charge. Worry can do nothing but steal your peace and keep you from enjoying your life as you're supposed to. I want you to rest, live in peace and enjoy each and every moment while I work to solve all of your problems, big and small.

Everything is within My control, but worry shows that you think there are some things that are not. When you worry, you're continually allowing your mind to revolve around your problems and you're constantly searching for answers that only I have. Pray for help with your worrying, ultimately choosing to focus upon Me instead of your problems. When you refuse to worry, trusting completely in Me, you are releasing Me to go to work and move heaven and earth to help you.

Casting the whole of your care [all your anxieties, all your worries, all your concerns, once and for all] on Him, for He cares for you affectionately and cares about you watchfully.

1 PETER 5:7 (AMP)

Always with You

I want you to trust Me. Beyond trusting Me *for* something, I want you to trust Me to simply be with you, helping you *through* … not always out. I want you to look to Me not only for the results you desire, but with a faith that simply desires Me.

In the midst of your requests, your prayers that are full of wants and needs, I want you to realize that I can give you all these things, but they are not always best. Many times I simply want to show you that I can take you through things instead of always bailing you out. You need to know that I will not always rescue you out of your circumstances, but I'll be with you through them, providing all that you need. If you truly trust Me, you can live your life, even through trials and troubles, with joy and peace.

I simply want you to maintain an attitude of faith, filled with praise and positive expectation. There is no blessing that I will withhold from you. You can trust in My perfect timing. There is nothing to fear, for I AM always with you. I'll forever guide you and comfort you, just believe that I will. Find peace in knowing that I AM in control, so you don't have to be.

Yes, though I walk through the [deep, sunless]
valley of the shadow of death, I will fear or
dread no evil, for You are with me;
Your rod [to protect] and Your staff
[to guide], they comfort me.

PSALM 23:4 (AMP)

Conquering Worry with Faith

Too often your worries fuel your fears and your faith loses its foundation. In order to experience My blessings, you're going to need to be willing to feel the fear and let go of your worries. If you continually give in to fear, allowing it to paralyze your faith, you'll never experience My very best in your life. Don't allow your worries to run your life; trust Me to.

It's easy to allow your worries to dominate your thoughts. They creep in unexpectedly, and it's difficult to get them under control. You must remember to take *every* thought captive. Consider what you're thinking and ask yourself if they are thoughts that I would be thinking. Do your thoughts line up with My Word? If you constantly give in to your worries, you'll be filled with depression, despair and disappointment. Faith brings you fulfillment, giving you My joy and peace to overcome your worries.

If you're overwhelmed by seemingly insurmountable obstacles, make the decision to conquer your worries first—with your faith—and then live confidently without fear. I AM with you in everything, so step out in faith and your fears will disappear.

God is with you in everything you do.

GENESIS 21:22 (NIV)

Winning over Worry

I know you're tempted to walk by sight and not by faith. Your circumstances seem to indicate that all hope is gone, and yet you fail to realize that worrying changes nothing. In this world you will have trouble, but you can live with joy and peace in the midst of it all. Your constant worry, which leads to disappointment, will leave you heartsick. But trusting in Me and counting on My miracles will transform you in ways that you cannot imagine.

You can win over your worries by hoping in Me. When your worries are weighing you down, I will help you to not only survive, but thrive. I want you to live joyously, free of anxiety, knowing that I AM holding you always. I want you to soar above your troubles, seeing things from the big-picture perspective through My eyes. I want you to fully trust that My hope will not fail you.

You worry that I've forgotten you, that I'm too busy to care, and you lose the faith that you were once living by. Come to Me in your worries. Allow My Spirit to give you revelation and let Me enlighten your heart. Then your hope will never be cut off. My plans for you entail countless blessings, so don't worry … My grace is endless.

There is surely a future hope for you,
and your hope will not be cut off.

PROVERBS 23:18 (NIV)

Holding Firmly to Faith

I know that you're used to promises being broken, but Mine never are. My promises to you are an anchor for your soul. The troubles of life will cause your soul to be turbulent, and you'll need to be secure in your spirit so that you can continue to walk in faith. It won't always be easy; what you see in your circumstances will give you more reasons to doubt than to have faith. Don't trust in what you see, trust in Me.

I AM your living hope—the hope that never changes, never wavers and is anchored in My faithfulness. When your hope is grounded in Me, there is nothing that can shake the foundation of your faith. Though the ground beneath you trembles, there is no reason for you to do the same.

I AM your security, the One who holds you within My grasp, and nothing can separate you from Me. If you're holding on to My hope, trusting in My love for you, you have a hope that is firm and secure. Remember that I have gone before you. I provide the way, so you should hold firmly to your faith, without wavering. I AM faithful. I have promised you I AM, and trusting in My truth will set you free from worry.

We must continue to hold firmly to
our declaration of faith. The one who
made the promise is faithful.

HEBREWS 10:23 (GW)

Weary in the Worry

It may seem that you endure more than you ever thought you could or should. Know that I AM at work within you through your suffering. I AM developing perseverance in you, in order that you might run with endurance to finish the race set before you. This life is not a sprint, but a marathon. I know your troubles seem endless, but they are not. I will always provide times of rest and renewal for your soul.

Though it seems like your problems are insurmountable, like a mountain you're climbing with no summit in sight, I'm steadily leading you to the top, preparing you for a revelation of My presence and power that will leave you in awe. There is no need to become weary and discouraged. I AM with you and will help you, giving you all the strength and grace you need.

Don't give in to self-pity. Trust in My sovereignty, knowing that everything is in My control. What you're facing is not by mistake. It is divinely orchestrated, preparing you to have a more precious view of the blessings to come. Eagerly await Me. Know that I love you with an everlasting love, I draw you with loving-kindness, and sometimes it is through trials and troubles. Don't lose heart, just be embraced by Mine.

Consider Him who has endured such
hostility by sinners against Himself, so that
you will not grow weary and lose heart.

HEBREWS 12:3 (NASB)

Persistent Presence

I know it's difficult at times to understand, and even harder to truly believe in, My omniscience. I AM everywhere at once. I go ahead of you, preparing the way and providing the resources for you to walk firmly in faith. The promise of My presence is eternal. No matter where you are, where you go and what you encounter, I will never leave your side.

Your assurance in My promises to you should be your courage and confidence. I know that sometimes fear and discouragement can get the best of you, but in those moments you must grab hold of My Word and trust completely in it.

Your heart is to be My dwelling place, the place where peace and joy constantly reside. Don't allow the distractions of the world to deter you from seeking Me continually. My love casts out all fear. It is in My presence, at My throne of grace, that My perfect love renews your hope and faith. There is nothing to fear; I AM always here. Rely on My strength as Christ dwells in your heart through your faith, enabling you to overcome any obstacle that threatens to overcome you.

> Do not be afraid or discouraged, for the LORD will personally go ahead of you. He will be with you; He will neither fail you nor abandon you.
>
> DEUTERONOMY 31:8 (NLT)

Don't Worry

Worry can get the best of you, and it often does. You tend to justify your worries by your circumstances and begin to question your faith. You see the comfort and prosperity of evildoers, and you begin to question My ways. The bait of Satan can deceive you to such an extent that you forget My promises, and you begin to worry.

Worry eliminates your worship, and your panic drowns out your praise. The enemy knows this. His goal is to move your eyes off Me and onto the circumstances of your life and the lives of others.

Trust in My judgment of your life's circumstances. Allow Me to repay those who have done evil against you, and find peace in knowing that though evildoers succeed for a time, in the end their path leads to destruction. Do not be deceived, but keep your eyes on Me.

You will be restless until you rest in Me. I have an infinite number of ways in which I show you My love and help in times of trouble. Trust Me, even through your suffering and uncertainty. I will right every wrong and wipe every tear. You will remember them no more. I AM with you, I assure you. Rest in what you know about My character, what I've revealed to you through My love.

Don't worry.

PSALM 37:1 (NLT)

Rest

Entering into Rest

If you are to enter into My rest, you must cease striving to relieve your weariness. I have endless purposes for your life that will require you to rest physically, mentally, emotionally and spiritually. It is not an option, it's a requirement. Faith is what will allow you to rest in Me, trusting that you don't have to worry about the details, but just walk in My will. I will lead and guide you each and every step of the way. When you're too weary from the journey, let Me carry you. I AM able.

You don't need to worry or reason over My plans. Just leave the details to Me. I AM responsible for leading you into My victory. All you must do is walk in faith. I don't want you walking ahead of Me, but with Me.

If you are experiencing anxiety and stress from the daily walk, it's because you're not completely relying upon Me. Your faith must overrule your emotions so that you can respond to your circumstances, instead of reacting to them. Resting in Me should be your number one priority. Nothing shows Me that you trust Me more than by entering into My rest, free of worry and firm in faith.

Those who entered His place of rest also rest from their work as God did from His.

HEBREWS 4:10 (GW)

Surrendering It All

The only way you can live with your soul at rest is to surrender your will to Mine. You've got to let go of all your expectations other than the expectation that I will embrace you continually. Without your submission to My will for your life, you will miss out on My best for you. You must do all that I command, obeying Me even when you don't understand, trusting without fully comprehending.

I know at times it may seem that all I've purposed you to do is too difficult, but you are never meant to do what I've asked you to do in your own strength. If you'll surrender to Me, I will strengthen you to accomplish My purposes. There will be times when you will find yourself exhausted from the faith walk and you'll need to enter into My rest. If I took time to rest from My work, so should you. That time of rest will refresh your soul so that you can continue the journey I have set before you.

Don't ever hesitate to give Me your all. Don't question My ways, and don't allow others to question what I've called you to do either. Do what you are able to do, allow Me to do the rest in and through you, and expect My supernatural power to accomplish the impossible. I'm holding you and everything else together. There is nothing to fear; rest in Me.

He is before all things, and
in Him all things hold together.

COLOSSIANS 1:17 (NIV)

Abiding in Faith

Whether your challenges in life are big or small, I want you to know that I AM here to help you. The things that seem big to you are small to Me. Whether you realize it or not, you need Me, continually, in everything.

I want you to have rest for your soul, to cease the struggle with life, and to find peace in the journey with Me. I want you to do life with Me, in Me, through Me, by Me and for My glory.

You'll need to invite Me into every area of your life so that I might work supernaturally in everything you face. You'll need to relinquish your fears, to surrender control and trust that I AM able to do the impossible, which you cannot. Apart from Me you can do nothing, but if you remain in Me, trusting and obeying, you can do everything.

Your desperate need for Me is not a sign of your weakness, but evidence of your strength: your faith in Me. Don't allow your worries to cause you to drift into self-sufficiency. Depend upon Me completely, and you'll find that I will enable you to do more than you had ever imagined.

> "I am the vine; you are the branches. Those who remain in Me, and I in them, will produce much fruit. For apart from Me you can do nothing."
>
> JOHN 15:5 (NLT)

Take a Break from Worry

I know it can be difficult to rest when life is continually keeping you from doing so. I want you to enter into My rest even when physical rest is difficult. Entering into My rest is simply trusting Me and letting go of your worries. I want you to focus on My Word when your faith is failing and you are weary and weak. My Word will strengthen you in ways you can't imagine. Fix your thoughts on Me and take a break from your worrying.

I want you to grow in your ability to trust Me, and you will need to experience difficult situations to teach you that. Walking in faith is a lifetime journey, not a brief walk. As you continue to grow in your faith, remind yourself continually to cast your cares on Me, to be anxious for nothing, and to trust Me at all times and in all things.

If you'll be diligent in your relationship with Me, you'll find yourself at rest more and more, even as the storms of life rage around you. I want you at peace, filled with My strength, assured that I have prepared a future and a hope that will not disappoint you. If you'll turn your troubles over to Me, you can rest.

We who believe are entering that place of rest.
As God said, "So I angrily took a solemn oath
that they would never enter My place of rest."
God said this even though He had finished
His work when He created the world.

HEBREWS 4:3 (GW)

Soul Rest

With all you must deal with on a daily basis—the troubles and temptations—I know that you need rest and refreshment for your soul. When you're weary and overburdened, come to Me and I will give you the rest you need. Relieve yourself of the burden of trying to be in control—ultimately I AM. I AM God of the universe, so let Me be God of your life. You simply need to rest and trust.

Most of the time you can't fix the problems you face because your situation calls for a miracle … the impossible … and only I can do that. Trust Me when you're in the midst of chaos and expect Me to get you through it, not necessarily out of it. Part of growing your faith is teaching you to be at rest in the midst of all your doubt and fear.

It takes great faith to refuse to walk by sight. I know what's best for you even though most of the time it seems like I don't. And though I may make you wait for the answers to your prayers, My timing is perfect. Wait with patient expectation, resting in Me, relaxed and assured that I AM at work, in control, and preparing to bless you in countless ways.

> Come to Me, all you who labor and are
> heavy-laden and overburdened, and I
> will cause you to rest. [I will ease and
> relieve and refresh your souls.]
>
> MATTHEW 11:28 (AMP)

Silently Submitted

Find rest in Me alone. Resting in Me provides you with the hope you need to walk in faith. I want you to rest in My presence so that you can confidently have hope. Only I can provide all that you need, so there is no use in putting your hope in anything or anyone else. The hope I give you when you rest in Me allows you to be filled with the peace you desperately need amid all the uncertainty in your life.

Circumstances are always changing, but I never do. If I'm the same yesterday, today and forever, then there is nothing to worry about and you can rest in My perfect love for you. Allow Me to work in your circumstances instead of tiring yourself by trying to accomplish what only I can. Your soul can find rest when your hope comes from Me.

I AM your rock and your salvation, the One who keeps your feet from slipping. You are secure in My care and I will be a shield for you, protecting you against the evil one. As you place your hope in Me and rest, My unfailing love will rest upon you.

My soul, wait only upon God and silently submit to Him; for my hope and expectation are from Him. He only is my Rock and my Salvation; He is my Defense and my Fortress, I shall not be moved.

PSALM 62:5–6 (AMP)

Protection

A Refuge and Fortress

My delays are not necessarily My denials. Sometimes I must redirect your desires so that your motives are right for what you ask. It may seem that what you're asking for is well within My will, but often I must orchestrate finer details to perfect My plan. Don't question My purposes for you; know that all I do is out of love.

Wait upon My guidance, and simply take refuge in Me until I assure you of the direction to take. I AM your fortress, keeping you safe and secure amid the battles that rage within your life. Trust that I AM completely sovereign, able to redeem your past, secure the present and fill you with hope for the future.

Though you can't always understand, you can choose to trust in My decisions for your life. I have purpose in everything I do. Though fear threatens to overcome you, challenging your faith and its foundation, you must stay focused upon Me at all times. When you are afraid, run to Me. I AM always a ready help in times of trouble. I will not only be your refuge, but your strength and your song.

I will say of the Lord,
"He is my refuge and my fortress,
my God, in whom I trust."

PSALM 91:2 (NIV)

Safe and Sound in Jesus

I know it seems the world is against you, and sometimes it very well may be. Your circumstances become overwhelming and you can't see a way through, much less out. Those who once seemed to care turned out not to, people who claimed to be your friend ended up being your enemy instead, and you thought you had control over things, but you just don't. Even with such despair, there is no need to fear. Your life is safe and sound in My hands.

Don't worry about those who talk behind your back, spreading rumors and false statements about you. I AM your defender. Nothing and no one can affect you that I don't first allow. And if I allow it, I will use it for your benefit. Let My justice overcome your desire to avenge. I will bless those who bless you and curse those who curse you.

I keep My Word. You must keep your own heart clean before Me and trust that though you will have negative forces come against you, they will not overcome you. I AM with you to deliver you. I AM your hope, your defense, and I hold your future in My hands. Nothing is too difficult for Me and I rule over all. No matter what happens, trust Me and you'll never be disappointed.

> No weapon that has been made to be
> used against you will succeed.
>
> ISAIAH 54:17 (GW)

The Rescuer

When you're facing fearful difficulties in your life, you need to cling to My Word to protect your mind and heart. When you're overwhelmed and falling into despair, recall all that I've done in the past. I've helped you before, I've rescued you, and I've promised I'll never fail you. Throughout your troubles, you'll need to keep focused upon Me, devoted to Me completely. Don't let discouragement keep you from Me.

Come to Me when you need Me to rescue you. I may not pull you out of the circumstance, I may simply carry you through as I develop your faith in and through the trials. Know that nothing can touch you without My permission. If I allow it, I will bring good from it. And when your faith begins to fail and you become weary in your walk, declare the victory. Have the vision of glory based on My promises. I AM all-powerful and all-wise. You can count on Me to rescue you. Wait patiently in faith for your miracle—it will not be one moment too late. Trust in Me, obey Me, and have the confident faith that I AM with you to deliver you.

> My eyes are always on the Lord,
> for He rescues me.
>
> PSALM 25:15 (NLT)

A Guarded Heart

I know your pain and the sorrow that pours out from your breaking heart. I know that your emptiness is overwhelming and your loneliness is consuming. I know that you feel as though there is nothing left within you. Empty is as close as you'll ever come to describing the state of your soul. Know that I remember every tear.

I see the defenses you've built to protect your heart from pain, which are now crumbling as you struggle to keep your mind from spinning into hopelessness. I know that you feel consumed with darkness, and the fear of all the unknowns immobilize you. I want you to know that I AM here. I will protect and faithfully guard your heart and mind.

I want you to find courage in My promises of protection, shelter, peace and redemption. Seek Me with all of your heart, mind and soul. I will give you peace. My peace will guard your breaking heart and troubled mind. I AM always watching over you, protecting you, guiding you, and pouring down my love, grace and mercy upon you … each and every moment of your life. Give me your heart, and I'll guard you with Mine.

The peace of God, which transcends all understanding, will guard your hearts and your minds in Christ Jesus.

PHILIPPIANS 4:7 (NIV)

In the Shadow

I know that in your deepest valleys and darkest nights, what you need most is My comfort and the assurance that I AM with you to protect you in every way. My faithfulness is your shield and rampart. There is no need to fear, for I AM near and I AM mighty to save.

As you seek My shelter, you will escape the chains of fear and find the peace of mind that you so desperately need. You must dwell in Me and trust in Me completely. If you will dwell in Me, you will remain in a constant state of peace and security. Nothing will move you. I'm asking you to live with faith that is active and expresses what you believe within your heart.

I want you to live out your life unreservedly under the umbrella of My will and purpose for you. If you live confidently in My will, at peace in knowing that I AM your defender and protector, you will find joy, purpose and confidence. Come to Me and I will overwhelm you with a sense of security. My protective care that will cast out all of your fears, so that you might find rest in the shadow of My wings.

> Whoever dwells in the shelter of
> the Most High will rest in the
> shadow of the Almighty.
>
> PSALM 91:1 (NIV)

The Blessing of Protection

I want you to have the confident assurance that I will bless you and protect you. I long to be gracious to you, and I naturally smile on you. My grace is always sufficient to keep you from whatever is not My will. My favor will give you hope through your hopelessness and strength when you are weary. I want you to know in your most desperate hour that I love you and want to bless you by giving you My peace.

Even when it looks like the odds are stacked against you, like there's no way out and you don't have the strength to go through, I will make a way. I will protect you along your journey of faith, providing all that you need in the moment you need it. Don't be afraid when your circumstances seem impossible. I'm using those impossible situations to reveal My power in a way that will conquer your fears and fuel your faith. When you are afraid, simply come into My presence and rest in My peace.

May the LORD bless you and protect you.
May the LORD smile on you and be gracious
to you. May the LORD show you His favor
and give you His peace.

NUMBERS 6:24–26 (NLT)

Diverting the Darkness

There will be times when darkness will close in on you and you'll feel helpless against the despair. But when you come to Me, I will protect you. My power will overshadow you, giving you security even when you must face the unthinkable in your life.

You will always have trouble in your life, but you do not have to give in to the hopelessness that tempts you to fall into fear and despair. You can have hope in Me. Though you will still have to endure through trials, I will be with you and you can be certain that My victory is sure, though it may not seem like it at the time.

You will be tempted to give up and give in, but you must not. Make the choice to hold on to your faith and trust in Me completely. Even when you're struggling with doubt, My Word will be a light for your path, giving you faith to face your fears. Through your difficulties you can be glad because I AM your refuge. My protection is over you so that you can have peace even as chaos surrounds you. You are My child and you have My favor. Rejoice in this knowledge.

Let all who take refuge in You rejoice;
let them sing joyful praises forever.
Spread Your protection over them, that all who
love Your name may be filled with joy.
For You bless the godly, O LORD;
You surround them with Your shield of love.

PSALM 5:11-12 (NLT)

Giving

Cheerful Giving

I know you're tempted to focus on yourself most of the time. It seems impossible to give to others when you have so many needs yourself. But know that I will take care of your needs. I need you to look for opportunities to give. Allow My love to flow through you.

The opportunities to give are all around you. Listen to others carefully. Seldom will others ask for what they need, just as you often forget to ask Me for what you need. But by being aware of people around you, your heart will naturally open up and you will more easily receive My grace. If you find yourself unable to help in the way your heart is leading you to, simply pray and ask that I will give you the resources and ability to help in the ways that I want you to in a given situation.

Giving is far better than receiving. You will find a joy in giving that you cannot experience otherwise. Selflessness will yield a fulfillment inside that brings happiness to you as well as others. Don't fear that you will not have enough of yourself to give and don't worry about growing weary: I will give you all the strength you need to cheerfully give as I'm asking you to do.

You must each decide in your heart how much to give. And don't give reluctantly or in response to pressure. "For God loves a person who gives cheerfully."

2 CORINTHIANS 9:7 (NLT)

Being a Blessing

I want you to focus on being a blessing to others. You are to be a vessel of My love and grace in order that you might know My heart better. Seeing others through My eyes draws you nearer to Me in countless ways. Selflessness will help you to overcome any discouragement you're experiencing.

If you focus on being a blessing to others, you'll find that you are happier overall. But the question is, do you really believe what I'm telling you? Do you truly believe it's more blessed to give than to receive?

I know that you need blessings and I will not withhold one good thing from your life. Learning to give and be a blessing is not always easy. There will always be challenges within and without. Sometimes people will try and discourage you from doing what your heart is telling you to do. Be willing to take a step of faith when I place a burden on your heart. If you make it a habit to bless others, you'll find that your spirit will be transformed in remarkable ways. When you make it a priority to seek out the needs of others, you will find yourself enjoying your life more and more.

"It is more blessed to give than to receive."

ACTS 20:35 (NIV)

Childlike Dependence

In order to enter the kingdom of God, you have to become like a little child. I know it goes against your natural instincts to be dependent—you want to have control and declare your independence. But you and I can never have the relationship we're meant to have if you're not completely dependent upon Me. It's the only way you can be assured of My presence and power. It's the only way you'll experience firsthand the miracles that I perform. If you place yourself in our relationship as My child, you'll be able to trust and not fear. You'll obey and not question. You'll have faith instead of being filled with doubt.

As My child, you have no need to worry. There is freedom in trusting Me, not fear. You will be amazed at what I can do for you. You'll be in awe at how I provide for you in unique ways. I will bring about blessings in your life in surprising and unexpected ways. All the things that are burdening you right now are things that I should be handling. Think about what is troubling you at the moment. Are you looking to Me as your Heavenly Father? Do you trust Me to provide in the ways you need?

Truly I say to you, unless you repent (change, turn about) and become like little children [trusting, lowly, loving, forgiving], you can never enter the kingdom of heaven [at all].

MATTHEW 18:3 (AMP)

Sowing and Reaping

It's not a hard principle to understand, but it *Is* a difficult one to live out. If you give more and more, sowing blessings in the lives of others, you will reap more than you can ever imagine. I know you understand the concept: If you sow, then you shall reap, but I want you to experience it fully by putting into practice what you already know.

If you are a blessing to others, giving in any way you can, I will bless you—you can count on it. And don't think that you have to give what you don't have. Don't always assume that I want you to bless others financially. I have given you gifts that are deeply spiritual. You can be an encouragement to someone, or you can offer to simply listen and relieve the burden that someone is carrying. You can show kindness to someone who seldom receives it.

You must continually be aware of the people I've placed in your life and the situations I've put you in. Everything I do is with great purpose. Each and every day I want you to look to Me and ask in prayer what I would have you do. I want you to be determined to be a giver, sowing into the lives of others, and I'll make sure you reap a harvest in your own.

Remember this: Whoever sows sparingly will also reap sparingly, and whoever sows generously will also reap generously.

2 CORINTHIANS 9:6 (NIV)

Give as You Have Received

When you are tempted to be stingy toward others or to wish them harm, it is because you are forgetting what I have given you: the blessings of salvation, the blessings that are in your life—all those things are gifts from Me. When you express gratitude for those things, it frees you up to give to others. Dwelling on how much you have been given will enable you to give to others.

Sometimes you pray to Me, calling upon Me to reply to your requests, yet I may be waiting on you to obey Me in taking a step of faith to help others. I work all things for good in your life. I want you to work all things for good in the lives of others as well.

You are an instrument for Me to bring heaven to earth, so don't miss out on the joy that comes from being a blessing to people and giving of yourself in whatever ways you can. You have the ability to change your reality and the reality of others by focusing on giving to others as I have given to you.

"Give as freely as you have received!"

MATTHEW 10:8 (NLT)

Lifting Burdens

I want you to constantly ask yourself if you're being fruitful. Are you focused on transforming the lives of others as much as you are on Me transforming yours? I want your life to make a difference. Your life can change countless lives in ways that go beyond anything you can comprehend, although you will rarely get a glimpse of the powerful impact you have. I breathe life into you so that you might breathe it into others.

It won't be easy, but forget about yourself and focus on others. Your primary focus should be to encourage, edify, comfort and bring help and hope into the lives of others. You are able to lift others' burdens just like I lift yours. When you are working with Me to fulfill My purposes and plans on earth, your faith will grow and our relationship will become more intimate—enabling you to trust Me more and in greater ways.

Don't underestimate the power that focusing on the needs of others will have in your own life. I AM all you need. I call you to show others that I AM all they need as well—that truth can lift any burden, and you can deliver that blessing.

Encourage one another and build each other up.

1 THESSALONIANS 5:11 (NIV)

Blessed to Be a Blessing

It is in giving My love to others that you will fully experience My love for you. You may not always feel like a blessing to others, but act in faith anyway. Being a blessing to others, giving of yourself in the most self-sacrificing ways, is the key to a Christian life. And I want you to live your faith aggressively and joyfully.

In Christ you have every spiritual blessing, so be assured that you have more than enough to give. If you're thankful for what I've given you, then show Me your thanks by keeping a continual cycle of blessing others in your life. My grace will give you all that you need, an endless supply, to obey Me in giving in the ways I'm asking you to. My grace will never run out, and it will be more than sufficient for you and for the needs of others.

If you freely give, without begrudging what you're giving, then I will bless you in all that you do. Work out your faith upon the foundation My Word has built for you, never doubt what I've commanded you to do, and My blessings will follow you all the days of your life.

Praise be to the God and Father of our Lord Jesus Christ, who has blessed us in the heavenly realms with every spiritual blessing in Christ.

EPHESIANS 1:3 (NIV)

Help

Remembering What You've Forgotten

Life can take some unexpected turns, leaving your faith in a state of shock and causing you to forget what you should remember and remember what you should forget. I find you continually doubting My provision, paralyzed in your faith because doubt has defeated any that you had. I do not have a short supply of miracles and I hear you when you call. I will not fail to help you in your time of need.

Too often you receive My miracles but fail to remember them. Or you constantly look for signs and miracles when you should be simply looking for Me. Don't have hope in the outcome of your circumstances, but instead put your hope in Me. Then you will never be disappointed.

Remember the miracles of the past, and not just your own: recall Me feeding the five thousand and healing the sick; don't forget David defeating Goliath and Jonah surviving being swallowed by a fish. These miracles are for you to remember, to assure you of My protection and provision. Whatever giants you're facing—relationship issues, financial ones, illness or emptiness—I will give you everything you need to defeat them.

"You have eyes—can't you see?
You have ears—can't you hear?
Don't you remember anything at all?"

MARK 8:18 (NLT)

If You Will Ask

I want to help you, but you need to ask for My help. I hear the faintest prayer, the gentlest plea, but you must lift your heart to heaven to acknowledge that you need My help. I don't want you to try and do everything on your own. When you do, you will become tired and frustrated. When you're overwhelmed, fearful of the future and facing uncertainties that cause you to doubt, simply sit quietly in My presence and ask for My help.

I know that often you think I'm too busy, and you only pray about the "big" problems in your life. I want you to pray your way through each day and completely rely on My help at all times. I care about every detail in your life. Choose to call upon Me in your hour of need and lean on Me to give you strength and power.

Pray and meditate constantly, nourishing your spirit through My Word. Remember to be thankful for all I've done and all I have yet to do. Whatever you need, whatever you're asking Me for, nothing is too big or too small for Me. And when you ask, trust that I have heard you and that I will answer. Trust in My timing and rely on My promises to carry you through. Don't doubt what your faith knows.

You don't have what you want
because you don't ask God for it.

JAMES 4:2 (NLT)

When You Feel Forgotten

I want you to tell Me exactly how you feel, to be honest with your heart. But as you do, don't forget to praise Me for being faithful to My promises. Bring a promise of Mine to Me when you pray to Me. Remind Me that you know My Word and I will open your eyes so that you might behold My face in the darkness. Be confident in Me. Expect My mercy and loving-kindness and allow your heart to rejoice and be in high spirits.

I know that sometimes it's difficult for you to truly express your feelings. I know you wrestle with releasing all your worries to Me. You especially struggle when you are angry at Me because you feel I've let you down. But when you release your heart to Me, opening it wide, I am able to heal your heart and bring comfort to you so that you can take one more step of faith.

Wait on My deliverance and trust Me with your deepest, most intense feelings. Even though you may have times of doubt, declare that you will trust Me, be diligent in praising Me, and expect Me to help you.

Oh LORD, how long will You forget me?

PSALM 13:1 (NLT)

Where to Go First

When you are in need, where do you run? To whom do you turn? Turn to Me first. You cause yourself so much unnecessary frustration when you depend on yourself and others instead of Me alone. No one but Me can see your situation from beginning to end. You need My perspective to obtain the help that you need. I can do the impossible, no one else can, so why wouldn't you come to Me before going to anyone else?

When you come to Me first, it shows that you absolutely trust Me. It draws you nearer to Me and your faith grows stronger. Everything I do in your life is to develop your faith, and coming to Me first when you face trouble will enable you to walk on a firm foundation.

Come to Me with your needs, knowing that I can do the impossible, assured that I can and will help you. Don't doubt My power to perform whatever miracles you need in your life. Whatever challenges you face, I AM able to overcome them all.

Praise be to the God and Father of our
Lord Jesus Christ, the Father of compassion
and the God of all comfort, who comforts
us in all our troubles, so that we can comfort
those in any trouble with the comfort
we ourselves receive from God.

2 CORINTHIANS 1:3-4 (NIV)

Going Through

Sometimes you may feel that you are stuck in your troubles, but you are not. I'm simply taking you through. You will always face difficulties, but you don't need to stop moving forward in faith because of them. No matter what, I will be with you, so there is truly nothing to fear. I AM with you to help you. Your adversities are not your reality, your faith in Me is.

I AM teaching you how to overcome adversity by taking you through things that will help you become stronger. If I were to simply rescue you out of your difficulties, you would not grow in the ways I want you to. You would not learn to press through and not give up.

You must choose to look at your trials and troubles in the way I do because growth doesn't automatically come from difficulties and your troubles don't always produce the transformation of your faith. You will have to make a conscious decision to see your situation as I do and know that I will be there to help you. I want you to stay faithful and refuse to give up.

The LORD Almighty is my strength.
He makes my feet like those of a deer.
He makes me walk on the mountains.

HABAKKUK 3:19 (GW)

Being Open and Involved

I want you to pray prayers that are powerful and life transforming, not only for yourself but also for others. I want you to be open and involved in helping work in others' lives. You are My representative; I depend on you to represent Me in all you say and do. But you cannot do it in your own strength—it can only be done in Mine. Bring others to Me in prayer and allow Me to do the rest.

You will need to keep your eyes open for opportunities to be My hands and feet to those around you. I don't expect you to do anything without My help. I want you to use the resources I've given you and the talents I've provided you with to encourage others and get involved in their lives in order to fulfill My purposes.

I will work in and through you as long as you continue to be open and willing to be involved and used by Me. I will never force Myself on you. I want you to have a natural desire to be loved by Me and to be a part of My plans. I will bless you as you're a blessing to others. Simply come to Me and ask Me to show you what to do and I will empower you in every way to do it.

Therefore, we are Christ's representatives,
and through us God is calling you. We beg you
on behalf of Christ to become reunited with God.

2 CORINTHIANS 5:20 (GW)

Set Up for Victory

There are always challenges in life, but there's no need for you to become overwhelmed by them. I want you to be completely confident in your faith, trusting in Me so that you can face your challenges head-on. It is My Word that will fully prepare you for whatever comes your way. Trust in Me, and I will make sure each step of faith you take sets you up for victory.

When you're overwhelmed, first acknowledge your desperate need for My help. You will need to focus upon Me and stay focused upon Me at all times. I don't want you to be surprised at the difficulties that come against you or unprepared for the spiritual battles they entail. The battlefield is in your mind, so you cannot fight this spiritual battle in a physical way. The Sword of the Spirit is your weapon against every thought of despair or doubt.

Your thinking can defeat you before the true battle has even begun. You have the mind of Christ, so allow His Spirit to live and think through you. I will help you and give you everything you need to face whatever challenges come your way. Without Me you can do nothing, but with Me you can do all things, so get ready and be prepared and know that victory is sure.

Get ready; be prepared!

EZEKIEL 38:7 (NLT)

Living with Purpose

Used by God

I can always use you to be a blessing to others. I want you to have an open and willing heart to help others when I need you to—it is vital to living out My purposes for your life. Nothing will bring you greater joy than being used by Me, so be ready to be a vessel of My glory.

Life can take some very unexpected turns that leave people in a state of confusion and drive them into a deep pit of despair. I have given you everything you need, and I want you to reach out to others, giving them the same hope you have in Me. It won't always be easy. Despair causes deep doubt. You will need to stand firm in your own faith and provide strength for those who are weary.

You must rely on the Holy Spirit to lead and guide you, to give you the strength and resources you need to help others in their time of need. Don't be overwhelmed and resist helping because you feel inadequate or because your own problems are too overwhelming to help others. I will be all you need. Focus on the needs of others and I'll take care of yours.

Let each of you esteem and look upon and be concerned for not [merely] his own interests, but also each for the interests of others.

PHILIPPIANS 2:4 (AMP)

Just Follow

Just as I chose twelve men to be disciples, so I choose you to be a fisher of men. The gospel is a gift to the world, one that I'm asking you to share. I need you to make My purposes in your life a priority. I need you to place Me above all else. You must follow in the path I've set before you. I have gone before you and prepared the way; just walk in it.

Following Me means letting go of your own path and steadily walking in Mine. When you're following Me, it may be inconvenient and uncomfortable, but I will be with you. No matter what I'm asking of you, you can trust that it will never be more than you can bear, and you will reap a great harvest if you sow continually.

I AM giving you the opportunity to experience the divine as you lead others to Me. If you live out the gospel, trusting Me to provide for you, the eternal impact you will have is exponential. I'm not going to ask you to do anything that I will not equip you to do, so simply follow Me, obeying My Word and living according to it. You will find others following after you so that you can lead them to Me.

Jesus called out to them, "Come, follow Me,
and I will show you how to fish for people!"

MATTHEW 4:19 (NLT)

The Example

I want everything you do in life to be meaningful. I have given you Christ as the example of how you should live, leaving no questions or doubt about how to walk in faith. He left you an example of humble, sacrificial, obedient service to others. Following Him will not be easy because I will always take you out of your comfort zone, causing you to depend upon Me more and more.

I need you to trust Me enough to make sacrifices in order to bless others. Trust that I will always take care of you, releasing you to focus on the needs of others. You are to be a servant to others so that they might see your humble attitude and devotion to Me.

When I lead you to give or to serve, it does not always have to be in response to a desperate need—it may be something proactive. I simply want you to give when I call you to, without hesitation or doubtful reservation. Having a heart that is helpful and giving will keep you from becoming greedy. We all need to feel loved, so just as I have loved you, love others in the same way.

*"I have given you an example to follow.
Do as I have done to you."*

JOHN 13:15 (NLT)

Any Time in Every Way

Sometimes it seems as though you want to help others, but you're not sure how. When you don't know what to do, just ask Me. I will answer you and direct you as to how you might both be a blessing to others and be blessed in return.

The most powerful thing you can do is to pray for others. Through praying for others you set aside your needs and desires and place others first. Nothing exemplifies your faith more than selflessness. But don't just pray, put feet to your prayers. Be kind and hospitable to those you pray for. Be patient through their faults and weaknesses. Forgive them, comfort them and encourage them with My hope and love.

Even relatively simple acts of love can make an enormous impact on countless lives. The little things can mean a lot. I just need you to be willing to do as I ask. Have a servant's heart, looking for ways in which you can be a blessing to others, even as you trust Me for the blessings you need.

Therefore, whenever we have the opportunity,
we should do good to everyone—especially to
those in the family of faith.

GALATIANS 6:10 (NLT)

Love Is a Verb

Love is a verb, not an emotion. Love *does*. Because My Spirit is within you, My love resides in you so that you are able to have a heart of compassion. Love will weaken if it is not active, so I bring opportunities into your life to fully express and give love to others. Your love is the evidence of your intimate connection to Me.

Although it may seem extreme, I want you to lay down your life for others. My desire is that you would allow Me to focus upon you and your needs and desires while you focus on others. I'm not asking you to do something that is more than you can handle; I'm just asking you to allow My love to flow in and through you.

Open your heart and leave the rest to Me. My love within you will motivate you to help the poor and needy, those who are alone and hurting. I want you to see everyone through My eyes and not your own. When you view life from an eternal perspective, it changes everything. It is in being a vessel of My love that you will find a peace and joy that goes beyond all your expectations—this is My way of allowing you to experience heaven on earth.

If someone has enough money to live
well and sees a brother or sister in need
but shows no compassion—how can
God's love be in that person?

1 JOHN 3:17 (NLT)

A Good Measure

There is nothing wrong with having hopes and desires, praying for what you want and expecting My answer, but I also want you to give and live selflessly—that is what produces the harvest of blessings you long for.

I promise to reward you if you diligently serve Me. I've made this promise not so that you would bless others to receive blessings from Me, but so that you would look forward to the reward of being obedient to My Word. If you look after the poor and needy, you will never be in want. What you do unto others, you do unto Me.

Focusing on the problems of others can help you to stop focusing so much on your own. It will help you to let Me handle your life as you invest in someone else's. As you serve Me and live passionately for My glory, I'll bring blessings into your life that you ask for and some that you would never have thought to. I will never withhold blessings from you if I see they are good for you, so simply focus on giving and you'll be given more than you can measure.

"Give, and it will be given to you. A good measure, pressed down, shaken together and running over, will be poured into your lap. For with the measure you use, it will be measured to you."

LUKE 6:38 (NIV)

Shining the Light

Loving and caring for others will help you learn to trust Me more and more, becoming fully assured that I am all you need in this journey of life. No matter the situation—relational, financial or otherwise—I have an infinite number of resources to provide what you need. When you turn to Me I will fill you with My light, and you will have less confusion, better clarity and more understanding in your life.

You are not meant to hide your light. Allow your light to break forth into the world. When you live your life in My glory, I bring healing and restoration to you that shines like a light in the darkness. I always go before you, paving a path that is safe and secure. I never want you to worry about the journey ahead; just live in the moment, trusting Me in every way.

My desire is that you would have such peace about Me sustaining your life that you would freely and readily pour yourself out for those in need. I will guide you continually, and even in times of desperation, I will satisfy you. I will give you strength in your weakness and hope as you live your life helping others and giving testimony to My grace and glory.

Then your light will break forth like the
dawn, and your healing will quickly appear;
then your righteousness will go before you,
and the glory of the Lord will be your rear guard.

ISAIAH 58:8 (NIV)

Sin

Guilt Removed

My love not only covers a multitude of sins, but also removes them. My love removes all unrighteousness and leaves you free to live a new life free of sin. You cannot hide your sin from Me, so you might as well bring it before Me and allow Me to cleanse you from it. You can never have peace if I do not remove your sins.

You may find yourself in a big mess, but I can wash your pain away and cleanse you, making you whiter than snow. No matter how terrible the circumstances may be, I AM able to bring good from what is bad. Trust in Me to love you through your faults and failures.

You don't need to make your wrongs right before you come to Me. You may be able to cover your sins temporarily, but you need Me to completely remove them and give you a new heart. Because of Christ, and the sacrifice He made on your behalf, you can come to Me fearlessly, confidently and boldly. My mercy is always available and My grace never runs out. Simply come to Me, ask for forgiveness, and receive My love while resting in My embrace.

He has removed our sins as far from us
as the east is from the west. The LORD is like
a father to His children, tender and
compassionate to those who fear Him.

PSALM 103:12-13 (NLT)

Faith like a Child

I truly want you to live an abundant life. I don't want you to live full of fear, stress, worry and depression. I want you to enjoy your life, and that is only possible if you are free of sin. Though you will always make mistakes, My forgiveness is readily available to save you from the sin that enslaves you.

Your childlike faith will bring you to My throne of grace, in the midst of your sin, so that I can cleanse and comfort you. I want you to trust Me completely with the sins that you struggle with. Nothing you've done can make Me love you any less. I know you're consumed with the guilt that comes with sin, but I can set you free from it.

My love conquers all. There is nothing that can separate you from My love, so come to My throne of grace and allow Me to set you free from the chains that hold you back from walking forward into the future I have for you … a future filled with hope and peace. You are My child, and I want you to have faith in Me to take care of you in every way. Live in simplicity; trust Me as My child.

"I tell you the truth, unless you turn from your sins and become like little children, you will never get into the Kingdom of Heaven."

MATTHEW 18:3 (NLT)

Forgiven and Forgotten

I not only forgive. I also forget your sins, past, present, and future. My forgiveness is ongoing and never failing. I know every wrong decision you'll ever make and every failure you'll ever endure, and I AM with you always.

When you find yourself overwhelmed with sin and consumed with guilt, turn to Me. I am willing to forgive and quick to forget. I want you to draw near to Me so that I might open your heart to receive the forgiveness I offer you. I'm not surprised by any of your mistakes; I'm well aware of all your faults, and I love you anyway. My love can take your pain and sorrow and heal you in miraculous ways.

Nothing can make your wrongs right, but My love can cover them all. It's your unconfessed sin that keeps you from experiencing the peace you're supposed to live in. Jesus was the perfect sacrifice, and when I look at you, repenting and asking for forgiveness, I don't see you or your sin, I see Christ. He has made a way for you to be reconciled to Me. So stop remembering what I've forgotten and stay focused upon My boundless love for you.

"I will forgive their wickedness, and I will never again remember their sins."

JEREMIAH 31:34 (NLT)

Don't Give In

Temptation will always be a daily part of your life. Continually strengthen your faith through My Word so that you can withstand it. It is vital that you recognize your enemy and that you learn to resist his evil schemes. Temptation is a reality, but you must not allow it to become a hindrance to your faith. Be on guard.

Sometimes temptations don't seem so obvious. The battle begins in your mind. You'll find yourself feeling overwhelmed, doubting that you're capable of doing what I've asked you to do and looking to yourself to solve your problems instead of looking to Me. In moments like these, you are filled with despair because there is no one to help you, and you become impatient in your relationship with Me.

You will need to defeat these thoughts with My promises to you. Don't allow yourself to be lured by the enemy's tactics. You'll need to continually wage war against temptation with My Word and refuse to give up. You'll be tempted to, but you must not. I will be your strength in your weakness, so when you feel a loss of peace, know that you're being tempted and turn to Me for help. Pray to Me, and I will rescue you.

"Pray that you will not fall into temptation."

LUKE 22:40 (NIV)

Uncovering Hidden Motives

There's always a reason you do what you do; it just may not be obvious. You often live in belief, but the motives behind some of your actions are not pure. My goal is to reveal your motives to you so that I can make your heart right. I want you to understand what you're doing and why. I want you to realize that at times your motives aren't in line with My will, and I must help you to have right motives so that you can receive the blessings I have in store for you.

Your impure motives can cause you stress and anxiety. I don't want you doing things to impress people or elevate yourself. You are only to lift Me up, and I will work the miracles and bring about the blessings. I want you to be led by My heart. Being led by pride, greed and other sinful motives will lead you astray. I want you to come to Me with an open heart so that I can expose whatever hidden motives lie within you. I want your burdens to be light. Trust Me to set priorities for you so that you will not be easily led off track from My very best for your life.

The Lord's light penetrates the human spirit, exposing every hidden motive.

PROVERBS 20:27 (NLT)

Forgive as You Have Been Forgiven

My love doesn't just cover one sin, it covers a multitude. I change hearts and lives through forgiveness, and you can too. I've paid a price so that you can be forgiven and forgive. I want you to love "above all things."

I know that forgiveness can often seem impossible, the offense unforgivable, but I've forgiven the unforgivable in you … and I'm asking you to do likewise. Do unto others as I've done to you. Some of the things you need to forgive may be fairly small, but many times you'll face forgiving the unthinkable. And it will seem painful and unfair.

I AM just, you must trust Me. I would never ask you to do anything unless I fully equip you to do it. When it comes to forgiveness you need only allow My love to flow through you. Open your heart. Remember all the ways I've forgiven you, not holding your sins against you. Trust Me to give you the ability to forgive all things in all ways, freely extending to others the love I give to you.

Most important of all, continue to
show deep love for each other,
for love covers a multitude of sins.

1 PETER 4:8 (NLT)

Fighting Sin Within

Sin begins within. And there's no quick-and-easy resolution to the struggle. I know your every thought, every temptation, and I know it's hard. You'll struggle with sin all of your life, and it will affect you in ways that you simply can't see—you'll need to continually fight the battle.

You can fight the battle within you and resist temptation by delighting in My law. The way you grow strong against the temptations you face is to draw near to Me. Sin cannot exist in My presence—I always conquer it. You will need to stand strong upon My Word and refuse to sin by being completely obedient to Me.

When you find yourself in a state of sin, quickly repent. By standing firm in your faith and repenting quickly when you sin, you will build up a resistance to the temptations that threaten you. Don't look for the strength to do this within yourself, for you'll find yourself vulnerable and weak. You must find your strength in Me, using My armor to protect you from the evil one. If you'll look to Me and focus upon Christ who has saved you, you'll win the battle and conquer every temptation. I'm with you to save you.

I don't really understand myself,
for I want to do what is right, but
I don't do it. Instead, I do what I hate.

ROMANS 7:15 (NLT)

Forgiveness

Freely Forgive

Life can bring about situations that you once thought were unthinkable, and you may find yourself needing to forgive what seems unforgivable. I know it's easy to internalize the anger and bitterness until your soul resolves it, but wrongs can seldom be made right and you're going to have to release it all, conquering the hurt with My love.

When you're betrayed and sinned against, you tend to give in to the fleshly emotions of anger that so easily arise. But I have offered you forgiveness for your sins, extending mercy and love, so I ask you to do the same for others. It's not negating the need for justice, but it sets you free from the chains of unforgiveness that can keep you trapped and unable to walk in the abundant life I intend for you to have.

I'm not saying it is easy to forgive others. The sacrifice of Christ was a brutal, fleshly and unjust suffering, but the end result was redemption for mankind. In light of His sacrifice, don't hold on to offenses; simply turn them over to Me and allow My justice and mercy to resolve and restore your breaking heart. Healing is in My hands.

> "If you forgive those who sin against you,
> your heavenly Father will forgive you."
>
> MATTHEW 6:14 (NLT)

Do Yourself a Favor

If you choose to harbor anger and bitterness towards others, you will find your soul tortured and unable to experience peace. I've exemplified forgiveness so that you have a clear picture of what it means and how it heals and redeems. Forgiveness is for you and the one you forgive. So do yourself a favor and forgive.

I know at times it seems that when you forgive, you're letting someone off the hook and they're getting away with their sin, but I AM God, you are not. My justice will pour down. Trust Me to do My job. By forgiving and letting go of the offense and the debt owed you, you are releasing your offenders and the situation to Me so that I can do what only I can do.

If you take revenge, then you have deemed your justice above Mine and you get in the way of My plans and purposes to redeem the situation. My throne is not big enough for the two of us. Let Me deal with the situation. Trust Me to handle it properly. Set yourself free to live in peace and allow Me to render justice by simply forgiving.

"Shouldn't you have mercy on your fellow servant, just as I had mercy on you?"

MATTHEW 18:33 (NLT)

The Freedom of Forgiveness

Forgiveness enables your faith to work. I've commanded you to forgive as I've forgiven you. Unforgiveness will hinder your faith and keep you from My very best in your life. I simply can't forgive you if you do not extend that same forgiveness to others. My grace is sufficient for you and for every other sinner.

Though forgiveness may seem painful, like you're losing control and allowing your offender to go free, the one you are really setting free is yourself. I want you to be happy, healthy and free from the pressure of stress that results from bitterness and resentment. If you'll quickly forgive, your fellowship with Me can flow freely and I can heal your heart.

Don't allow the enemy to convince you that you must maintain control. Unforgiveness will be a foothold that will become a stronghold for Satan, keeping you from the blessings I long to give you. Know that there is no end to the blessings in your life if you'll trust in My Word and obey My command to forgive. You won't be able to do it in your own strength, but you can do it in Mine.

"If you do not forgive others their sins,
your Father will not forgive your sins."

MATTHEW 6:15 (NIV)

Receiving Forgiveness

I know that it's difficult to control your feelings and emotions when you've been wronged. But you can't make decisions based upon your feelings; they will lead you astray. I've given you a free will, but you'll need to choose to trust My will more than your own. You will need to trust in My Word with all of your heart—then you'll begin to live by what you know instead of what you feel.

I know that you will be tempted, and there will be times that you'll fall into sin. I still love you. Come to Me and repent, and I will forgive you, setting you free from the burden of guilt. When you receive My forgiveness, there's no reason to keep remembering what I've forgotten.

I want you to be filled with joy and live free from the guilt of sin. Always remember that where sin abounds, grace, forgiveness, love and mercy abound much more. There is nothing that can separate you from My love, so live in the Truth that My love covers a multitude of sins. Allow My grace to strengthen you to press on with joy into the future, filled with hope that I have prepared for you.

Should we keep on sinning so that God
can show us more and more of His
wonderful grace?

ROMANS 6:1 (NLT)

A One-Way Street

I know that when you've been betrayed and hurt in ways you never thought possible, you naturally react with revenge, anger and bitterness. I know you want to protect your heart by withdrawing from your offender through isolation, but you need to face the situation with My love so that you can forgive and experience peace again.

The idea of waiting for the offender to make things right is usually futile. When I ask you to forgive, I'm simply asking you to let go of the offense and turn the situation over Me. Sinners often "know not what they do."

Your decision to forgive will allow My love to flow and enable them to come to Me. They may not, but you can be a catalyst to their saving grace. Best of all, if you release them from their debt of sin, you will experience peace and joy again. I'll heal your hurting heart and there will be no need to look back on the road you've traveled in pain. Forgiveness is a one-way street, so keep looking to Me and continue moving forward in faith.

Jesus said, "Father, forgive them,
for they know not what they do."

LUKE 23:34 (ESV)

How to Forgive

I know that although I've forgiven you and I've set the example of how you are to forgive, it can still seem confusing. You may struggle with what you're specifically supposed to do and if you've really forgiven in the way you're supposed to.

First and foremost, remember how you've been forgiven—how I loved you in the midst of your sin, how I embraced your repentance, and how I set you free from the guilt. I want you to receive more and more of My grace, enabling you to forgive as I have forgiven you.

Allow Me to render justice and let go of your desire to get even. I know that life is not fair and you endure things that you never thought you could or would. But I'm with you, and if you'll leave justice to Me, you can be sure that I will settle the score. All I ask is that you approach your offenders with My love, responding to evil with good.

I want you to do good to those who hate you and bless those who curse you, while praying for those who mistreat you. You'll know that you've truly forgiven when you can look at your offender and empathize, through My love, with their pain and not just your own.

Be kind and compassionate to one
another, forgiving each other,
just as in Christ God forgave you.

EPHESIANS 4:32 (NIV)

Paid in Full

One of the hardest things you'll ever have to do in life is forgive someone, trusting Me for justice instead of demanding your own. If I have forgiven you in all your imperfection and disobedience, you can forgive others as well. My love and grace is all that's required—rely on My strength in your weakness.

Forgiveness is not just for the benefit of your offender; it's mostly for you. You may never hear an apology, you may never see the wrongs in your life made right, but you must let it go. I want you to live a life full of blessings, fully consumed with My peace. Bitterness and resentment will steal that peace.

You must always remember the price—the sacrifice of Jesus—that was paid on your behalf, and rest in that miracle. Your sin debt was paid in full; I will never ask you to repay what you cannot. All I'm asking you to do is extend to others that same love and grace I've offered to you. It won't be easy to love those who hate you or to bless those who curse you, but you must do it anyway. When you are struggling to forgive, come to Me in prayer. My mercies begin afresh every morning.

"To you who are willing to listen, I say,
love your enemies! Do good to those who
hate you. Bless those who curse you.
Pray for those who hurt you."

LUKE 6:27–28 (NLT)

Trusting God

From Faith to Faith

No matter what you face in life—every obstacle, every decision—do all things with faith. My purposes and plans for your life include situations that will cause you to press on in your faith and draw nearer to Me. There is no need to doubt, for faith overcomes every fear.

Faith—trusting in Me fully—enables you to enjoy your life completely. Living by faith is not based on feelings and emotions, it is a decision that must be made each and every moment of your life. It's a conscious, deliberate choice to place your trust in Me. I've never said faith is easy; you're believing without seeing, and your human nature struggles with truly trusting a God you cannot see. But you see Me in ways that you seldom recognize.

In exercising your faith, praying diligently for what you want and trusting Me for what is best, you are looking expectantly for Me. If you seek Me, you will find Me. I AM faithful in the big things as well as the small things. I want you to step out in faith today and every day, trusting Me for the impossible, relying on Me through your faith, and resting in the promises I've made you.

In it the righteousness of God is revealed
from faith to faith; as it is written,
"But the righteous man shall live by faith."

ROMANS 1:17 (NASB)

When You Don't Understand

There's a reason that I've asked you not to rely on your own understanding. My ways are higher than yours, and are mostly beyond your ability to comprehend. If you always understood My ways, there would be no need for you to trust Me. And your dependence upon Me is essential to the perfection of your faith.

Even with all the overwhelming uncertainty you face, you can trust Me. I want you to learn to live with unanswered questions. I may never give you the answers you want, but you can be assured that I know all, and I'm able to fully see your life from beginning to end. The sin in the world can disrupt the path, but not My purposes.

Come to Me when you're uncertain, unsure of what the future holds. I will fill you with hope so that you can face each day expecting My blessings. Very seldom will you ever be able to see My hand at work, but you know My heart … trust in that alone. Even when you face a staggering series of crises and losses, trust in Me anyway. Believe that I AM always sovereign. You will only experience the peace you desperately need when you stop trying to understand it all and simply trust Me more.

Though He slay me, yet will I wait for and trust Him.

JOB 13:15 (AMP)

Trusting God in the Fire

You worry too much about what people think and what they will say. You must be willing to obey Me at any cost. I've given you My Word to guide you, and it is filled with My promises to be with you and save you.

Whatever miracles you need in your life I AM able to perform. There is nothing that can separate you from My love, My protection, and My power—you are Mine. If you know in your heart what is right, if the Spirit has led you into My will, walk confidently. Simply fear Me above all else and I will be your strong tower. When you're too weak to walk the path I've set before you, come to Me. I will always help you. I will give you the strength and peace you need to take each step of faith.

You will encounter fires of affliction because it's a fallen world. But I AM with you, and I will meet you in the fire. If I'm with you, what is there to fear? What is it that I cannot do? Is anything too difficult for Me? I am able to save you from whatever it is you need saving from. The question is: Do you believe that truth?

If we are thrown into the blazing furnace,
the God whom we serve is able to save us.
He will rescue us from your power.

DANIEL 3:17 (NLT)

With You in Trouble

I know that at times it's difficult to trust Me. You are haunted by the pain of the past and filled with fear about the uncertainty of the future. But you can trust Me. I want to take care of you, providing for you in every way, but your unbelief ties My hands. My power works under the law of faith.

If you'll stop trying to take care of yourself, you will release My power in your life. I won't battle you over control of My throne. I want to be God in every area of your life, delivering the promises I've made you. I've promised to be with you in trouble and save you from whatever is not My will for your life. I will lift you up in due time. Rely on My help. Call to Me in the day of trouble and I will deliver you.

Simply humble yourself before Me and your faith will beckon My grace. I'm not asking you to try harder or to do anything but believe that I can and will do the things I've promised in My Word. Trusting in yourself will only lead to strife, but trusting in Me leads to peace that surpasses all understanding. Just call to Me and I will answer you.

"When they call on Me, I will answer;
I will be with them in trouble. I will
rescue and honor them."

PSALM 91:15 (NLT)

Removing Spiritual Roadblocks

I know that you go through periods of questioning, doubting and even blaming Me for the unpleasant situations in your life. I only want your heart to be open and honest with Me. When your heart grows cold toward Me, filled with unbelief, simply turn back to Me. Do not let the spiritual roadblock of disbelief and doubt keep you from opening your heart to Me.

It's easy to get stuck in bitterness towards Me when you suffer through the unthinkable, enduring what seems unimaginable. But your anger only closes the door on Me. I'm the only One who can help you, heal you, and comfort you. Run back to Me; I AM waiting. Know that all I allow in your life I will use for good. Things may look impossible, but you cannot allow your faith to walk by sight. I know what is best for you. You may stumble, but I won't let you fall. I will uphold you with My righteous right hand. Do not be dismayed, I AM your God, I will strengthen you, I will help you—you will see My glory if you'll only believe.

As for me, it is good to be near God.
I have made the Sovereign LORD my
refuge; I will tell of all Your deeds.

PSALM 73:28 (NIV)

The Measure of Faith

Your first response to any situation should always be prayer. When you pray to Me, you invite Me into your circumstances. Asking for My help is evidence of your faith. There is tremendous power in prayer, and you have been given the privilege of coming boldly to My throne of grace. Know that I can and will meet every one of your needs.

I don't want you to merely pray for an escape from your problems, but realize that I can take you through difficulties, strengthening your faith in the process. Often you will have to wait on Me and My perfect timing, but I will always perform My miracles when they will have the greatest impact on your life and in the lives of others.

Your attitude of thanks as you wait glorifies Me and is a powerful testimony of My faithfulness to those around you. Expect a breakthrough in your situation, especially the impossible. There is no reason to doubt Me. Don't allow fear to steal your destiny. Release your fears through faith and simply trust in Me.

Because of the privilege and authority God has
given me, I give each of you this warning:
Don't think you are better than you really are.
Be honest in your evaluation of yourselves,
measuring yourselves by the faith God has given us.

ROMANS 12:3 (NLT)

Trusting God's Love

Don't allow yourself to drown in your doubts—you have every reason to trust Me and be confident and positive regarding every situation in your life. Don't concentrate on your weaknesses and inadequacies, but instead focus on My strength. I want you to live your life boldly, honestly, and full of hope.

My promises enable you to live without worry and to feel safe and secure. I have amazing plans for your life. I can do more than you can hope for or imagine, so keep hoping. Rely on My Word to get you through each day. When you're uncertain and filled with fear, come and find freedom at My throne of grace. You can always come to Me and express your true feelings.

I want to have a relationship with you in which you are open and honest and able to even express your anger toward Me. My mercy will meet you where you are and My grace will always be more than sufficient to embrace your pain and sorrow. My love goes far beyond your feelings, and your faith in Me, regardless of what lies before you, enables you to experience peace in the midst of the chaos. Your faith in Me, believing against all odds, brings about My greatest miracles.

… In Whom, because of our faith in Him, we dare
to have the boldness (courage and confidence)
of free access (an unreserved approach to
God with freedom and without fear).

EPHESIANS 3:12 (AMP)

Doubt

Overcoming Doubt

Never allow fear to overcome your faith. You will have doubts, but never choose to walk in any other direction than faith. I'm not angry with you when you doubt, and I know that at times your faith will falter. But I want you to turn to Me in your disbelief. I will help you.

Faith is required throughout your life because My power is released as you show your confidence in Me and My Word. Obstacles are an opportunity to experience My faithfulness, so don't doubt just because difficulties come. These are the times when I show Myself strong. With every circumstance you encounter, you must choose whether or not you'll trust Me to direct and guide you into My best for your life. Don't rely on your feelings or depend on your emotions.

Pursue Me in prayer and wait patiently for My answers. I don't want you to miss My blessings for you by making mistakes, by becoming anxious and moving ahead of Me. Yet even if you travel a road I never intended for you to go, I will meet you there. If you call out to Me, I will come to you and redirect your steps into My perfect will. All that's required is faith.

"My righteous ones will live by faith. But I will take no pleasure in anyone who turns away."

HEBREWS 10:38 (NLT)

Stepping into the Unknown

Faith will always require you to step into the unknown. If it didn't, it wouldn't be faith. I use your circumstances to stretch your faith, and oftentimes it's in those difficult places that challenge your faith that you'll encounter doubt. But don't give in to it, simply see it as a catalyst to strengthen your faith.

I'm full of surprises and I'm completely dependable. I'm not always predictable, but I'm forever faithful. So trust in My Word, focus upon My promises, and rest in knowing that I AM sovereign. I want you to come to Me, seeking My help, but also realizing that you need to be persistent in your desire for your faith to grow. Growth may take you places you never thought you could go or would want to.

Faith will seldom be easy because it requires you to step into the unknown, and uncertainties tend to bring about fear. Yet, there is never anything to fear. I AM always with you. I'll ask you to do things that seem unreasonable, and I'll often require that you step out in ways that seem impossible. Rely on My strength and power, and watch your faith step out upon the water.

Peter answered, "Lord, if it is You, order me
to come to You on the water." Jesus said,
"Come!" So Peter got out of the boat
and walked on the water toward Jesus.

MATTHEW 14:28–29 (GW)

Hidden in Mercy

I've assured you that troubles will come. Whether they are unexpected or expected, they threaten your faith, especially when they entail illness, job loss, financial crises or relationship failures—scenarios that can bring the greatest faith crumbling to its foundation.

Some of the storms in life can be short-lived—quick showers with distant thunder that awakens your fear for but a moment. Other storms bring about hurricane-force winds and leave a path of destruction that seems irreparable. Don't allow the storms of life to move you. I will protect you. My mercy will hold you. All you must do is hold fast to your faith. In the midst of the storms of life, I want you to remain calm, focusing on trusting Me. I can do what you cannot—the impossible.

Don't try to go through the challenges of life on your own. Instead run to Me for shelter. Call upon Me in trouble and I will help you. Too often you strive for a way out of the storm, only to drive yourself into another one. Trust Me to fill you with peace and rely on Me to protect you from all that tries to come against you. The key is focusing upon Me and resting beneath the shadow of My wings.

Have mercy on me, O God, have mercy!
I look to You for protection. I will hide
beneath the shadow of Your wings
until the danger passes by.

PSALM 57:1 (NLT)

Doubt and Worry

Doubt stirs up your worries, so know that in order to overcome them, you must first face your doubt with faith. You are My child; therefore there is no need to worry. Don't focus on your problems, let them drive you to My throne and stay focused on Me. Trust in My ability to help you. You can win over your worries—simply turn to Me to help you.

Worries can be endless because life brings about challenges that are impossible for you to handle, and uncertainty about the future gets the best of you. But your worries have no truth to them. You worries don't dictate your future, and most of what you worry about never transpires. If you're filled with fear, confused about what lies ahead and unable to take another step of faith, rely on My promises to you.

I've assured you that I AM with you always, that there's nothing to fear, and that I'm a ready help in times of trouble. I want you to cast your cares upon Me—every thought, burden and worry that is filling you with fear. Let Me handle what you cannot, and trust Me for the miracles you desperately need.

"Can all your worries add a single moment to your life?"
MATTHEW 6:27 (NLT)

Believing the Promises

I want you to be consumed with My grace. I want to bless you beyond anything you can hope for or imagine. I want you to constantly live in My favor, fully trusting that I AM working all things together for good.

I know it's not always easy to believe what I've promised, especially when your fears cause you to believe otherwise. So you'll need to stay focused upon My Word continually. There are far too many challenges in life for you to face them alone and without the assurances that I've given to you. Refuse to give in to fear and doubt. Remain confident in My promises and know that I AM perfect and good in all I do.

Don't try and figure out your circumstances, reasoning them out and giving in to disbelief. I want you to believe that I am loving and good … then you'll see. I want to save you from the doubt that so diligently seeks to destroy you. Your faith needs to believe what it knows, relying on what I've promised and fully trusting in My faithfulness. Never allow your faith to walk by sight. Believe that you will see My goodness in your life and wait expectantly for all I've promised you.

I believe that I will see the goodness of the Lord in this world of the living.

PSALM 27:13 (GW)

Always on Your Mind

Not knowing what lies ahead tends to open the door to fear. Faith should slam the door on doubt and defeat the impending despair. When you're filled with worry, unable to see a way out and with no desire to go through, remember My faithfulness.

It's easy to allow your mind to wander, to be overcome by the worries of the world, but I have not given you a spirit of fear—I've given you a spirit of power and love and a sound mind. Rest in My promises and focus upon My faithfulness. There will be good times and bad, but I AM with you through them all—sometimes to rescue you in them, oftentimes to show you My constant presence and power in your life by taking you through them.

I will be your strength in your weakness, as I always have been. My grace and power in your life have gotten you this far, and I will not leave you nor forsake you. If you're facing the unthinkable and staring into the face of the impossible, recall how I have brought you through the unimaginable before and know that My power has not diminished, and neither has My love for you. You have trusted Me before, it's time to trust Me again.

> I recall all You have done, O LORD; I remember Your wonderful deeds of long ago. They are constantly in my thoughts. I cannot stop thinking about Your mighty works.
>
> PSALM 77:11-12 (NLT)

Without Wavering

I never change. I'm the same yesterday, today and forever. Your life will change direction continually, but I will guide you constantly. There will always be uncertainty, but I AM with you through it all. Don't allow your feelings and emotions to affect your faith. Walking upon the foundation of My Word creates the stability you need when the ground is shaking beneath you.

All of the decisions you make, the small ones, the big ones and all of those in between, should be guided by My Word. I want you to be confident that even amid the chaos, I will continue to work in and through your life to bring about My perfect plans and purposes. You will seldom be able to control the circumstances in your life, but you can respond to them without hastily reacting. Trust in Me and continually meditate upon My Word. Lean on the Holy Spirit to teach and guide you and allow My promises to transform your heart and mind.

Your circumstances should never steal your peace and joy if they are truly found only in Me. Any other peace and joy is temporary and easily lost through changing circumstances. Prepare your heart for the changes that are to come in your life by believing in My Word and never allowing yourself to waver in faith.

> Declare me innocent, O Lord, for I have
> acted with integrity; I have trusted in
> the Lord without wavering.
>
> PSALM 26:1 (NLT)

Blessings

Blessed with Every Blessing

I want you to bless others just as I have blessed you. I want you to have a continual cycle of blessing in your life, and that requires you to bless others.

When life becomes difficult and you feel as though you have nothing left to give, make an effort to give something … anything. Your time, your presence and your prayers transform lives and hearts in unseen ways. Don't allow yourself to believe the lie that you have nothing to offer. I have created you uniquely and placed you in specific circumstances so that you might have a powerful impact with the distinct spiritual gifts I've given you. But you won't be able to be a blessing on your own. I will empower and equip you to do all that I'm asking you to do.

Never will I leave you or forsake you. As you look for opportunities to bless others, I will look for ways in which I can bless you. Rest in My promises and be a witness to others so that they too might be blessed by My love and faithfulness. I'm opening heaven to you, and I'm ready to bless you for being a blessing.

All praise to God, the Father of our
Lord Jesus Christ, who has blessed us with
every spiritual blessing in the heavenly
realms because we are united with Christ.

EPHESIANS 1:3 (NLT)

Asking for the Blessing

I love you beyond anything you can comprehend, and I want to help you in every way. But you need to come to Me and ask Me for all you need and desire. I've designed prayer so that when you feel overwhelmed, you need only lift your voice to heaven and I will answer you. I hear the faintest cry from your heart and I know all of your troubles and trials, but when you come to Me, you are acknowledging that you need Me; you are showing Me your humble heart.

When you're upset and frustrated, tempted to force circumstances to happen instead of waiting on Me, you find yourself on the wrong path. In your desperation, simply call upon Me and I will lead you, guide you, protect you and provide for you in ways you could never imagine. I deeply care about everything that concerns you, so allow Me to bless you. If you'll choose to come to Me, obey Me and lean on Me to give you strength, My power will enable you to walk into the victory I have prepared for you.

Pray and meditate on My Word at all times. It will give you hope when you're hopeless. I want to encourage you when you're discouraged and filled with despair. I will help you in any way you need it; you just need to ask.

You don't have what you want
because you don't ask God for it.

JAMES 4:2 (NLT)

The Blessing of Pain

Pain serves a purpose. I use every obstacle you face to strengthen you so that you are better prepared for the challenges in life that lie ahead. I know what I'm doing when it comes to your sanctification.

If I chose to remove all the challenges in your life, you would never grow in your faith—you'd never learn to truly trust Me in every way. Through every difficulty I permit, I reveal something that needs to be strengthened or trans-formed in you. Your weaknesses are never revealed when "all is well" and life is free of trouble. Trials and tribulations show your true character and display the strength of your faith.

As you walk with Me, I orchestrate your life, the good and the bad, so that you will be strengthened in faith, lacking nothing. I know that in your weakness you desperately want Me to make a way out instead of a way through, but My ways are higher and better. I want you to be strong and stand firm in your faith when it is threatened by the enemy, so you will need plenty of practice to overcome fear and defeat the doubt. Know that I AM with you and I will help you in every way. I AM your God.

> "Don't be afraid, for I am with you. Don't be discouraged, for I am your God. I will strengthen you and help you. I will hold you up with My victorious right hand."
>
> ISAIAH 41:10 (NLT)

Don't Lose Heart

Y ou'll want to give up and give in when your soul is enduring more than you ever thought it could. But you can't lose heart. I can do the impossible, and you need to expect the impossible in your life.

Don't allow life to overwhelm and defeat you. I uphold you with My righteous right hand. I AM dwelling within you, and that means My power is as well. Nothing can frustrate My perfect plans for your life, so there is nothing for you to fear. I want you to experience My peace and joy in all things and at all times. Let nothing move you. No matter what you're going through, My grace is sufficient.

When you're tempted to worry and doubt My provision in your life, remember that your problems may appear to have power over you but they have no power over Me. I have promised you a future filled with hope, so refuse to settle for anything less than peace, joy, and the glorious riches in Christ that are yours. If you'll rely on My strength to get you through every difficulty and never give up, you will experience every blessing you've asked for and more.

You will have success if you are careful to observe the decrees and laws that the LORD gave Moses for Israel. Be strong and courageous. Do not be afraid or discouraged.

1 CHRONICLES 22:13 (NIV)

Receiving through Faith

I see you continually trying instead of trusting. I need you to be completely reliant on Me if I'm to perform miracles in your life. You try to create your own changes, but only I can create the change you need from the inside out. You need to let Me be God in every area of your life.

I know how desperate your needs are. I know how your heart longs for all its desires, and I want to give you peace that I will not withhold one good thing from you as you trust in Me. Give up your desire to control your life and allow Me the joy of transforming your life from glory to glory. It's up to you to live from faith to faith. I will give you peace to remain calm and secure through all of life's storms. Just trust Me to take you through them.

It's not about what you can do in the situations you face; it's about what I have done for you. I want you to focus on My heart, not My hand. Your faith will bring about the blessings you desire. Live each moment in peace, joy and confidence. Trust Me with your life, for every blessing depends on your faith.

The promise is received by faith.
It is given as a free gift.

ROMANS 4:16 (NLT)

Blessing Your Neighbor

I've created you specifically to accomplish things that no one else on earth can. Your spiritual gifts are unique so that you will be equipped to bless others in a particular way. You are made for a purpose. Don't compare yourself to others; the only thing that matters is how I see you.

I will orchestrate circumstances for you to uniquely use your gifts—trust Me to bring the right opportunities to you. The paths I pave for you may not always be easy. They may present challenges that require Me to do the impossible, but I need you to trust that I know what I'm doing.

I want you to lay aside your fears and trust that I will equip you to do what I'm asking you to do. All that I do is for good, even though it may not seem like it at the time. I have blessed you so that you will be a blessing to others. Just rely on My strength and allow Me to work in and through you.

In His grace, God has given us different gifts
for doing certain things well. So if God
has given you the ability to prophesy,
speak out with as much faith as
God has given you.

ROMANS 12:6 (NLT)

The Blessing of a Hope-Filled Future

You tend to lose track of your blessings. I know it's easier to see what you're lacking, rather than what you have, but focusing on all the ways in which you've been blessed can provide hope when all hope seems gone.

Hopelessness can lock you into a prison of your past. Your doubt and despair keep you from moving into the future with faith, and you can easily begin to live a life of discouragement. My Word will set your thoughts straight, transforming your mind and enabling you to see a hope-filled future. You need to let go of your past, focus upon the ways you've been blessed, and move into the future I have for you.

Don't allow discouragement and despair to keep you from My very best in your life. I have blessed you in the past, but I have so much more I want to do in and through you in the future. Even if you're faced with what seem like hopeless situations, rely on My promises to give you new insight into your circumstances. I want you to always wait for Me hopefully and expectantly, depending fully upon Me, assured that I have plans for you ... to give you a future and a hope.

The Lord is good to those whose hope
is in Him, to the one who seeks Him.

LAMENTATIONS 3:25 (NIV)

Listening to God

More Than Meets the Eye

I know it's easy to walk by sight instead of by faith. What you see seems so much more real than what you don't. But the spiritual realm is just as real as the physical. Your humanness gets in the way of discerning spiritual realities, so you need to be continually connected to Me through prayer to see them. I will give you spiritual understanding. Ask and keep on asking. When you call upon Me, I will answer.

The Spirit will lead and guide you, teaching you things that you do not know. You will not always have a complete vision or full understanding, but I will lead you step by step. I want you to be at peace knowing that you are being led by My Spirit, instead of making decisions based on your own finite knowledge, emotions and desires.

My guidance is a gift to you, helping you to avoid the pits of destruction. But you must come to Me. You must pray and ask Me to develop and increase your discernment so that you will have more and more peace. Things aren't always what they seem, so pray that I will give you revelation … and I will.

Let those who are wise understand these things.
Let those with discernment listen carefully.
The paths of the LORD are true and right,
and righteous people live by walking in them.
But in those paths sinners stumble and fall.

HOSEA 14:9 (NLT)

Are You Listening?

I don't always speak to you in the same way. You want to hear Me audibly, but rarely do I speak so directly. More often than not, I will speak to you through others, in circumstances, and by the simple beauty of the world around you. So look for Me and then listen carefully.

It is vital that we have an ongoing intimate relationship so that I can lead you into My perfect will for your life. Your struggles and difficulties can come between us from time to time, and I need you to draw nearer to Me during the times when the troubles of life try to drown out My voice. You'll need to daily make the decision to quiet the noise around you and focus on being sensitive to My still, small voice. I will speak to you about everything—not just the big things in your life, but the small things as well.

I will often give you desires within your heart and then find ways in the world around you to lead you in the direction I need you to go. So don't wait for My audible voice. Listen with all of your senses. Find joy in knowing that I AM with you, always desiring to speak to you. All you must do is listen.

> You will hear a voice behind you saying,
> "This is the way. Follow it, whether it
> turns to the right or to the left."
>
> ISAIAH 30:21 (GW)

The Way You Should Go

My plans and purposes for your life won't always seem obvious. As I lead and guide you, you will not always have a full understanding of what exactly I'm asking you to do and why. I just need you to listen to Me and obey.

Faith is going to take you in directions you never imagined, and new paths will be opened before you as I work in and through your life. Often things won't make sense. You'll struggle with whether or not you trust Me. Your emotions will get the better of you from time to time, and you'll have to draw nearer to Me in order to allow My voice to speak over your own. My grace will be all you need as I take you through trials and troubles, so there's nothing to fear.

Your greatest challenge is going to be to trust Me when you can't see the very next step in front of you. I know it's hard to walk by faith, but that's why I'm with you always. I will speak to you. I will lead you. I will guide you. My plans and each step you should take will be clear. Just be patient, don't demand My answer before it's time. I will speak to you when the impact is perfect and powerful.

"I [the Lord] will instruct you and teach you
in the way you should go; I will counsel
you with My eye upon you."

PSALM 32:8 (AMP)

Full of Surprises

You tend to look for Me to be predictable, but I'm full of surprises. Don't allow your fears to keep you from hoping in the impossible. I want you to live an outrageously exciting life, learning to walk by faith and experiencing My joy and peace along the way.

I will continually ask you to step into the unknown. I use the uncertainties of your life to develop your trust in Me. So don't draw back in fear just because you're required to step out of your comfort zone. Situations that cause fear are also opportunities for your faith to become stronger and ultimately victorious. When you're tempted to doubt the direction in which I'm taking you, uncertain if I will perform the miracles needed to fulfill My plans and purposes, dig deep into My Word.

You won't ever have Me all figured out, but you can be assured of My character and faithfulness through My previous promises fulfilled throughout history and in your own life. Don't worry about the details of the direction I'm taking you; leave those to Me. Just trust in My voice, know My Word, rely on My promises to fuel your faith, and know for certain that you'll be blessed for your desire to follow Me.

Jesus said, "Blessed rather are those
who hear the word of God and keep it!"

LUKE 11:28 (ESV)

Listening for Truth

It's easy to get lost in all the things that are wrong in life. Pain tends to overshadow joy. You will have troubles in this life—it's a fallen world. But I've given you My promises to keep your faith focused upon truth, not the lies the world presents you.

Don't be deceived by your feelings and emotions, and don't allow yourself to give in to despair. You will have to make a choice in your most difficult moments as to whether you will live within My joy or yield to discouragement and depression. There is always a positive route and a negative route when it comes to your thinking. My truth will enable you to think positively, with hope, when you are overwhelmed with negative circumstances.

You always have a reason to hope if you're placing your trust in Me. As I perfect your faith through trials and troubles and work in and through you to accomplish My purposes, I want you to enjoy life. I want you to live each moment to the fullest, focusing on My promises to you, assured that I will provide and protect you in every way. Live in My peace and let My joy be your strength.

> The thief comes only in order to steal and
> kill and destroy. I came that they may
> have and enjoy life, and have it in
> abundance (to the full, till it overflows).
>
> JOHN 10:10 (AMP)

Stepping Out

Faith will always cause you to live on the edge between the known and the unknown. I ask you to walk by faith and not by sight so that you might come to know Me more intimately, so that you will see, firsthand, My mighty power. Faith calls you to action, to join Me in fulfilling My plans and purposes. So when I call you, be ready to go where I lead you.

You will need to walk closely with Me, listening for My voice continually. I will always be with you to lead, guide and direct you. There is nothing to fear, because I've gone before you and prepared the way. As you seek Me, I will fill you with desires that will guide you onto the path I want you to take. I'll open up doors of opportunity so that you can be a witness to others.

I only ask that you lift Me up, and I will draw all men unto Me. Know that I will give you a deeper desire to be used by Me as you gain a glimpse of the powerful impact you are having on eternity. Trust Me to help you step out in faith and you'll reap blessings beyond all you can imagine.

I heard the voice of the Lord, saying,
"Whom will I send? Who will go for Us?"
I said, "Here I am. Send me!"

ISAIAH 6:8 (GW)

Provision

Don't Waste Your Time

It's easy to get overwhelmed with the worries of the world, but it's only a waste of your time. I don't want you to be anxious about tomorrow because I've only given you enough of My grace for today. I want you to have faith for the future but live in the present hope right now.

I will give you all the strength you need in the moment you need it, and I want you to use that strength to live out My purposes for your life, not worry. I don't want you to miss out on one of My blessings, and worry will rob you of My blessings. If you rely on My promises to you and live in the hope they offer, you will not need to waste your time worrying.

You will never have all the answers, but you can have the confident assurance that I will do what I've promised to do and you can trust Me to equip you with all you need for today, tomorrow, and every day thereafter. Receive the fullness of My grace today, in this moment. Focus on Me and on the here and now. There's no need to worry about the future; everything is fully under My control.

"Don't worry about tomorrow, for
tomorrow will bring its own worries.
Today's trouble is enough for today."

MATTHEW 6:34 (NLT)

Parting Waters

If you thoroughly study My Word, you'll find impossible situations made possible in mighty ways. The miracles recorded were not just for those who experienced them, but for you to find hope and assurance that I can and will perform miracles in your life as well.

When your back is against the wall and there is no solution to your problems in sight, I will part the waters and provide you with a way of escape. I might take you through the parted waters, and fear may accompany you, but I will be with you just as I was with Moses and the Israelites through the Red Sea.

I AM aware of every detail in your life and I know when you're trapped with no place to go. Trust Me to always provide for you and protect you against all the evil that comes against you. Rely on Me and draw near to Me during your times of despair and you'll be amazed at the miracles I will show you. And when I have rescued you, there is celebrating to be done. Rejoice in Me and My love for you. Know that the impossible situations in your life are by My design. I want to show you My mighty power and My great love for you.

Moses stretched out his hand over the sea, and the LORD drove the sea back by a strong east wind all night and made the sea dry land, and the waters were divided.

EXODUS 14:21 (ESV)

The Provision of Peace

I see your life from beginning to end, and I want to bless you with every good thing. But sometimes the "good" things come after great trials and tribulations. Don't be deceived by what you see. I work more mightily in your life when I see you walking by faith. Stand firm and keep trusting Me; there are great rewards ahead.

You might need to sacrifice hopes and desires in the short term in order to reap long-term blessings. Pain and sorrow can yield way to great peace and joy when you believe in My promises. I may discipline you by orchestrating situations in your life that will be overwhelming and challenging, taking your faith into hard places. This is not to discourage you or fill you with fear, but to challenge your faith and perfect it.

I want you to rely on My provision and learn to trust Me more fully. When you're unsure about the future and unable to find the courage to take a step of faith, come to Me and I will help you. I will provide peace and fill you with strength so that you might walk forward into the future I have prepared for you.

No discipline seems pleasant at the time,
but painful. Later on, however, it produces
a harvest of righteousness and peace for
those who have been trained by it.

HEBREWS 12:11 (NIV)

Provided with Protection

Nothing can ever separate you from My love. Nothing could make Me love you more or less than I always have and always will. I want you to be assured of My protection. I want you to feel safe and be free of fear. The world has many troubles, many of which you will endure, but I ultimately oversee everything I allow in your life.

I want you to find peace in knowing that I have given My angels charge over you, to guard you, to protect you, and to watch over you in every way. There will be situations you face that you will not understand because they bring you pain and sorrow, but you are not always aware of how I have protected you from even greater tragedy.

I AM your keeper and I will never leave you or forsake you. I hold your life with My righteous right hand and I will keep you always. I always have a plan and I am always working in your life, whether you realize it or not. I want you to rest in My peace, knowing that I have everything under control. I never sleep nor slumber. I AM always watching over you, so there is never anything to fear. I want you to relax, let go of your worries, and know that I AM holding you.

He will give His angels charge concerning you, to guard you in all your ways.

PSALM 91:11 (NASB)

Divine Nature

I have made you to share My divine nature. I want you to receive and share My nature through the promises I've made you. When you develop godly habits, you will come to recognize My provision for you. Through your humility, you'll see that your dependence upon Me yields blessings, big and small, in your life. I will often empty you so that you can be filled, so do not fear when you feel as though life is falling apart. It's really just falling into place … into My plan.

I want you to fully be Mine, yielded to Me and My will at all times. I want you to be identified as Mine and I want My blessings to flow through you continually. Don't try to understand My ways or try to figure out the future. Just live in this moment and know that you're right where I want you, even if you're filled with despair.

I often remove idols in your life so that you might come to My throne. I want you to live a self-sacrificing life, always giving and always being satisfied by your relationship with Me alone. Trust in My love for you.

Because of His glory and excellence, He has given us great and precious promises. These are the promises that enable you to share His divine nature and escape the world's corruption caused by human desires.

2 PETER 1:4 (NLT)

Meeting All Your Needs

I know it's not easy to trust Me to provide for all your needs. Sometimes you think things are just too impossible; at other times you think your needs are too small for Me to care. But I've promised to provide for all your needs.

You can plan and prepare for your journey of life all you want, but you will need Me. You burden yourself by trying to do everything on your own. You wonder how I can possibly provide for more income, and you struggle with how it is I can work within someone's heart to restore a broken relationship. But I've told you not to lean on your own understanding. Your journey, your story, is one that you can write on your own, or you can allow Me to write it.

I assure you that My plans for your life are far more amazing than anything you can hope for or imagine. So, instead of trying so hard, instead of carrying all your burdens alone, come to Me and let Me help you. A humble heart will move My hand in miracle-working ways. When you're tempted to doubt, and fear and despair threaten to consume your faith, draw near to Me and rest in My love.

He has not left Himself without testimony: He has shown kindness by giving you rain from heaven and crops in their seasons; He provides you with plenty of food and fills your hearts with joy.

ACTS 14:17 (NIV)

The Great Provider

I AM your great provider. There is nothing too difficult for Me, and there's no miracle that I can't perform. In troubled times, saturate your mind with My promises. They will give you hope when all hope seems gone.

My truth will help you to rise above your distress and drive you deeper into your faith. I never run out of resources to help you in times of trouble. I want you to know that My grace will always be sufficient for your every need. I restore and redeem. Trust Me to be faithful in every way that you need Me to be. When you're fearful and feeling alone, come to Me in prayer and ask for My help. Focus on what is true and believe that I'm at work in your circumstances.

Do not allow yourself to give in to the fear that comes with not feeling in control. Remember that I AM always sovereign, always in control. You can be certain of one thing: I will provide you with everything. So live in the hope that I've given in My promises and cling to the measure of faith I've given you. I will take you from glory to glory as you live from faith to faith.

Command those who are rich in this present world not to be arrogant nor to put their hope in wealth, which is so uncertain, but to put their hope in God, who richly provides us with everything for our enjoyment.

1 TIMOTHY 6:17 (NIV)

God's Word

Set Free through Truth

You live in a fallen world, filled with deception and lies that challenge your faith and fill you with fear. But I have given you My Word—truth that can keep you on the path of righteousness. When you're confused, come to Me, listen for My still, small voice, and listen to the truth that I will speak to you.

Life can take you in many different directions, but My truth leads you down paths that bring blessings in your life. It doesn't mean that you will not encounter trial and troubles, but you will have the solid foundation of truth that will make your faith stand firm in the face of fear. My Word will keep you from losing hope when all hope seems lost. When you start to doubt that I love you and care about you, My Word will assure you of the truth that I AM with you always and I will never leave you.

It's truth that will give you the strength you need to take another step of faith, to trust Me to help you no matter what you're going through. When you're trapped in disbelief and struggling in your faith, My truth will set you free from the chains of fear and doubt. So don't live captured by the lies of the world. Break free through truth and live the life of joy and peace I intend for you to live.

> "You will know the truth, and
> the truth will set you free."
>
> JOHN 8:32 (GW)

No Empty Words

Do not take My Word lightly. I've spoken to you through the Bible so that you might have instructions for life, keeping you on the path of righteousness. My Word does not contain empty words, but words of life.

Your spiritual life hinges upon My Word. You must live by My Word, abiding in it and allowing it to sustain you. It has life-giving power. The power contained within My Word is the foundation of your joy. It is what will give you hope when hope is gone and fill you with peace when you are in the midst of chaos and destruction.

When life becomes frustrating and you're struggling to make meaning of it all, you can come to Me and I will speak to you through My Word. I will shelter you under it and provide for and protect you as I've promised you. I want you to learn to breathe My Word with every breath you take. I want you to claim every promise I've made as fulfilled in your life. If you will grasp the power of My Word and lean upon it, you'll find yourself experiencing more victories than you ever thought possible.

Take to heart all the words I have solemnly declared to you this day, so that you may command your children to obey carefully all the words of this law.

DEUTERONOMY 32:46 (NIV)

By Day and By Night

Y ou tend to allow your thoughts to manage the direction of your life instead of demanding that My truth dictate it. If you make meditating upon My Word a habit, then obeying it will become a natural response rather than a challenge. Trusting in Me doesn't come easily; you must use discipline in studying My Word and do it consistently.

You have many habits—some good, some bad—and you need to pray that I would search your heart and reveal to you what areas of your life need to be worked on. You may not always like what I show you, but I have your very best interests at heart. I want you to live life to the full, experiencing My greatest blessings. Lean on Me completely so that you do not live in the bondage of bad habits that tend to lead you off My course for your life.

My Word will help you take every thought captive, enabling you to live obediently to My law. You will always see victory if you realize that My law has been given to you not to keep you in bondage, but to set you free from the lies of the world. I want you to live full of faith and free of fear, never missing the endless blessings that I have stored up for you.

They delight in the law of the LORD,
meditating on it day and night.

PSALM 1:2 (NLT)

To Keep You from Stumbling

At any given moment you will need to make critical decisions that could change the course of your life. You can easily be deceived, which is why you must walk by faith, trusting in My Word.

I always want you to look to Me first when you are making decisions in your life. Whether they are small decisions or big ones, I want to be involved in every step you take. I have a plan for your life, to give you a future and a hope, but you'll need to walk closely with Me, listening carefully to My direction. You may get off course from time to time, but I AM always with you and I can put you back on the right path when you wander away from Me.

I AM always looking after you, so I always know where to find you even when you lose your way. My desire is that you would study My Word so thoroughly that you would have My eyes to see with and My thoughts within you at all times. I want you to have peace along the journey of life, even when you face uncertainties that cause you to fear. I've given you My Word to direct you so that you can live confidently and contentedly, knowing that you are Mine.

Great peace have those who love Your law,
and nothing can make them stumble.

PSALM 119:165 (NIV)

My Good and Pleasing and Perfect Will

I know it's easy to fall into the ways of the world. Your thought patterns so easily fall in line with those around you, and it's difficult to walk by faith. But in order to live by faith, you're going to need to think My thoughts and take every thought that is not in line with My Word captive, making it obedient to Christ.

More often than you'd think, you'll need to renew your mind. It can get cluttered with the lies of the world and tainted by your circumstances. You'll need to continually dig deep into My Word. It will take energy, effort and time, but studying the truth I've spoken to you will keep you from falling into the traps of the enemy.

Discipline yourself to develop good thought patterns that come from trusting in My promises to you. Don't be too hard on yourself; it will take some time to train your mind to constantly live in My hope. Don't feel overwhelmed, just take one thought at a time and let Me help you transform it so that I can lead you into the life I have for you that is good and pleasing and perfect.

Don't copy the behavior and customs of this world, but let God transform you into a new person by changing the way you think. Then you will learn to know God's will for you, which is good and pleasing and perfect.

ROMANS 12:2 (NLT)

Thinking Clearly

You can't allow your mind to wander. You must control your thoughts and make sure they align with My Word. I don't want your thoughts causing you to stumble as you run the race I've set before you.

I want you to stay focused upon Me so that you don't go astray. Your thoughts can so easily take over your life. You worry about things that will never happen and make decisions based on fear. I want you thinking clearly, through My Word, so that you will stay on the path of My will for your life.

Don't assume that if the road is easy, you're going in the right direction. Most of the time the paths I take you down entail challenges that will frustrate your faith. I will use these times to draw you nearer to Me, to teach you to rely on Me in every way, and to help you learn to rely on My Word to guide and direct you.

Don't become discouraged if your vision gets clouded by your feelings and emotions. Simply seek Me and ask Me to help you to see things clearly. I will give you the grace to hear Me and to obey Me. Keep looking up when life's got you down and confused. I will surely help you.

So prepare your minds for action and exercise self-control. Put all your hope in the gracious salvation that will come to you when Jesus Christ is revealed to the world.

1 PETER 1:13 (NLT)

Deeper Devotion

My Word is not simply to teach what to do and not to do; its purpose is to lead you into a deeper devotion with Me. My Word is sweeter than honey because it brings a sweetness to your life and fills you with satisfaction and joy. I want you to crave My Word and long to be near to Me.

I want your time spent in My Word to be enjoyable, to bring a satisfaction to you that the world cannot. The world leaves you temporarily satisfied in the flesh, but spiritually you are left empty, and I want to fill you to the full. You are often too easily pleased because you base your pleasures on your fleshly desires. But I want you to live deeper. I want you to experience the supernatural in your physical world.

I don't want you to be satisfied by the simple pleasures of life. It is through My Word that you will come to know that things are so much deeper than what they appear on the surface. My promises are sweeter than honey and filled with hope, so come and listen to My voice. Taste and see that I AM good.

How sweet are Your words to my taste,
sweeter than honey to my mouth!

PSALM 119:103 (ESV)

Believing God

Faithfulness over Failures

I don't ever want you to feel that just because you've failed in the past means that I can't use you to fulfill My purposes. I use broken people to alter the course of history, so if you're broken, rest assured that you're in a place where I can use you. I just need you to believe in Me and then believe in yourself.

The struggle between your failures and your faith can keep you from accomplishing all that I desire you to do in your life. When I call you to join Me in fulfilling My purposes for your life and the world around you, I'm not asking you to do it all in your own strength. I know that what I ask of you often requires the impossible, and that's the part that I do. I'm just looking for you to open your heart and mind, do what I ask you to do, and then leave the rest to Me.

I know that you will have fears and doubts, feeling inadequate to do what I'm asking you to do, but I will honor your faithfulness and I will never put you to shame. I will provide every resource you need to obey My will for your life, and I will empower you to be courageous, faithful and victorious.

> Moses protested to God, "Who am I to appear before Pharaoh? Who am I to lead the people of Israel out of Egypt?"
>
> EXODUS 3:11 (NLT)

Blessings and Burdens

I don't want you to lose faith just because you go through difficult times. I know it can be confusing when you're enduring pain and sorrow and it appears as though unbelievers suffer little. Don't be fooled by what you see. As a believer, you may encounter more troubles because you are not living as the world wants you to. You're living according to My will, and that's not always easy in your fallen world. But I AM with you.

Hard times do not negate My mercy and grace. I AM always at work on your behalf. You may not always be able to see what I'm doing as I work behind the scenes of your life. But you can trust Me and believe that your burdens will lead to blessings. I use all things for good.

I need you to believe, even during your most difficult days and hardest nights, that My love and wisdom are doing what is absolutely best. Your faith cannot walk by sight; you must trust in My love for you and My power to fulfill every promise I've made you. In your suffering, I never leave you. I AM with you. Believe that no matter what happens, I can work all things together for good.

"In that way, you will be acting as true children of your Father in heaven. For He gives His sunlight to both the evil and the good, and He sends rain on the just and the unjust alike."

MATTHEW 5:45 (NLT)

Boldly Believing

Life is full of pain, sorrow, limitations, failure, injustice and disappointment, but all of your circumstances are within My providence. I AM always working all things together for good.

Things may not always seem like they are going to work together for good, but you can trust in My promises to you. Most of the time it's the toughest circumstances that strengthen your faith the most. I want you to learn to not just have faith and hope in an expected outcome, but to have hope in Me, knowing that I will do what is best for you. I can't promise it will be easy or pleasant, but I can assure you that I love you and I always have your very best interests at heart. When troubles come your way, I want you to get to the point where you don't immediately worry, but look to Me and wait upon Me to work within your circumstances. When you encounter difficulties I want you to not be filled with doubt and disbelief, but instead be assured that if I've allowed it, I will use it for good. I want you to have peace at all times and in all ways, so trust in the promises I've made to you and decide to believe each and every one of them.

My being in prison has given most of the believers more confidence in the Lord, so that they grow bolder all the time to preach the message fearlessly.

PHILIPPIANS 1:14 (GNT)

Continuing in Faith

There will be many unanswered questions in your life. Even when you are obedient to Me and walking in My will, you may not experience the feeling of peace and tranquility. Often, the opposite is true. Your obedience can lead to trials because the deeper you go in your faith and the further you come into My kingdom, the more likely you are to meet resistance.

As you walk out your faith in your daily life, you'll be tempted to rely on your feelings as to whether something is right or not. But your responses to life and the circumstances you face should be made by seeking My Word and testing to see if your decisions are in line with My will.

The direction may not always be clear, so often you will need to be patient and wait until I provide a clear path for you to take. Sometimes you will agree with the guidance I give you, at other times you will be tempted to question My ways. I want you to believe that I AM sovereign and loving, but I don't want you to simply believe it because I say it, I want you to look at those who have gone before you and have witnessed, firsthand, My faithfulness. You can trust Me.

They strengthened the disciples in these cities and
encouraged the disciples to remain faithful.
Paul and Barnabas told them, "We must suffer
a lot to enter God's kingdom."

ACTS 14:22 (GW)

Perfect Peace and Rest

There are so many ways in which life can come crashing in on you, but there is no reason to fear. Whether you have walked down the wrong path in life or been forced down it for reasons you had no control over, I AM with you and I will deliver you.

I know that in difficult times you seek peace and rest, and there are two ways I can answer those prayers: I can remove the troubles, or I can give you a calm spirit in the midst of them. More often than not I want to take you through your troubles so that you can learn to trust in and rely on Me.

I want you to pray to be rescued from your trials and tribulations, but I want you to also trust Me if I decide it's best to take you through them. Don't lose faith and stop believing in Me just because I don't answer you in the way you want Me to. Don't give in to doubt as you struggle to walk forward in faith. Simply step out and believe My promises to you. Pray, listen as I speak to you, and trust in what I've told you. There is nothing to be afraid of, for I AM with you and nothing is too difficult for Me.

They were all terrified when they saw Him.
But Jesus spoke to them at once. "Don't be afraid,"
He said. "Take courage! I am here!"

MARK 6:50 (NLT)

A Higher and Better Perspective

Don't give in to negative thinking. I know it's easy to when your job hangs by a thread, your finances have fallen apart, or your relationships just aren't working anymore. But if you focus on what is wrong, you develop unhealthy emotions, anxious thoughts, and a fearful spirit. And you lose your faith.

I see your life and the circumstances of the world from a much different perspective. I see the big picture, and that changes everything. I want you to see through My eyes, so I've given you My Word, which contains My thoughts. I don't want you relying on what you see or what others tell you. I want you to come to Me. I want you to glimpse your life and your situations through My eyes.

From heaven's standpoint, the impossible is possible. From My perspective, anything can happen at any time because I'm sovereign, in control, and able to do all things. My power reaches outside of time and space and I do not operate within the physical world. And that means that I can change human hearts and provide resources that don't exist one moment, but do in the next. I'm full of surprises, and they are always for good. Believe in My vision for your life, trust that I know what is best, and rest while I work.

"As the heavens are higher than the earth,
so are My ways higher than your ways
and My thoughts than your thoughts."

ISAIAH 55:9 (NKJV)

Believing That You Have a Blessing to Give

In order to be blessed, you need to be a blessing. And you're going to have to trust Me when I say that I need you to bless others when you don't feel like it or when you are certain you have nothing to offer. Trust Me when I say that if I bring an opportunity into your life to bless someone, I will equip and enable you to do it.

You are a vessel of My mercy and grace, and I intend to use your life each and every day for My purposes. You will need to continually surrender to My will and obey all that I command. I invite you to test My faithfulness. If you will follow My plan for giving and surrendering your life to Me, I will bring about miracles in your life that go far beyond all you could hope for or imagine.

I want you to step out of your comfort zone, trusting Me more and more. I want you to step into the impossible and see that I make *all* things possible. I want you to personally witness My faithfulness so that your testimony will be sure and strong, unshakable and longstanding. I want your faith to be a solid foundation that blesses others.

"Test Me in this way," says the Lord of Armies.
"See if I won't open the windows of heaven
for you and flood you with blessings."

MALACHI 3:10 (GW)

Salvation

Deepest Mercy

Everyone falls short of My glory. Yet My grace sheds mercy on all those who come to a place of repentance. I want you to always remember the price that has been paid for your sins—past, present and future. Those sins, once forgiven, can so easily return, so My mercy is new every morning.

When you come to the Cross, you can leave your sins at the foot of it and be cleansed. Your sins have been nailed to the Cross, the price has been paid, and there is no longer any room for guilt or shame. Let go of what I already have and work diligently at building an intimate relationship with Me. You will need to draw close to Me each and every moment of your life, clinging to My Word and diligently living out the faith you profess.

You cannot live the life you're called to in your own strength, but you can rely on the strength that Christ gives you, so that you can experience My glory. You have been justified, now you must be sanctified, changed from glory to glory. Live in the joy I've given you. You've been redeemed.

Since, therefore, we have now been justified by His blood, much more shall we be saved by Him from the wrath of God.

ROMANS 5:9 (ESV)

More Grace

You tend to forget My grace. You receive My mercy but fail to accept My grace. My desire is that you would allow My grace to fill you to the full, until you overflow. I want you to know My love for you in ways you can't imagine.

My grace shows up when you look to Me for all you need. My resources are limitless, but your lack of faith limits them in your circumstances. I don't require your life—your behaviors and actions—to be perfect for you to receive My grace. I only require you to have faith in Me. I only ask that you come to Me and allow Me to love you completely, with your failures, faults and everything in between.

I have made you, I will perfect you, and I will take you from glory to glory as you live your life from faith to faith. Do not put any distance between us, simply because you know that you've fallen short of My glory. Draw near to Me at all times, good and bad, and receive My grace, the favor I will always give you, even when you least deserve it.

He gives us more grace. That is why
Scripture says: "God opposes the
proud but shows favor to the humble."

JAMES 4:6 (NIV)

See for Yourself

Your salvation is personal. No one can explain it to you and you can't fully explain it to others. You can let your light shine before men, showing them My glory, but ultimately I give the grace that saves.

Something happens when you live the saved, surrendered life—you start to desperately want others to be saved as well. My Spirit comes alive within you when you are saved, creating the desire to lead others to Me. At the point you believe in the sacrifice made for you, your eyes are opened to see those who also need to be saved. This is the evidence that I AM alive in you, using your life for My purposes, enabling you to live in the Kingdom and bringing others into it.

My plan of salvation is such a personal, intimate one. No one has the same story. No one knows Me in the exact same way you do, and no one knows you in the ways that I do. I have designed a life of faith to be unique, so that you are aware that I AM your God. I want you to witness, firsthand, My power in bringing about miracles. I want you to see for yourself that I AM God and there is no other.

Come and see for yourself.

JOHN 1:46 (NLT)

Saved Once and Forever

Although I "save" you from temptation and difficulties over and over again, the price for your salvation was paid once and for all. You do not need to be continually saved. When you come to Me, trusting in My sacrifice to save you from your sins, I restore and redeem, making all things new through your repentance.

I've made it possible for you to come to Me and receive My grace, right where you are, even in the shadow of all your sins. I want you to stop often and think about what an amazing miracle it is for Me to wipe the slate clean, to leave your sin behind, and to enable you to live a completely new life. It's not a temporary fix, it's a once-and-forever saving grace that sets you free from your past and enables you to walk forward in future glory.

It's the blood of Christ that purifies you and makes you whiter than snow. Know that it is Jesus and Jesus alone who has enabled you to come to Me and My throne of grace. Recognize the power that has saved you. It is because of My great love for you that we will spend eternity together.

Therefore He is able, once and forever, to save those who come to God through Him. He lives forever to intercede with God on their behalf.

HEBREWS 7:25 (NLT)

Dead and Gone

Whether you realize it fully or not, the person you once were is dead and gone. You were made alive in Christ when you first believed. You are completely saved, but every day you must yield to Christ. Christ in you can accomplish more than you can ever imagine. Don't miss out on the life I have purposed you for.

You can try and live this life on your own, or you can realize that you were never meant to. You are not capable of working the miracles that need to be performed or able to acquire the resources needed to bring them about—only I can do the impossible. Yet I allow you to join Me in bringing My kingdom to earth.

When you live diligently in your new life, realizing your responsibility and allowing Me to help you carry your burdens, you help others see the salvation I am offering. Whatever it is you do or say, do it all to My glory and you'll experience a life of faith that goes beyond all you ever dreamed of.

> My old self has been crucified with Christ. It is
> no longer I who live, but Christ lives in me. So I live
> in this earthly body by trusting in the Son of God,
> who loved me and gave Himself for me.
>
> GALATIANS 2:20 (NLT)

Proclaiming Salvation through Suffering

No matter what is going on in your life, I want you to rejoice in Me. When your back is against the wall and life is falling apart around you, sing praises and realize that there's a reason for all I allow. Through worship, you'll rid yourself of worries and your eyes will be opened to My ways.

Though you wish there was another way, trials and troubles test your faith like nothing else can. Through testing, the state of your faith is truly revealed. I use crises to clarify your faith and to cleanse your heart, so don't think that your struggles are in vain. I have saved you and I want to strengthen and perfect your faith so that you might help others be saved. When unbelievers look upon your life and all that you endure, seeing strength when there should be weakness and joy when there is only visible pain, I AM glorified. And when I'm glorified, My light pierces the darkness, enabling those who don't know Me to see Me, inviting them to ultimately come to Me. So don't see your suffering for only what it appears on the surface, see it as being necessary to perfect your faith and call others to Me.

I want you to know, my dear brothers and sisters, what has happened to me here has actually served to advance the gospel.

PHILIPPIANS 1:12 (NIV)

God's Power

Limitless Power

You tend to doubt Me because you compare My abilities with your own. As your circumstances become more difficult, you assume that if you can't figure things out, I can't either. You struggle endlessly to make sense of what doesn't and in the process you not only give up on yourself, you give up on Me.

You so easily forget that My ways are higher than your ways. I work outside of time and space and I AM able to do the impossible through My supernatural abilities. There is nothing I cannot do. So when your life seems to be falling apart at the seams, let go of your desire to sit on My throne and instead allow Me to do what only I can do.

You might be in a pit, but I can pull you out. Your boat may have drifted far off course, but I have an anchor of hope to keep you from being lost at sea. And you can let go of the rope you're barely hanging on to because I'm holding on to you. You can stop the struggle and rest while I work. You may have run out of options, but I never do. Your victory will come when you realize the limits of your own abilities and grasp the limitlessness of Mine.

I did this so you would trust not in
human wisdom but in the power of God.

1 CORINTHIANS 2:5 (NLT)

Glory Revealed through Creation

There are days when I just want you to sit back and fathom the intricate design of the universe. You can get so caught up in your daily troubles that you forget My power and My constant presence in your life. I give you the very breath you breathe and the orbital speed of the earth and everything in between. Just to keep you on the earth is a miracle of My hands.

At times when you doubt My presence in your life, I want you to witness all that I've done in creation. My power is evident in the complexity of the atmosphere. If I can keep the world in motion, shouldn't you be confident in trusting Me with all that concerns you on a daily basis? You may not see a burning bush, but I have worked plenty of miracles in your life. I want you to be looking for Me in everything, at all times. Just because I don't show up how you think I should or work in the ways that you expect Me to does not lessen My omnipotent power and constant sovereignty. Embrace the revelations I've made to you through My Word and the creation around you. Open your eyes so that you might witness My glory.

The heavens declare the glory of God;
the skies proclaim the work of His hands.

PSALM 19:1 (NIV)

Shining Brightly

I have never, and will never, ask you to walk this life alone. I AM with you. In the moments when you feel as though all hope is gone and you are consumed with loneliness, I want you to simply look up and acknowledge My presence. In the darkness, I will be your light. I will put My light inside you to shine in a dark world.

I know that at times the troubles of life can dim your light and often seemingly put it out, but My Spirit is within you and your light will shine brightly even when you are unaware of it. You are called to be "the light of the world," a light that should not be hidden, but should shine brightly.

I AM the One who illuminates your spirit through My own. I AM your light, so let Me shine through you by surrendering your life to Me each and every moment of your life. If you are humble and surrendered, I can work in and through you to draw others to Me and display My glory. My light can pierce through any darkness, just be ready and willing to stand firm in your faith, amid the darkness, and join Me in penetrating the dark corners of the world.

Once you were full of darkness,
but now you have light from the Lord.
So live as people of light!

EPHESIANS 5:8 (NLT)

Walking in Power

My power is unprecedented and unfathomable. I AM able to do the impossible, and in My perfect will I work miracles that break all possibilities. There is no heart that I cannot heal, no burden I cannot lift, no guilt and shame that I cannot cover with grace, and no pit so deep that I cannot bring about a rescue. I AM all you need. I meet you right where you are, accept you in your sin and shame, and begin restoration and redemption.

It is vital that you see Me as God in your spiritual life as well as your physical one. Just because you cannot see Me in the way you think you should does not mean that I AM not there. I AM closer to you than you can ever imagine.

I'm within you, transforming you, increasing your faith, using My mighty power to bring you from glory to glory. Only in My strength can you walk in faith and accomplish all I've asked of you, so don't for a moment try to walk alone. Trying to live life relying only on yourself and your limited resources will only cause frustration and lead to failure. In Me, with My power, you can do all things.

Who is a God like you? You forgive
sin and overlook the rebellion
of Your faithful people.

MICAH 7:18 (GW)

Power in the Name of the Lord

There is power in My name. I AM not only always with you, but surrounding you on every side. I AM your protector and provider. I AM the strong fortress that you should run to. I will keep you safe, so come to Me.

You can confidently call upon Me in times of trouble and continually rest under the shadow of My wings. I AM a God who delivers, but I AM also a God of miracles who allows you to go through impossible circumstances so that you can experience My mighty power.

In the midst of the unthinkable, I want you to trust Me even when it seems as though things are moving in the wrong direction. You will only get a glimpse of My hand, but you have My Word to reveal My heart.

The world may seem as though it's coming against you, but there is nothing to fear. If I AM with you and for you, who would dare to be against you? Who or what has more power than I do? I want you to pray diligently, "God, deliver me." If you will only ask, I will answer.

The name of the Lord is a strong tower;
the righteous run to it and are safe.

PROVERBS 18:10 (NKJV)

Demonstration of Power

Surrender to Me so that you might be filled with My power, enabling you to accomplish the plans and purposes I have for your life. The surrendered life makes others thirsty for Me. Your life of faith on display is the greatest demonstration of My power.

You don't need to always "witness" as you think of it. Sometimes you will hardly need to interact at all. Just live the life of faith, allowing Christ to live in and through you and embracing the Holy Spirit to lead and guide you. I want you to have an open heart, sensitive to the people and situations around you, looking for opportunities to be a living testimony to others. Spend time each day in prayer, seeking My will and asking for My help to enable you to stay within it.

I will give you all the courage and strength you need to lead people to Christ. Follow My promptings and I will do the rest. Only I can save a life, but you have been called to live in such a way that others will seek Me. If you will become filled with Me, you'll find yourself living a life that brings heaven to earth.

My message and my preaching were very plain.
Rather than using clever and persuasive speeches,
I relied only on the power of the Holy Spirit.

1 CORINTHIANS 2:4 (NLT)

Victorious Living

I have commanded victory in your life; all you must do is live it out. I haven't asked you to do anything but trust Me. Stand firm in your faith and believe what I've promised you. There is no reason for your soul to be downcast or filled with fear, for I AM with you and I will deliver you.

I've told you that you are more than a conqueror through Me and through My love, so live that way. Don't give in to doubt and despair. They are nothing but lies of the enemy trying to keep you from My very best blessings in your life. I want you to live full of joy in the midst of trouble, knowing that My power alone can save you.

Hold fast to your faith and believe that I work all things together for good. All evil was defeated at Calvary, and I've promised you that there is victory at the end of the story. Cling to My promises and let nothing move you. When you're down, look up and remind yourself of Who I AM and what I've done. Remember what I've declared: You are a conqueror, a victor in Christ, and you can live in joy because I will give you strength.

Thanks be to God, who gives us the victory through our Lord Jesus Christ.

1 CORINTHIANS 15:57 (ESV)

The Faith Walk

Chosen to Be Holy

Jesus came to earth for more than the reason of sacrificing Himself for your sins. He came to be an example of the life of faith. If you choose to follow His example, you will be able to lead more people to a place of salvation. There is no greater calling.

Your heart must be surrendered, willing to obey Me regardless of the price. Your life is to bring Me glory and to lead others to My throne of grace. I want you to rely on the Holy Spirit to fill you with meekness, humility and love. If you will feed on My Word, you will be a branch that bears much fruit.

This is My desire for you: that you would continue to grow in your faith, surrendering as a servant to Me, learning to love with My love, and walking in the peace I give to you. If you will fulfill your calling, using the unique talents and gifts I've given to you, you will be a key to the kingdom of heaven being enriched and enlarged. Know that I can do all things in and through you, so I'm not asking you to do it all alone. But I AM asking you to daily make the choice to surrender and be holy because I AM holy.

Since God chose you to be the holy people
He loves, you must clothe yourselves with
tenderhearted mercy, kindness, humility,
gentleness, and patience.

COLOSSIANS 3:12 (NLT)

Guidance for the Life of Faith

You were created to make an impact on earth for My kingdom. Your faith is dead without works, and I have uniquely designed you to live out your faith by doing good. You'll need to focus on the purposes for your life each and every day. Draw near to Me as you awaken and allow Me to speak My will to your heart.

I want you to have a foundation of faith that drives everything you say and do. My Word will fill you with hope and help lead and guide you as you live out your faith. I never want you to rely on your own insight and intuition; you are to fully rely on the Holy Spirit to provide you with direction as you are faced with choices and challenges in your daily life.

Remember when you are overwhelmed and feeling as though the road ahead is too rough, I AM with you to make your paths straight and smooth. I will provide you with the resources necessary to fulfill My will and I will make sure that My grace abounds along your journey. I will supply you with all your needs when you rely on My strength and not your own.

Whoever speaks must speak God's
words. Whoever serves must serve
with the strength God supplies so that in
every way God receives glory through
Jesus Christ. Glory and power belong
to Jesus Christ forever and ever! Amen.

1 PETER 4:11 (GW)

Peace in the Midst of Pain

The greatest example of your faith is when you are able to praise My name and give thanks in the midst of trials and tragedies. I know that it's difficult to live with joy when you're going through unspeakable pain. I know that when your heart is breaking, it's hard to believe I AM with you and love you, but I AM and I do. Always stay focused on Me and I will keep you calm through all the chaos.

My eyes are always upon you. I AM watching every detail of your life and overseeing all that concerns you. There is no reason to fear or worry, so do not be discouraged.

Don't think that just because you suffer or hard times threaten your faith's foundation that I have lost My power. You will go through many difficulties to walk into the blessings I have in store for you. Don't be deceived by your circumstances, look to Me, rely on My promises, and relieve your frustrations, fears and fretting. Glorify Me in the midst of it all and I will help you to have peace through pain, suffering, loneliness and despair; peace right in the midst of it all.

The apostles left the high council rejoicing that God had counted them worthy to suffer disgrace for the name of Jesus.

ACTS 5:41 (NLT)

Always Abounding

I know that at times you grow weary in your work. You want to put Me and My purposes first, but things don't always go the way you planned. You're consumed with providing for yourself instead of allowing Me to do so. I want you to stop trying and start trusting.

When you're walking in My will, often doing so without immediate reward, I know you question whether or not it's all worth it and if what you're doing really makes a difference. But I've promised that your work will be rewarded, and I keep all of My promises. I promise you that your labor is not in vain. I AM using your calling to draw you near to Me and to teach you to trust Me.

Plant the seeds of the gospel with all you say and do and I'll take care of the rest. Don't give up when you grow weary—press through and press on and know that in due season you will reap a harvest if you do not lose heart. When you are weak, rely on Me for your strength—I will carry you when you're too weak to carry on. I will fill you with hope when all hope seems gone. I will give you peace in the midst of the chaos. My grace will abound always.

As for you, be strong and do not give up,
for your work will be rewarded.

2 CHRONICLES 15:7 (NIV)

A Chosen Vessel

I'm not concerned with how inadequate you might feel to accomplish My purposes. I'm looking for you to trust Me to work in and through you. I'm asking you to live out your faith by simply being a vessel in My hands.

I want you to live faithfully, choosing to walk in My will, and to worship through your worries. I'm simply asking you to walk with Me and to lead others to Me. I want you to continually dive deep into My Word so that you will be filled with light. You'll find guidance and hope in My promises and you'll be able to endure more for My glory than you can ever imagine. I want you to lay down your heart before Me, surrendering all that you are to Me and allowing Me to use you for My purposes.

You long to be fulfilled, but fail to understand that it is in serving Me fully that you can find the joy your soul seeks. I'm not worried about your faults and shortcomings; I know them all. I designed you, and those are by design. Everything I do is with purpose. So live daily as a vessel of My love, mercy and grace and I will work supernaturally, using your life, to bring about miracles that go far beyond anything you ever dreamed of.

"Go! I've chosen this man to bring My name to nations, to kings, and to the people."

ACTS 9:15 (GW)

Upside Down and Inside Out

I orchestrate opportunities every day and every moment of your life so that you can be a witness to how My grace has turned you upside down and inside out. The same mercy and grace that has saved you is meant to save others and wash their sins as yours have been cleansed. I want your life to be the light that leads others to Me through the darkness.

I don't want you to be discouraged about your witnessing. Your only responsibility is to share the Good News; it's the supernatural power within it that saves lives. All I ask is that you do your part and leave the rest to Me. I want you to be a living testimony to all that I've done in your life. I want others to look at you and see Me.

Sometimes no words are needed when your faith is radiant and truth is evident in the way you live. The greatest testimony you can give is living out My Word in all your thoughts and actions. You'll find that others want to know where your joy comes from when you're going through unthinkable pain. They'll wonder why you have peace when your life is falling apart. In that moment their heart will search for Me. Let My grace shine in and through you; that's all I ask of you.

"Go rather to the lost sheep of Israel.
As you go, proclaim this message:
'The kingdom of heaven has come near.'"

MATTHEW 10:6-7 (NIV)

The Response

I know it's not always easy to accept My call on your life. You get overwhelmed, believing that somehow I'm asking you to give up life as you know it. You believe My call will entail sacrifice that causes you to endure more than you want to. And in some ways you're right, but you can't see the reward that I can see.

Every soul on earth needs a Savior, and the saving grace that is within you as My child is a bright light in a dark world. I AM only asking you to be surrendered to Me each and every day, looking for the opportunities I place before you that will lead lost souls to Me. At times I will ask you to face difficulties that bring no immediate benefit, but the joys to come will last forever.

Don't be afraid that you cannot fulfill My will; I will help you. I will equip you with all you need and fill you constantly with the light you need to draw others to Me. Don't underestimate My plans for your life. I have created you to accomplish more than you can ever imagine, and your response to My call on your life enables Me to fulfill that call. Will you live the surrendered life, bringing glory to My name and blessings to your life?

"You are the light of the world."

MATTHEW 5:14 (NIV)

Mercy

Endless Mercy

My mercy is endless, My love forever, and My grace unending. My mercy covers sin and sets free those who are captives of sin. My favor is there when you least deserve it, so don't be afraid that My grace is limited to your behaviors and state of mind. I love you no matter what.

In the midst of your sin, I wait eagerly for you to return to Me. You'll lose your way from time to time, but I always provide a way back. I know you fear My judgment and are worried that you've wandered too far or sinned too much. But My love is for bringing you back to Me.

I assure you that My grace will embrace you the moment you turn to Me. My mercy transcends every situation in your life. No matter who you are or what you've done, I long for you to fully receive My love and mercy. Draw near to Me, sit quietly in My presence, and allow Me to embrace you. Don't worry about making your wrongs right before you come to Me; Christ has already done that for you. Simply come to Me with a humble heart, ready and willing for transformation and healing, and leave the rest to Me.

Give thanks to the LORD, for He is good!
His faithful love endures forever.

1 CHRONICLES 16:34 (NLT)

The Great Escape

I know you praise Me for the blessings I give to you, but I also want you to praise Me for the escape that My mercy provides. One day, as I have promised, the day of Great Tribulation will come. But I will remove you from My wrath. You will be saved through My mercy.

I have given the book of Revelation to be a source of comfort to you when that time comes. I want you to know that you can live without fear or concern because you will not suffer but be brought into My kingdom. I have set you free from your sins through your repentance and acceptance of My sacrifice for them. I have dealt with your sins before so that you will not suffer. I want you to daily be thankful for this blessing alone.

I know at times you feel overstressed and under blessed, but there are blessings within My mercy that you will never be aware of. I protect you from more evil than you realize. I keep you from a permanent state of desperation and despair. I hold you close and protect you with My love. My mercy does so much more than you will ever know, but you can be thankful for it, right now, as My mercy covers you.

> "Because you have obeyed My command to persevere, I will protect you from the great time of testing that will come upon the whole world to test those who belong to this world."
>
> REVELATION 3:10 (NLT)

Mercy in the Morning

Before you arise, call out My name. Each and every day, every moment, you need Me. And you need My mercy. So begin each day with praise. Thank Me for all I've done and all I haven't done, through My mercy. I want you to be content in all circumstances, trusting in and relying upon Me to meet all of your needs, while working miracles to fulfill your desires.

My goodness begins before the day, My mercy carries you into the night. If you'll seek Me first, each and every day, you'll find yourself more focused and fulfilled. You'll be content with what I've given you and be sure that I will always take care of you. I want your life to exude joy in the midst of all the uncertainties of life. You're not supposed to have everything figured out—if you did, you'd have no need for faith. I want you to set your heart and soul to seek Me always.

When you begin first thing in the morning, you set the stage for your day. Through your praise, you establish a firm foundation of faith and you can face whatever you must with courage, strength, wisdom, patience and peace. I tell you that joy comes in the morning because you will find My mercy there.

I will sing of Your strength, in the morning I will sing of Your love; for You are my fortress, my refuge in times of trouble.

PSALM 59:16 (NIV)

Blessed beyond Measure

I need you to stop during the day and remember the mercy that has been given to you ... fresh every morning, enabling you to walk in the grace that has saved you. If you will focus on all that I AM and all that I've done to give you joy and peace in a world that is filled with trouble, you will experience the confident faith you are meant to have.

You will need to submit to Me continually and confess any sins constantly. Don't compromise our time together; our relationship must come first. Though I have delivered you from hell, you still walk in a dark world that is in desperate need of My light. I have saved you by My mercy because I love you.

Don't allow your circumstances to get the best of you, to distract you from all the blessings in your life. I AM continually using My mercy to lead you into blessings, some that you experience immediately, some that will take some time to fall into My perfect will. All you must do is trust in My love for you. Praise Me for the gift of salvation and the blessings that come from being My child. My mercy toward you is great, so come to My throne of grace boldly and receive the fullness of My glory.

Your mercy toward me is great.
You have rescued me from the depths of hell.

PSALM 86:13 (GW)

A Reflection of Mercy

Sin deserves punishment. You pray for mercy for yourself and judgment upon others, but My love doesn't work that way, but I need you to open your heart to My love and be a reflection of My mercy.

I know that it's not easy to show mercy when you're going through unthinkable pain and suffering. I know that you want to walk in My love, but it just doesn't seem that simple. Your broken heart overwhelms you as you try to understand the why questions of life. Understand that there are just some things that you will never understand.

My plans go far beyond your comprehension. I don't want you to understand everything, I want you to trust Me in and through it all—the good and the bad. Remember that I've given you grace, favor that you don't deserve but that is readily poured out on you. Recall how you've been mercifully forgiven and that it is necessary for you to show the same compassion that I've shown you to others who don't deserve it either. In your bitterness and resentment, do not retaliate, but make the choice to be merciful, always forgiving and reflecting My love by offering mercy.

The wages of sin is death, but the gift of
God is eternal life in Christ Jesus our Lord.

ROMANS 6:23 (NIV)

Infinite Care

Every gift from Me is good and perfect. I AM only good, and I long to bless you in unthinkable, uncountable ways. It is from the fullness of My grace that you can experience the peace that surpasses all understanding and walk in faith through a world of doubt.

Each and every day you have the choice to receive all that I want to give you. My favor is upon you at all times and in all ways, so live with that knowledge. You can't measure My love and My mercy cannot be contained. I put infinite care into every blessing I bestow. There is purpose for all I do and everything I allow. Trust Me to know what is best for you. And when I don't show up when you think I should and in the way you expect, trust Me anyway.

Fuel your faith by listening to My voice through My Word and make the decision to believe what I've promised. Your feelings and emotions will often get the better of you, so you can't walk by sight. Count on My blessings, expect My glory, wait patiently, and then receive My grace.

Every good present and every perfect gift comes from above, from the Father who made the sun, moon, and stars. The Father doesn't change like the shifting shadows produced by the sun and the moon.

JAMES 1:17 (GW)

Merciful Promises

My promises are your hope when all hope seems lost. My Word is your assurance that I AM with you to deliver you. I have promised you more blessings than you can count. Cling to every one of them so that you might live in the victory you're meant to.

It is through prayer that My promises will lead and guide you as you face the challenges of life. My promises help you to see your challenges as opportunities. Your prayers should be based on My Word to you. I want you to come to Me boldly, standing upon the promises I've made to you, assured that I will fulfill them. My promises are precious to your life, your soul and your spirit—more valuable than you can ever imagine.

Don't miss out on the miracles in your life because you fail to seek out My promises to you. I've designed My Word to speak directly to you in every area of your life. I speak through it and bring about My glory as you trust in it. Don't live your life based on the lies of a dark world. Instead, trust in the good things I've promised to you. Bring My promises to Me in prayer and watch what I will do.

You are God, O Sovereign Lord. Your words
are truth, and You have promised these
good things to Your servant.

2 SAMUEL 7:28 (NLT)

Wisdom

The Only Way to Joy

It's not always easy to be obedient to My Word. I know that yielding your will to Mine is difficult at best. But you need to understand that it's your obedience that leads to joy in your life. Disobedience causes distress and unnecessary separation from Me. I want you to be filled to the full.

Ask Me to search your heart and reveal any area of your life in which you're disobedient. Have an open mind to what I will reveal and be ready to repent and ask for My help in order to get you back on the path of righteousness. I will always help you. My Spirit will lead and guide you, and there is never anything to fear at My throne of grace. It is vital that you come to Me each and every day so we can examine the state of your faith.

I want you to have a desire to run to My will and receive the joy that comes from being obedient. You have nothing to lose and everything to gain if you will only walk in My will and allow Me to direct you in My perfect plan for your life. Your obedient submission will fill you up with the joy your soul longs for, so be determined to be obedient so that your joy will be made complete.

God gives wisdom, knowledge, and joy
to anyone who pleases Him.

ECCLESIASTES 2:26 (GW)

The Helper

I want you to read My Word and be filled with supernatural insight and wisdom that will illuminate the dark places in your life. As you read My Word, pray that I would open your eyes that you might see wondrous things from My law.

I have given you My Spirit to help you in your walk of faith, to give you wisdom and understanding as you strive to walk in My will. I want you to have insight into the big decisions in your life as well as the small. I want you to take steps of faith confidently, without hesitation, knowing that I AM with you because the Spirit has helped you to make right choices.

With so many directions to take and countless paths to follow, you need to rely on My Word and the Holy Spirit to keep you walking in My will. Don't be afraid of the unknowns; I have gone before you as I lead and guide you. There is nothing to fear if I prepare the way. I know all that lies ahead and all that must be left behind.

"The helper, the Holy Spirit, whom the Father will send in My name, will teach you everything. He will remind you of everything that I have ever told you."

JOHN 14:26 (GW)

Take the Word to Heart

I've fulfilled many of My promises, but have foretold many more yet to be fulfilled so that you might live in peace and comfort. I want you to be prepared for the time when Christ returns, assured of the outcome and comforted by My promises to you.

I know you wonder about the future, sometimes overwhelmed by uncertainties. At other times you are filled with joy because I show you the path of victory clearly. You won't always be able to know what lies ahead, but I will give you the strength you need to take each step of faith, knowing that I AM in control, overseeing every detail of your life.

Don't allow fear of the unknown to keep you from continuing to pray for vision. I will often give you glimpses of My glory. If you'll focus upon Me in every situation, I will open your eyes to see what I see. As you discern My will, cling tightly to My Word. Don't just read it or listen to it, obey it so that all might be well with you. I will bless you as you walk obediently, trusting in the ways that I lead you, even when you don't understand them. Trust in Me with all your heart, walk in faith, and watch what I will do.

God blesses the one who reads the words
of this prophecy to the church, and He
blesses all who listen to its message and
obey what it says, for the time is near.

REVELATION 1:3 (NLT)

Life's Instruction Book

In order for you to stand strong against the lies of the world and the deep darkness that constantly threatens you, you must continue in the things you've learned in My Word. It is your Instruction Book for life, all you'll ever need for wisdom and understanding in your walk of faith.

You will face situations every day where you will need discernment to know the proper direction to take, and I've provided a way through My Word. You will hear My voice through it and I will guide you, specifically showing you which way to go. The Holy Spirit will help you to hear My voice clearly and give you the strength to be obedient. My Word is a sword, able to cut through the lies and enable you to live in truth in a deceitful world.

It is so easy for the enemy to capture your mind if you're not grounded in Scripture. Do not be caught unawares. Your enemy prowls around looking for someone to devour with his lies. Be careful and watchful, always focusing upon My truth, standing firm in your faith in the face of your fears. My Word will stand forever. Trust in My Word at all times and let nothing move you.

Take the ... sword of the Spirit,
which is the word of God.

EPHESIANS 6:17 (NIV)

Wholeheartedly Devoted to the Word

Y ou must come to know My Word so that it lives within you and acts as your anchor of hope. When you're facing frustrations and problems, I know that it is easier to question My ways than to be confident in them. My truth will cut through the lies and strengthen you to claim the victory in every battle.

Seeking Me cannot be something you do when you have time. You'll never *have* time, but you can *make* time. I have given you My Word to be a light on your path—use it and hold it in front of you at all times to illuminate the path ahead of you. Let My Word lead you and be your guide; not just when you're in need, but at all times and in all things.

Consistently seek Me. Wholeheartedly commit yourself to My Word and you will find the continual peace, joy and fulfillment that your soul and spirit so desperately needs.

Commit yourselves wholeheartedly to these
words of mine. Tie them to your hands and
wear them on your forehead as reminders.
Teach them … Talk about them … at home
and when you are on the road, when you are
going to bed and when you are getting up
… so that as long as the sky remains above
the earth, you and your children may flourish.

DEUTERONOMY 11:18–21 (NLT)

The Source of All Wisdom

Trust Me in those times when your trials are unbearable and you're not sure if I'm there or if I even care. Choose to believe that I'm in control, even when life is not. Take your eyes off the situation you're worried about and refocus them on Me. Examine your faith and pray that I will increase it.

Each time you are oppressed or encounter opposition, I have the opportunity to work miracles and lift you up. When something in life is taken from you, it gives Me the chance to give you "secret treasures" to prove that I AM God. I want you to draw near to Me and rest under the shadow of My wings while I work in and through your circumstances to fulfill the desires of your heart.

When you're overwhelmed, unsure of which direction to take and filled with fear about the future, call to Me and I will answer you. I hold *all* wisdom and insight into whatever you are going through. Though I cannot fully answer all of your questions, I will give you the strength and confidence in just knowing that I know them. Trust Me through your doubt and in the details. I've assured you the victory. Believe what I've promised.

There is no wisdom, no insight, no plan
that can succeed against the Lord.

PROVERBS 21:30 (NIV)

Trust and Rest

The first thing you should know about faith is that it won't answer all of your questions in life, and it won't solve all of your problems either. Faith is about trust, not about being certain. Faith gives you what you need to take one more step in the darkness, by the light I have given you through My Word. I'm not asking you to walk in blind faith, I'm asking you to believe in who I AM and trust in what I've promised.

The strength or weakness of your faith is directly proportional to your belief in what I've promised through My Word. Faith has nothing to do with feelings—it should never be based on what you see. If you're walking by sight, and not by faith, you're not trusting in Me. If there is no trust, your heart will be restless instead of resting in Me. Don't miss out on the blessings that are just beyond your fears. I've promised that I'll never leave you—there is nothing to fear. If I AM for you, nothing can be against you.

Though doubt knocks, let your faith answer. Trust and rest in Me, and I will do more than you could think possible. It is your faith that moves My heart *and* My hand.

I trust in Your word.

PSALM 119:42 (NIV)

Gladness

The Joy of Encouragement

Each and every day, I give you blessings. I want you to be a blessing and share My grace with those whom I place in your life. It may be a brief encounter; it might be a relative that has been lost for some time and is not receptive to the gospel. I want you to be ready to put yourself and your priorities aside and be the servant I've called you to be through My grace and mercy.

I know it's not always easy to set yourself and your priorities aside, but it's necessary if you want to live a life of faith. The more you give of yourself, being emptied in every way, the more I can fill you. The more you encourage others in their faith, the stronger your faith will be.

It's not easy to be strong in faith at all times, especially when you're facing difficulties and challenges, but if you will encourage each other, you'll be stronger. Work diligently at lifting others up, assuring them of My power and provision, and I will make sure that all of your needs are met. Trusting fully in Me means believing that as you focus on others, I'll focus on you and all your concerns.

> When he arrived and saw what the
> grace of God had done, he was glad and
> encouraged them all to remain true
> to the Lord with all their hearts.
>
> ACTS 11:23 (NIV)

Glad Praise

Thanking Me is not the same as praising Me. I want you to be thankful, conscious of the benefits and blessings you've received. When you're thankful, you're focusing on all that I've done for you. I want you to spend time being glad for all the great things I've done in and through your life.

Once you've given thanks, your prayer will naturally turn to praise. There's a time for simply focusing upon Me. Not My hand and what I have done, but My heart—who I AM. You will strengthen your faith and experience great peace when you make an effort to constantly remember that I AM holy, righteous and just, merciful and mighty, and always sovereign.

It's easy to allow your thoughts to drift into your trials and troubles, so you must be truly focused through the process of prayer. Spend time alone with Me, allow yourself to ascend, forget about your worries, and receive the fullness of My glory. Be glad that I have done great things and will do so much more. Praise Me for My power and pray that you would fully receive My grace.

> "This is how you should pray:
> 'Father, may Your name be kept holy.
> May Your Kingdom come soon.'"
>
> LUKE 11:2 (NLT)

Joy in the Waiting

My promise to you is to give you a future and a hope. You seldom realize that I spend time thinking about you, looking after all that concerns you and working behind the scenes of your life to fulfill My promises to you.

I know it's not always easy waiting upon Me to intervene in the circumstances of your life, but there's purpose for the waiting. I'm growing your faith, teaching you to be full of joy and expectant with gladness. I know the dire situations in your life, those things that fill you with fear and uncertainty about the future, but I've promised to deliver you, to protect you, to rescue you. There is nothing to fear.

Be glad that I AM with you. And while you wait, be consumed with My grace as you trust in My Word. Recall the ways in which I've performed miracles in your life in the past. Strengthen your faith by focusing on all that is right in your life, instead of what's wrong. I want you to be grateful that I love you, that I care about you, and that I will move heaven and earth to answer your prayers. Trust in Me and rest in the joy that is found in Me alone.

O LORD my God, You have performed many
wonders for us. Your plans for us are too
numerous to list. You have no equal.
If I tried to recite all Your wonderful deeds,
I would never come to the end of them.

PSALM 40:5 (NLT)

The Rock

I never change. I'm always the same—your Rock. I cannot be moved and neither should you. Your faith should be strong and unmovable when you're trusting in Me to provide for you and protect you. Give thanks to Me at all times, regardless of your circumstances.

You can thank Me because I AM good all the time. I pour out My mercy and consume you with My grace. In your praises you can have peace and gladness, knowing that I will render justice and rescue you from the fear of defeat.

There is nothing too difficult for Me. There is nothing I can't do—no miracle that I can't perform in your life. I AM all you need and everything is under My authority, so there is nothing to fear no matter what you must face in life. Although there are many reasons to give thanks to Me and praise My name, I want you to find joy and gladness in the most basic thing: that I AM God … all-loving, merciful and mighty.

The LORD lives! Thanks be to my rock! May God,
the rock of my salvation, be glorified. God gives
me vengeance! He brings people under my authority.
He frees me from my enemies. You lift me up
above my opponents. You rescue me from
violent people. That is why I will give thanks
to You, O LORD, among the nations
and make music to praise Your name.

2 SAMUEL 22:47-50 (GW)

Contented Dissatisfaction

Y ou tend to focus on the circumstantial obstacles in your life. Your faith walks by sight and you don't recognize that your greatest distraction is doubt. Doubt is what causes your faith to stumble into despair.

All doubt starts with one thing: discontent. Discontent creates mumbling, and mumbling rattles the chains of hell to join you in a chorus of self-pity and feelings of betrayal. This ends with a declaration that I just simply don't care about you or your life. The fallen world in which you live continually feeds your negative feelings, and faith is hard.

Refuse to doubt. Refuse to worry ... and "consider it pure joy" (James 1:2). Rejoice in faith, by resolution and by reckoning. Be content to be dissatisfied in your flesh. When you don't know what to do, keep your eyes on Me and lay aside everything that keeps you from stepping forward in faith. Be patient, stand firm and watch My victory unfold.

Since we are surrounded by so many examples
of faith, we must get rid of everything
that slows us down, especially sin that
distracts us. We must run the race
that lies ahead of us and never give up.

HEBREWS 12:1 (GW)

Your Shepherd for Today

You tend to look too much into the future, focusing on tomorrow when I've only given you this very moment. I don't want you looking ahead; I want you to trust Me for each step. I AM the same yesterday, today and forever. If I cared for you yesterday, and I AM with you today, then you can rest assured that I will be with you in each and every tomorrow. There is no reason to worry. I will either shield you from the suffering you so desperately fear, or I will give you strength beyond all you can imagine so that you might bear it. Set aside all of your anxious thoughts and worries, and be at peace.

I AM your Shepherd. I lead, guide and care for you in every way. I AM your Shepherd on Sunday, on Monday, and every day of the week. I AM your Shepherd every month of the year and wherever you are. I AM your Shepherd during the raging storms of life and when there is peace. I AM your Shepherd in times of abundance and when there is little. I AM your Shepherd in moments of joy and through seasons of pain. Never look ahead at the challenges of life in fear. Let each moment arise in its own time, live in the now, and you will find the grace that is always sufficient for your every need.

The Lord is my shepherd;
I have all that I need.

PSALM 23:1 (NLT)

All These Things

As you're seeking joy, blessing and an abundance of My favor, you'll need to reorganize your priority list. It is when you surrender your will and embrace Mine that your purposes align with My plans. Then I begin to open the floodgates of heaven to pour out blessings for you (see Malachi 3:10).

Part of building your faith is realizing that My purposes come first and then everything else will fall into place when you make My priorities your priorities. When you follow My plan for your life, you are making wise use of your time and you are taking steps to experience My very best. I have promised that you will reap what you sow— sow those things that are eternal and I will take care of all that concerns you here on earth.

Trust that I know what's best. Believe that I have your best interests at heart. Know that I AM with you and can accomplish all things. I have infinite resources that go far beyond all that you can imagine. I work in and within you and your circumstances in order to bring heaven to earth. Trust Me to take care of you, to give you the desires of your heart, and be glad.

"Seek first His kingdom and His righteousness,
and all these things will be given to you as well."

MATTHEW 6:33 (NIV)

God's Sovereignty

Absolute Rule

If you'll fully believe that I reign, your thinking will change dramatically in every situation you face. You will have more hope, courage and confidence. You will walk more firmly in your faith, without wavering. You will live with great peace, knowing I'm in control.

Sometimes it seems you fully believe in My sovereignty, but when tragedy strikes, you put Me on trial and the questioning begins. You believe I can control some things, but that I have somehow lost My grasp on others. The truth is that I'm always sovereign over all things at all times.

Don't doubt what I've promised you. Don't lose faith, simply walk in it. Don't try and reason everything out. You have limited understanding. That is why you need faith. When I've promised you something, you can step out in faith and simply take Me at My word.

Trusting Me may not be easy, but it makes all things possible, so don't allow your worries to drown out your worship. Praise Me for all I've done and all I have yet to do. Then watch and wait for My promises to be fulfilled in your life.

> Let the heavens rejoice, let the
> earth be glad; let them say among
> the nations, "The Lord reigns!"
>
> 1 CHRONICLES 16:31 (NIV)

Abundantly Satisfied

Your faith must come to a place of being satisfied with My will. I won't always lead you down the easiest path because overcoming obstacles and facing your fears strengthens your faith. I know what is best for you. I AM with you to perfect your faith, so keeping you from struggles would keep you right where I found you, and I just can't do that. I love you too much.

Being satisfied will often mean that you must be emptied of everything. Too often the path you're walking on is not the one I intended and I will need to realign your life with My will. I will need to transform your thinking through My Word and you will need to draw near to Me, discerning My voice and being obedient in every way.

My blessings are beyond number and My grace cannot be contained. I want you to reap it all. As you are transformed by My promises, you'll find your life starting to fall in place. You'll experience more peace and less fear. You won't worry about the unknowns and what lies ahead because your faith will stand firm. Don't for a moment live unsatisfied. Know that you can be abundantly satisfied if your hope is in Me alone.

"My people will be filled with
My blessings," declares the LORD.

JEREMIAH 31:14 (GW)

Ultimate Authority

I know you're tempted to believe that I'm sovereign over some things but not others, but I AM sovereign over all. Nothing happens in your life and in the universe without My permission. I oversee it all, so you can have peace knowing that I control the chaos.

When you're fearful of the circumstances that seem to be controlling your life, trust in My truth that assures you that I AM in control. There is no detail of your life that I AM not aware of and no challenge that goes beyond My power to overcome. Don't walk in fear, trying to make sense of what you simply can't. Be determined to trust Me, even when you are tempted to doubt. Choose to have faith. Even when you're faced with situations that are truly threatening your future and your well-being, remember that I've promised to give you a future and a hope.

Trust that I've promised you that never will I leave you or forsake you. There's no reason to worry if you're relying on the promises I've made to you. I cannot lie; I AM only truth, and if you'll walk on that foundation, you will realize that by surrendering and submitting your will to Mine, victory is sure to follow.

All authority comes from God, and those in positions of authority have been placed there by God.

ROMANS 13:1 (NLT)

Settled in Heaven

You tend to worry because you think life is full of uncertainties, but My Word has assured the outcome of life and My Word is settled in heaven. My truth is eternal. It has never and will never change. I hold all authority over heaven and earth, and that includes your life.

It may often seem as though things are out of control, as if you're stumbling through your faith and not sure that what you believe in is worth it, but you must press through the doubts and trust that I AM sovereign. Don't allow the lies of the world to deceive you and keep you from My very best for your life. An obstacle can be an opportunity for Me to bless you. Trust Me to oversee the details of your life. You must decide to not lean on your own understanding; just rely and trust in Mine.

Don't allow others to taint your thoughts with their own and don't give in to your fears, even though it's easier to. Truth is measured by My Word, not the opinions or advice of others. Allow My Word to guide you, bringing you into alignment with My will. Never for a second do I step off My throne. Come to Me and I will comfort you in the chaos and give you peace.

Your word, Lord, is eternal;
it stands firm in the heavens.

PSALM 119:89 (NIV)

Filled Up

You stress and worry because you're trying to make decisions without Me. You fail to ask for My help and assume I'm not able to. If I'm in control, if you truly believe that, why wouldn't you come to Me and allow Me to do what only I can—work miracles?

When you allow Me to lead and guide you, I will fill you to the full with My love, mercy and grace. Your lack of fulfillment comes from trying to fill yourself with the things of the world instead of Me. Allow My Spirit to work within you, revealing the things that need changing in order for you to walk in My will for your life. The changes may take time or they may come instantly, but if you breathe in My Word, I will fill you with true life.

I want you to live the abundant life, not filled with just things, but filled with the Spirit. My Spirit will lead and guide you, restoring your strength and enabling you to continue along the path of righteousness. When you are weak, I will be your strength. When you are empty, let My living water fill you to the full, until you overflow.

The LORD will guide you continually,
giving you water when you are dry
and restoring your strength. You
will be like a well-watered garden,
like an ever-flowing spring.

ISAIAH 58:11 (NLT)

Don't Miss the Miracle

You'll often find yourself between a rock and a hard place, yet you fail to realize that I AM that Rock. I work miracles, just as I did at the Red Sea. I am able to part the seas and even move mountains, if necessary. Why do you doubt? Why won't you watch Me prove Myself faithful?

When you're stuck, not sure what to do and which direction to take, look to Me immediately. This is My universe, and I can do miracles that go beyond your ability to ever comprehend.

I'll never fall short of My glory; I *always* have the victory. But if you continue to doubt, walking by sight instead of by faith, you hinder My heart. I'm looking for someone to believe. I've given you so many promises that should enable you to live a life of peace and joy, but seldom are you experiencing that abundant life. I've said that I will fight for you, you need only be still. But being still requires action; it requires faith. It's not a matter of *if* I can work the miracles you need in your life, but how. Watch in faith so you don't miss it.

Sing to the LORD. He has won a glorious victory.

EXODUS 15:21 (GW)

In Awe of Majesty

Y ou should have a sense of My majesty every moment of your life. I have created the earth to draw you near to Me and cause you to stand in awe of Me. There is no other God but Me, and I hold the universe in My hands.

At times you forget Who I AM: all-powerful, the Creator of the universe, and Lord of all. I AM your heavenly Father, able to move heaven and earth in response to your faith. I have given you the Holy Spirit to lead and guide you, giving you supernatural wisdom so that you might live the abundant life you're supposed to live. I've given you My voice through My Word, so that without seeing Me, you know Me.

I want you to walk in the fullness of My peace and joy instead of the doubt and despair the world tempts you to live in. It is in your worship of Me that I hear your heart's cries. Keep crying out to Me; I always hear you. I bottle each tear, collecting them all, waiting for the moment when I will pour them down out of heaven in the form of joy. I will do whatever it takes so that you will continually find yourself in reverence and awe of My amazing grace and boundless love for you.

The highest angelic powers stand in awe of God. He is far more awesome than all who surround His throne.

PSALM 89:7 (NLT)

Making Decisions

Truth That Is Always the Same

The Bible, My Word, is how I've given you truth. Truth never changes, just as I AM the same yesterday, today and forever. When it comes to righteous living, the same practical solutions and law for living apply to you as they did in the Old and New Testament days. Truth is for all people at all times; to lead and guide you, to enable you to live the abundant life.

You never need to wonder about how I view the various situations in your life. I have given you My Word to lead and guide you in to My will. My Word is alive, and it will speak to you with the help of the Holy Spirit. Don't be overwhelmed, believing My law to be too difficult to understand or follow. My Word has supernatural power. Allow it to transform you from the inside out.

Embrace My correction as you open your heart. Know that all sin is forgivable and My hold on you is unbreakable. Don't allow the lies of the world to taint and distort your thoughts. You will be tempted in all the ways you never want to be, but I AM with you. You can face and conquer anything and everything that threatens your faith by standing firm in My truth.

All Your words are true;
all Your righteous laws are eternal.

PSALM 119:160 (NIV)

Seeking Wisdom

You can know what to do by relying on the power of My Word to lead and guide you. Sometimes that means taking a step of faith, and at other times it means not taking a step at all. I want to have an ongoing conversation with you so that I can keep you on the straight and narrow path.

You often decide to speak to Me about some things, but not others. I want to be involved with every single detail of your life, the things you perceive as small as well as those that are big. Why would you ever pass at the chance to speak to Me, to ask for My wisdom? I'm the God of the universe, sovereign over all things. I know the past, present and future, and only I know your life from beginning to end.

Don't rely on yourself, and don't rely on others; come directly to Me. Let nothing keep you from Me. Don't be distracted or swayed by the ways of the world. There will be decisions that will dramatically alter your life, and you will not always know which ones they are. So bring everything to Me. Speak to Me, call upon Me, and I will answer you.

> You are my rock and my fortress.
> For the honor of Your name, lead
> me out of this danger.
>
> PSALM 31:3 (NLT)

The Routine of Faith

You can't walk in faith "sometimes". Faith is a routine, a way you live your life, continually. You can't rely on Me sometimes, but not others. Ours must be a consistent relationship that entails continual communication in order to perfect your faith and enable you to walk in My will for your life.

I want you to be dedicated to spending time with Me regularly. I will use My Spirit to work in and through you as I transform your thinking to fulfill My will. The only way I can use your life is if you continually surrender to Me, allowing Me to empty you of yourself, filling you with My power, presence and peace.

In order for you to be effective, you will need to live and breathe My Word. It will be your guide when you need direction, your strength when you are weak, and your peace amid chaos and uncertainty. If you consistently seek Me in all you say and do, you will more easily walk the path I have prepared for you. Faith doesn't make things easy, but it makes all things possible. And your faith must be grounded in My Word. If you will live out your faith based on the promises I've made you, the impact your life will have on others will be incalculable.

Keep a close watch on how you live and on your teaching. Stay true to what is right for the sake of your own salvation and the salvation of those who hear you.

1 TIMOTHY 4:16 (NLT)

Day after Day

Yᵒu can't walk by faith sometimes and not others or you'll find yourself going down paths you never wanted to. I always intend for you to walk the path of blessings. It may not always be easy, but ultimately when you're following My will for your life, My victory is a sure outcome.

When you're spending time with Me in prayer, I want you to fully speak your heart, but also listen attentively so that you might hear Me speak to you. Sometimes it's vital that you simply sit in My presence, quietly waiting and resting in the assurance that I AM with you always.

You will need to constantly search My heart so that I can speak to yours. I will always lead and guide you through My Word; I will teach you how to think the way I think and to view your circumstances in the way I do if you will trust in My ways instead of your own. Don't ever stop coming to My throne of grace. Don't make a decision or take a step without seeking My will first. Faith is about living life one day at a time and continually seeking Me day after day.

They listened eagerly ... They searched the Scriptures day after day to see if Paul and Silas were teaching the truth.

ACTS 17:11 (NLT)

Praying for Help

Obedience to Me is not easy, but it is necessary to live the life I've called you to. You will need to pray for My help to be obedient, to give you a strong spirit, to overcome the temptations that come your way. The world will try to get you off course, but I will be ever constant, always calling you back upon the path I intended for you.

You will find yourself weak in times of trouble and I will be all you have and all you need to walk out your faith. Daily prayer for obedience will help you keep your eyes focused on Me. Nothing can protect your mind from the temptations that encompass you except for My Word. If you will continually seek My will for you, searching the Scriptures and attentively listening for My voice, you will find all the guidance and direction you need to be successful wherever you go.

Don't allow yourself to walk by sight. Stand firm in your faith and walk upon the straight and smooth path I've made for you. Don't be tempted to get off track, to follow the ways of the world instead of My own. Be careful, be strong, be courageous, and know that I AM with you.

"Be very strong and courageous. Be careful to obey all the law My servant Moses gave you; do not turn from it to the right or to the left, that you may be successful wherever you go."

JOSHUA 1:7 (NIV)

Live by the Word

My Word can be heard, but living by it makes it come alive. I want you to live in a way that makes My Word come alive in you. I want you to continually stop and consider all the blessings I've given to you. Praise and worship me as you walk through your daily life.

My Word has been given to you as instructions for your life. Every situation you face in life has been covered in the Scriptures. Each miracle I have performed in the past is to assure you that I can and will do the impossible. Don't believe that miracles aren't for you. I will do the impossible in your life, just as I've done in the lives of others.

My desire is that you would live with a grateful heart and a joyful spirit, no matter what you're facing in life. But you must allow My Word to sink deep within your spirit and soul, enabling you to live righteously by faith.

I AM with you to strengthen you through My Word, to give you the courage and power you need to resist all that comes against you. My Word is alive and active, sharper than any double-edged sword, penetrating even to dividing soul and spirit and leading you onto the path that's everlasting.

Teach me Your ways, O Lord, that I may live
according to Your truth! Grant me purity
of heart, so that I may honor You.

PSALM 86:11 (NLT)

The Last Word

If you are to live successfully, reaping the rewards of being obedient to Me, My Word must be the first and last thing you focus on each day. It must be the authoritative standard for your life. It must be the compass that leads you throughout your life, the benchmark you use in every decision and action in life.

Most of your troubles occur because you have made choices based on your own reasoning or the thoughts and opinions of others. But the ways of the world are not Mine. The world is unreliable and will lead you in directions that are contrary to the ways I want you to go.

You need My Word to be the standard in your life—it will never lead you astray. It will always lead you into My glory. It will never fail you, and neither will I. My Word is flawless, settling the issues of your life. My Word must be the ultimate authority, leading and guiding your mind through all of the decisions you must make in life.

Look to Me, listen to Me, and trust in My Word, being obedient whether or not it makes sense. Walk purposefully in faith, never relying on your sight, and I will always have the last word in your life. The victory is Mine.

He who has compassion on them will guide
them and lead them beside springs of water.

ISAIAH 49:10 (NIV)

Turn to God

Grace to Endure

You'll never experience My grace unless you need it. My faithfulness is not proved by the absence of trials and troubles, it's seen most clearly when your faith is tested, when you question My ways and doubt My love. It's in your weakness that I am able to show you the fullness of My power and the reality of My presence.

You will see My faithfulness in your pain and suffering and in those moments you will find My grace to be sufficient. I want you to have a very real and deep understanding of how grace works in your life, and I will use all the situations in your life to give you a greater revelation of My grace. I want you to come to a place in your faith where you are filled with more joy in the presence of My grace than in the absence of troubles and worries.

I want you to embrace the pain and sorrows of life, realizing them to be more than what they appear on the surface. I want you to be assured of My presence and power in your life at all times, knowing that the greatest indicator of My faithfulness is in the midst of your troubles. I AM with you and will give you all the grace you need to not only survive, but to thrive and live in My joy through it all.

"My grace is all you need. My power
works best in weakness."

2 CORINTHIANS 12:9 (NLT)

A Purpose for Everything

I can direct any evil to ultimately lead to good. My goal is My glory, and sometimes evil will dwell within circumstances that I will ultimately overcome in victory. Don't be fooled by what you see, but instead determine to walk by faith.

All too often you'll be tempted to believe that just because there is tragedy and evil in the world, I AM less than all-powerful. Your doubt tempts you to conclude that if I were all-loving, I would not allow evil. But I've made it clear that evil is a result of sin. You can so easily be deceived when you're not fully trusting in Me. Look at all the ways I've saved you in the past, and know that there are so many more times that I have done so, though you were not aware of it.

Know that the things that burden you, the ways in which you're struggling, are opportunities to show Myself stronger and more powerful than ever before. Call upon Me in the day of trouble and I will answer you, delivering you and bringing about good from all that is evil. I have purposes for all I do; trust that I do and watch the miracles I will bring about in your life. Just when you think things are falling apart, you'll look back upon your answered prayers and find that they were simply falling into place.

"I have appointed you for the very purpose
of displaying My power in you and to
spread My fame throughout the earth."

ROMANS 9:17 (NLT)

The Final Say

I've spoken the final words in your life; the Scriptures say it all. From beginning to end, it is My Word that finalizes every priority, hope and plan I have for your life. I have given you My Word so that you might have the strength to endure and believe until the very end, come what may.

No matter what difficulties you're facing in your life, know that I AM always with you. I will not forget you, leaving you desperate and lost. I will give you all that you need in the moment you need it.

I know about your hopes and dreams, I know My perfect plans for your life, and I will bring them together in a plan for your future that will ultimately go beyond all you can hope for or imagine.

When you're drowning in despair, unable to live by faith, you must turn to Me. As long as you're alive, I need you to confidently approach My throne of grace, relying on Me to meet your needs and fill you with faith. Trust completely in My promises to you so that you might have hope and peace as you face the unknowns. My Word, the truth, has the final say about whatever you're going through, and you can rest assured that you will see My glory.

It is God who arms me with strength
and keeps my way secure.

PSALM 18:32 (NIV)

You Can't Live without It

I know your world drives you to a place of instant gratification. You act upon your impulses, and they lead you down paths you were never meant to travel. However, everything depends on self-control, the fruit of My Spirit that enables you to live according to My will.

Success in life is based on your obedience to Me. The control you have over your body, motives and purposes is the only way that you can walk by faith in Me and live the life I've called you to. But you can't do it on your own. You need Me for every step you take. You'll need My Word engrained within you so that when there are decisions to be made, you will know which direction to take.

I want you to live confidently in Me, knowing that I AM with you to lead and guide you through every detail of your life. Stay connected to Me, leaning on Me at all times so that you might reap the rewards of My blessing in your life. Trust that if I lead you in a direction that is contrary to the way you desire to go, I know what I'm doing and I have your very best interests at heart. I will not withhold any good thing from you. Strive to have the self-control that doesn't demand your own way, but fully trusts in Mine.

The spiritual nature produces ... self-control.

GALATIANS 5:22–23 (GW)

Put Your Problems into Perspective

You tend to allow your troubles to be the focus of your life, and desperation is the result. Bring every single one of your problems to Me and allow Me to handle them. There is nothing that I can't do—nothing.

Don't forget that I sustain you through troubles and strengthen you to endure your trials. And remember that it's the testing of your faith that develops perseverance. I have purposes for all I allow in your life. The trials and tribulations are all a matter of perspective. Everything becomes small in light of My greatness. I just need you to change your perspective, viewing everything you're facing through My eyes and not your own.

You struggle for answers to prayer when the answer may lie within you—changing your perspective can overcome any adversity. Remember that I'm big enough and powerful enough to take care of your burdens and calm your worries. I AM the answer to all of your problems. I will help you in your failing health, the brokenness of your relationships, the despair from financial crises, and in the midst of the sin you're drowning in. I AM enough.

"I am the LORD God of all humanity.
Nothing is too hard for Me."

JEREMIAH 32:27 (GW)

Living Power

You fail to realize that My power lies within you. I've given you My Spirit, which enables you to be filled to the full with the truth that sets you free. My Word is there to instruct you and guide you, but it's also for miracles of healing, encouragement, and hope when all hope is gone. Nothing equals the power of My Word.

A whole new world will open up to you if you will believe what I've told you, that My Word is "living and powerful." My Word comes to life through your faith. Hide My Word in your heart. Rely on the power of My promises to set you free from the chains of depression and despair. Trust in My Word to provide for you spiritually and physically.

I reach into your world to do the impossible. I need you to believe that I do that. I need you to rely on Me in ways you think you can't. I need you to trust in Me for things that you're not sure you can. Your life is a manifestation of your faith, or a lack thereof, in Me; so examine your faith and take a look at where you are. Are you trusting in Me completely? Is your faith wavering? Cling to My Word, let it come alive in you, and let its power transform your life and lead you into the blessings I have for you.

The Word of God is living and powerful.

HEBREWS 4:12 (NKJV)

Hold on to the Word of Truth

Don't compromise what I've taught you through My Word. Stand fast and hold on to what you know is truth. The temptations in your life will be great and many, and you will need to be prepared for them through the power of My Word. Let it be your first defense and your great offense against the lies of the world.

When your faith is challenged and you're not sure where you stand, stand firm in what I've promised you. I will never fail you, but the world will. I want you to live in My truth without compromise. I AM to be your Rock, the One you run to when in doubt. As life takes hold of you and threatens to drag you under, it is My grip that will save you.

Know that you are Mine; I will hold you and often carry you, but you must trust Me. You must trust My faithfulness—My love for you and My ability to move all of heaven and earth to deliver you. Don't allow the ways of the world to tempt you to stray from what I've taught you through My Word, your Instruction Book for life. Standing firm in the faith that you have in My promises will enable you to win the battle of faith and live the abundant life I intend for you.

Stand firm and hold fast to the
teachings we passed on to you.
2 THESSALONIANS 2:15 (NIV)

God's Faithfulness

A Sense of Majesty

If you will only take a moment to recognize My mighty power that is enveloped in My love, your worries will be fewer, your peace will be consuming, and you will have a sense of awe in My majesty.

When life becomes turbulent, you so easily forget who it is that allows—and calms—the storms of your life. I will never abandon you. I have promised you My power and presence in your life, and I AM faithful. Never have I failed to fulfill one of My promises, so you can trust that they will be fulfilled in your life as well.

Your worship brings you into a place of understanding of who I AM and all that I AM. Come into worship more often. Sit at My throne and be quietly aware of My love for you. Know that every detail of your life is in the palm of My hand. Every situation you face, every obstacle that threatens your faith, is under My control. I have made a promise to either take you through it all or deliver you out of it. I know what I'm doing; trust that I AM Almighty God, the faithful One. Rest in that truth.

God is terrifying in the council of the holy ones.
He is greater and more awe-inspiring than
those who surround Him.

PSALM 89:7 (GW)

Fulfilled Faith

I have made you promises that demand your faith and My faithfulness. You should continually claim them for your life, applying them to each and every situation you face. You can have confident faith, believing in My promises and trusting in Me completely.

Do not allow your doubt to get in the way of your faith. My timing is seldom yours, and My faithfulness will come in My perfect time. Though My promises seem slow to be fulfilled, you can be assured that they will never fail. I want your faith to always be active and alive, ready to act when I ask you to take the next step. The way may not always be clear, but you can be assured that I AM with you each step of the way.

There is never a reason for you to fear. I will never leave your side, not even for a moment. Don't allow doubt and despair to silence your faith. Shout out in praise, confident that I AM faithful to My Word and every promise I've made for your life will be fulfilled in due time.

We must continue to hold firmly to
our declaration of faith. The one who
made the promise is faithful.

HEBREWS 10:23 (GW)

Returning in Power and Great Glory

My faithfulness does not simply cover the fulfillment of My promises in your daily life. Rather, there is a master plan, an ultimate promise in which I am leading you to in faith: Christ's return. Your faith in this promise is the touchstone of your faith. Everything hinges on you living with a moment-by-moment awareness of the Second Coming.

Your hope of eternal life is based on the promise of Christ's return, and your faith keep you looking and listening for that glorious day. He will appear at a time of which you are unaware, and your faith will bring you into His glory. Your life is about nothing less than that one day when you will take off your crown and lay it at His feet.

Each moment of your life, lived out in faith, culminates in the coming of the Son of Man in power and great glory. When your life seems mundane, trivial with trials and seemingly meaningless, rest in who you are in Christ. Let each day be one that honors Him for the sacrifice made, and know that your faith leads to a victory that overcomes the world.

"Then will appear in heaven the sign of the
Son of Man, and then all the tribes of the
earth will mourn, and they will see the
Son of Man coming on the clouds of
heaven with power and great glory."

MATTHEW 24:30 (ESV)

Faithful in Temptation

At some point in your life, you will face unexpected temptations that will challenge your faith in more ways than you would like. But if you remain in Me, I will remain in you and no temptation will overtake you.

As life moves at a faster pace than your faith can keep up with, you must take control of each and every moment, keeping your thoughts under My control. Your faith will keep you focused on Me when the temptations of life are pulling you in opposing directions. When you're in the midst of the struggle and you don't know what to do, keep your eyes on Me.

Let nothing move you, and never give in to the fear. Know that through all that you will face, all the temptations that come your way, I will never allow you to endure more than My grace can uphold. I will always make a way out. So cast out all fear and defeat your doubt through faith, look to Me, and I will lift you out of the pit of destruction so that you see My glory.

No temptation has overtaken you except what is common to mankind. And God is faithful; He will not let you be tempted beyond what you can bear. But when you are tempted, He will also provide a way out so that you can endure it.

1 CORINTHIANS 10:13 (NIV)

Assurance about Everything

I never fail. Each and every promise that I've made to you is a capsule of grace, given to meet specific needs in your life at specific times. And it's My all-sufficient grace that will carry you through all of life's uncertainties, assured that every promise I've made will be fulfilled.

My promises are the basis of your life of faith. I have made specific promises that meet every condition and contingency in your life … cling to them. Depend upon them with each and every breath you take, because without My promises, you have no assurance about anything. Without My faithfulness, you have no hope, no security, no comfort and no peace. But if you are trusting in My Word, you have everything in endless supply.

Allow My grace to consume you each moment of every day. Not one word of My promises will fail. You can rest and rely on them at all times and in all ways. My promises mark the parameters of My grace. They define Me—all that I AM, all that I have done and all that I will do. I will do what I have promised, and nothing less.

There has not failed one word of all His good promise.

1 KINGS 8:56 (NKJV)

Always Held

You don't need to feel My presence to be assured that I AM with you always. Faith that doesn't walk by sight will carry you through the times when fear overcomes you and you wonder if I'm there or even care. Beyond your senses, the truth that My everlasting arms are underneath you will keep you from stumbling in your faith.

When you are overcome with despair, I want you to immediately run to Me. No matter what you're going through, however big or small, I AM over it all. I AM able to do what you cannot and accomplish what you never thought possible. And I will always allow situations in your life that will strengthen your faith. I will call you to step out in faith in ways you never wanted to, but I am perfecting your faith, sanctifying you.

I want you lacking in nothing, dependent upon Me for everything. Though I may be silent, I am always at work. I never slumber. So leave your worries and cares to Me and allow Me to work in your life in the ways that I desire. Trust Me to do what is best. Never lose sight of the fact that I AM your God. You are Mine, and nothing can separate you from Me.

The eternal God is your refuge,
and underneath are the everlasting arms.
DEUTERONOMY 33:27 (NIV)

A Ready Help

Every day is a battle—physical and spiritual—and you will find yourself in the trenches of prayer. It is there, poised in prayer and praise, that you will realize that although you cannot win the battles alone, in Christ you are more than a conqueror.

Every battle is won upon your knees, so don't try to stand and fight on your own. I have assured you that the "earnest prayer of a righteous person has great power and produces wonderful results" (James 5:16, NLT). Find shelter under the shadow of My wings and strength in My promises to you. Know that you are never on the battlefield alone. I AM always with you, a ready help in times of trouble. Don't struggle with fear and doubt, allowing your faith to waver. Simply come to Me; victory is yours when you bring your battle before Me.

I will enable you to fight the fight of faith, strengthening you in every way for whatever you must face. I have all power, I oversee every detail of your life, and there is nothing that I can't do. Cling to My promises and stand firm in your faith. Take up the whole of My armor "so you will be able to resist the enemy in the time of evil. Then after the battle you will still be standing firm" (Ephesians 6:13, NLT).

With us is the LORD our God to help us and to fight our battles.

2 CHRONICLES 32:8 (NIV)

Deliverance

A Voice from Heaven

You may find yourself in so deep that there appears to be no way out. You may be drowning in despair, with no hope of ever being saved, but I AM the One who saves. Pray in faith and wait confidently for your deliverance.

When I think of you, when I look upon your life, My heart sings a song of deliverance, a song of joy over you. When you're frightened and afraid, I AM your hiding place. I have promised to protect you at all times and in all ways. Praise Me even when there seems no reason to; trust Me even when it's hard. I have plans for you that are better than you would ever believe, so hope in Me and watch Me do more.

I AM with you through every step to lead you into My glory. In every obstacle and struggle, the victory is Mine. Don't allow the unknowns to cause you to fear. Simply stand firm in the promises I've made to you and trust in My faithfulness. There is no reason to fear, no reason to doubt. I AM surrounding you with protection and giving you My grace. I AM all you need, and your victory song should resound within your heart as it does in Mine.

You are my hiding place; You protect me from trouble. You surround me with songs of victory.

PSALM 32:7 (NLT)

Always Listening

I know at times you feel as though I'm not listening, but I AM. I hear in your heart what you're too weak to convey. I know your every hurt and every fear. Yet, though I know it before you say it, I want to listen. I want to hear you speaking to Me in prayer. Your voice beckons Mine.

When you're facing the unthinkable, while your heart is breaking, cry out to Me. I AM here. I want to embrace you and pour out My love on you. But I want you to recognize your need of Me. I want you to clearly see that you were never meant to walk this life alone.

Don't always assume I'm not there or don't care when troubles and trials come your way. Know that I use the good and the bad to bring about My perfect plans in your life. Trust that I know what I'm doing. No matter how dire your situation, I have a plan for your deliverance.

I hear your cries for help, every one, and I will answer you. When the moment is perfectly right, when I'm certain that you are ready for the miracle and it will have its greatest impact on your faith, I will move. But until that moment, rest in My grace and continue to walk firmly by faith.

> I cried out to the Lord in my great trouble,
> and He answered me.
>
> JONAH 2:2 (NLT)

An Overwhelmed Heart

It's hard for Me to watch you give in to your worries, filled with panic and anxiety about what tomorrow may bring. I hold all of your tomorrows. Instead of being overwhelmed by the troubles of life, I want you to be overwhelmed by Me; My love, mercy and boundless grace.

I AM with you for one reason ... to deliver you. No matter where you are and what you're going through, call to Me and I will answer you. In your weakness, I will be your strength, and I will give you all the faith you need to take you from glory to glory. I AM the Rock, the One who is immovable and faithful.

No matter what your needs, I AM a ready help in times of trouble. And there is NOTHING that I cannot do. That obstacle you think is insurmountable, I can overcome. I AM full of surprises and I move suddenly, in unexpected and unbelievable ways. Trust in My power to deliver you *through* whatever you're going through, not just out of it. I can use every situation in your life to bring about greater faith within you. So let me work in your heart, and remember to look up when life is bringing you down.

> From the ends of the earth I call to You,
> I call as my heart grows faint; lead me
> to the rock that is higher than I.
>
> PSALM 61:2 (NIV)

Humbly Exalted

When you are humble before Me, you set yourself up to be exalted by Me and blessed beyond your imagination. If you will recognize that I AM God and you are not, I am able to lift you up in due time. Trust that I will.

I don't want you to strive for success, working endlessly to create a future that is separate from My plans for your life. My desire is that you would follow the path that I have set before you—the straight and narrow path, the one that leads to victory and deliverance.

I want you in a place of dependence upon Me, clearly understanding your need for Me in every area of your life. I want you to live not with an attitude of entitlement, but one of humility. Let go of your desires to do more, be more and have more. Know that I will supply all of your needs according to My glorious riches in Christ Jesus.

My timing is not your timing, so don't doubt My grace or question My ability to perform miracles in your life. Stay in a place of confident expectation, fully assured that I will lift you up, bring you out and deliver you.

Be humbled by God's power so that when the right time comes He will honor you.

1 PETER 5:6 (GW)

Continued Hope and Praise

I always want to find you filled with hope and praise for Me. When I look into your life, I want to see you filled with My joy and strength. Your hope is based on your faith, and your faith comes from fully trusting in My Word.

When you find yourself walking in darkness, experiencing life among the unrighteous, you must continue to hope and to praise Me. It will not come easy. You will struggle to have hope when all hope seems gone. However, the more you hope, the more you praise, and the more you praise, the more you'll have hope. Your praise will keep your hope alive and your hope will become the reason to praise.

Though you're weary, you can still be filled with hope if you trust in My deliverance. In those moments when you find yourself lacking in praise, ask yourself what you're hoping in. If your hope lies in anything or anyone other than Me, you have no true hope and those hopeful moments will be short-lived. If you're unsure of your hope, simply shout out and praise Me; I always hear you and My grace will fill you with hope.

As for me, I will always have hope;
I will praise You more and more.

PSALM 71:14 (NIV)

Peace, Protection and Promises

No matter what you're going through, you're never alone. And I AM always a prayer away from delivering you. So keep praying and be expectant for My answers.

You may find yourself in unthinkable situations, going through unbearable pain and suffering, but you are not beyond My rescue. My hand is mighty to save. Often I will allow you to go through deep valleys so that you might recognize your need of Me. I desire to draw you nearer to Me, to perfect your faith, and to sanctify you.

I know you want answers now and I know that you are growing weary and weak, but I can carry you through. I will bring you peace in your despair, protection in your fears, and promises that will assure you of My presence and power.

You may be tempted to doubt when nothing seems to be happening, but when all hope appears to be gone, I will show up. Don't have expectations about how I will bring about miracles in your life; don't worry about the details. I've always got everything under control. It's not a question of whether or not I will show up, it's simply how.

Praise to the God of Shadrach, Meshach,
and Abednego! He sent His angel to rescue
His servants who trusted in Him.

DANIEL 3:28 (NLT)

Brought Up and Out

Everyone needs My deliverance. There are always pits of darkness from which you will need deliverance—sinfulness, pain, and suffering. But deliverance will not always come right away; all too often you will have to wait for it. If you are patient, I will hear your cry and I will place you upon a firm foundation.

In your trials I hear you praying for Me to do what you want and when you want, but that's asking Me to step off My throne and allow you to rule. I know that your needs are urgent—that time is not on your side—but you can rest assured that it's on Mine. I control time and space, and I will never be too late to deliver you from the pit of destruction. Your great enemy wants you to give up hope and to give up your faith in Me, but you must resist the temptation and never give up hope.

Know that your prayers will be answered according to My will and within the boundaries of My love. I will deliver you into the fullness of My glory. You must trust in Me even when there seems to be no reason why you should. Press past your feelings and cling to the truth that is found in My promises to you. Hold fast—help is on the way.

I waited patiently for the Lord to help me,
and He turned to me and heard my cry.

PSALM 40:1 (NLT)

Burdens

In Constant Prayer

If you will pray to Me about everything, you will be more aware of My presence in your life. Praying to Me constantly will help release your burdens and enable you to experience peace in the middle of chaos.

I want you to remember that you can pray at any time. Anywhere you are, you can pray. I have instructed you to be unceasing in prayer because I want you to keep open communication with Me at all times. When you're in constant fellowship with Me throughout your day, you will be able to more confidently walk in faith and resist the temptation to doubt.

There are times to be diligent and focused, times to be set apart to pray, but all too often you will need to offer up quick, simple prayers. And all prayer is effective and heard by Me, every word uttered moves My heart to answer. As you pray, offer praise and thanksgiving as the evidence of your faith. I have never meant for you to carry your burdens alone, I want to carry them for you. I AM your helper, the One who holds your life in My hands—trust Me, talk to Me and allow Me to be your God.

Pray in the Spirit at all times and on every
occasion. Stay alert and be persistent in
your prayers for all believers everywhere.

EPHESIANS 6:18 (NLT)

Living in Wholeness

Y ou can completely relieve your burdens by talking with Me and allowing Me to carry what you cannot. I will either relieve your burdens or direct you to the next step of faith and help you carry them. Don't try to deal with your burdens by yourself, or ignore them, thinking they will go away. Bring your burdens out into the open, into My presence and into My hands.

When you come to Me, I will often bring others into your life who will comfort you and encourage you in your faith. I AM with you, but I also use others for My purposes in your life, just as I want to use you to accomplish My purposes in the lives of others. I will bring others into your life whom you can trust, who can hear My voice clearly when you cannot.

When you are overwhelmed with the troubles of life, you will need others to be a source of strength and hope in your presence, there with you and in the flesh. At the same time, My Spirit will strengthen you in your inner spirit, giving you peace and rest, releasing you from your restlessness and bringing about hope and restoration.

Carry each other's burdens, and in this way you will fulfill the law of Christ.

GALATIANS 6:2 (NIV)

No Excuses

It's easy to get caught up in life and the problems it brings and want quick fixes. But seldom are the quick fixes in life fixes at all. Even My miracles can take time and require patience.

Your burdens may be the result of external sources or they may be because of mistakes you made or decisions that were taken without consulting Me. Either way, you can take responsibility for what you can, and I will help you through it all. I'm aware that there are things that are beyond your control and I realize that the evil in the world can wreak havoc in your life. There's no need to make excuses.

It's important to look at your situation from a realistic viewpoint and begin seeing it through eyes filled with truth. As long as you continue to make excuses, there will be no progress in your situation. But if you'll bring your burdens to Me, owning your responsibilities in them and allowing Me to handle the rest, there will be transformation for you in the physical world and the spiritual as well.

My love for you never changes. There is nothing that you can do that will make Me love you less than I do right now. You are Mine and I AM your God. My grace will be all that you need in every moment.

Turn your burdens over to the
LORD, and He will take care of you.
He will never let the righteous
person stumble.

PSALM 55:22 (GW)

Ready for Anything

There's no need for you to be overwhelmed when troubles come your way. I AM with you. I have promised you there will be trouble, but as you walk by faith, you must refuse to be overcome by fear and worry.

In order to face life's challenges head on, you'll need to have your mind set on Me. Your faith must be fixed so that you are not caught off guard or unprepared. You must declare in truth that you "can do all things through Christ." Your mind leads your life, so think upon My truth and live within it. Don't allow your thoughts to get caught up in "what ifs." Stand firm in what I've promised you and don't get lost in wrong thinking patterns that only lead to self-defeat. I want you to live a life of faith that is strong, powerful, encouraging and victorious. You have the mind of Christ, and I work all things together for good. So rest in those truths.

Whatever obstacles you must face on your path of life, do not allow yourself to be discouraged or defeated; just remember that apart from Me you can do nothing. Cling to My promises in times of trouble and be encouraged. I will help you and give you everything you need. All you must do is be ready and prepared to work out your faith in the way I call you to.

Get ready; be prepared.

EZEKIEL 38:7 (NIV)

Heavy Burdens

I see you carrying more than you should, burdens that are Mine to bear. There are some things that are just too heavy for you to carry, and it's vital that I help you.

If you will bring your troubles to Me, I will comfort you and give you peace to make you feel secure. I know that as you struggle with the ongoing troubles of life, you need rest for your soul. I can give you that rest. But I want you to bring your weariness to Me; I want you to lay your burdens at My feet.

There are answers you simply don't have. You can't know what lies ahead in the future, so you need Me to lead and guide you. Nothing is too hard or heavy for Me, so allow Me to answer your faith with My faithfulness.

Don't for a second doubt what I've promised you; I cannot lie. I have promised to help you in every way, and every promise I've made is a promise for you. I will daily bear your burdens as you lift up your life to Me in prayer and supplication, with thanksgiving. And know that when you do, I will give you My peace, the peace that surpasses all understanding.

Praise be to the Lord, to God our Savior,
who daily bears our burdens.

PSALM 68:19 (NIV)

Brought Out

I know it seems as though life's troubles will never end and what you're enduring is simply too much to bear … and it is, but I AM here to help you. You tend to get busy with life and forget Who holds your life together. Your fears tell you that life is falling apart, but My promises to you say something entirely different.

I know that there are troubles that surround and consume you, but there is no need to be distressed or in despair. I will never forsake you. I want you to enter into My rest, walking courageously by faith, allowing Me to strengthen your heart as you place your hope in Me. When you're feeling down, you need to look up. Your help comes from Me, for I made heaven and earth. And though you may walk through darkness, I AM with you and I will revive you. All you must do is simply cast your burdens upon Me, and I will sustain you and keep your faith firm.

At My throne of grace there is peace for you—not the fleeting peace of the world, but My peace that finds strength in weakness and comfort in pain. So don't let your heart be troubled; don't allow it to be afraid. My grace is enough and My mercies are unending.

"I am the Lord your God who brings you out from under the burdens."

EXODUS 6:7 (NKJV)

For Your Own Good

My commandments were never meant to burden you, to cause you to feel hopeless and helpless, but to save you—from yourself. The temptations of the world can drive you in directions that are contrary to My will for your life and bring about burdens that will sink your soul into a state of despair.

I know there are commands within My Word that seem trivial, unimportant or irrelevant, but I assure you that every command I've made has a purpose. I've not overlooked anything that might affect your life and My will for it. And I'm not asking you to be obedient in your own spirit, in your own strength, but in Mine. I will give you all that you need to walk obediently in faith. When you're struggling to obey My commands, come to Me so that I can help you. When you call upon Me, I will answer you.

Wait patiently and expectantly for My direction. Stand firm in your faith and wait upon My Spirit to fill you and move you into obedience. Don't fear failure, but trust that I will be there to help you in every way. Believe that if I've commanded you to do something, it's for good reason, even when it doesn't seem to make sense. In the end, you'll fully understand My ways and My love.

Loving God means keeping His commandments, and His commandments are not burdensome.

1 JOHN 5:3 (NLT)

Contentment

Avoiding Strife

When you do all that you can to keep strife out of your life, you will live in peace and you'll freely receive My blessings. But with strife, there is no peace, joy or blessings. Conflict creates chaos within your faith and keeps you stagnant and struggling through each and every moment of life.

If you're experiencing continual difficulties in life, feeling like you're lacking My power and blessings, look at the relationships in your life. Could it be that there is ongoing strife—a lack of My love—flowing into these relationships that is causing the continued struggles in your life? Until we get to the root of the problem, your progress will be stalled.

Whatever your situation, there is Scripture to help you through. It may mean loving your enemy. It may mean self-sacrifice for the sake of My will. But I will enable you to do what I've asked you to do. I want you to be in unity with Myself and with others so that My love and power can freely flow. When we are one, you can overcome the strife in your relationships.

Behold, how good and how pleasant it
is for brethren to dwell together in unity!
… It is like the dew of [Mount] Hermon
coming down on the hills of Zion;
for there the LORD has commanded
the blessing: life forevermore.

PSALM 133:1, 3 (AMP)

Seeking Peace

I know you want success, a life of joy, peace and great blessing, but there are actions of faith that are required for answering that prayer. There are principles that are required for you to fully enjoy the life you've been given.

The power of life and death is in your words, so you'll need to keep yourself from speaking evil. You can cause misery to yourself and others by what you say, so choose your words carefully and rely on the mind of Christ to guide your voice. As you walk in faith, it's vital that you're relying on Me to help you make decisions, to give you direction that is in alignment with My will. And if you end up on the wrong path, allowing sin to make its way into your life, turn to Me, repent and I will help you back onto the path of righteousness.

Nothing can separate you from My love, and within My love, there is peace. Seek peace with Me and with others so that you might enjoy life. You need only come to Me so that I can unleash My breakthrough power, freeing you from the chains that are keeping you from fully enjoying life.

People who want to live a full life and enjoy good days must keep their tongues from saying evil things, and their lips from speaking deceitful things. They must turn away from evil and do good. They must seek peace and pursue it.

1 PETER 3:10-11 (GW)

Standing Still

Y̶ou tend to believe that life is nothing but a battle, a struggle in a war that you can't win. You forget that the victory is already Mine … and yours. You need only stand still.

When you're filled with fear and your first reaction is to fight, remember that I AM the One who saves. Your faith in Me should remain firm, confident and undismayed. I've given you My word that I will fight for you. All you must do is hold your peace and remain at rest. Though it seems contrary to logic, you need to stand still to win the battle. I simply want you to show your confidence in Me by relying on Me to deliver you.

Be content within the confines of your troubles and realize that I AM with you to rescue you. The victory does not come in creating your own battle plan, incorporating your own logic and reason, and moving ahead of Me. Winning the war is about winning within. I need you to lay it all at My feet, recognizing Me as God. Choose to stop fighting and trust Me to fight your battles for you. You need only stand still and watch My mighty hand work the miracles you're praying for.

Stand firm then, with the belt of truth buckled around your waist, with the breastplate of righteousness in place, and with your feet fitted with the readiness that comes from the gospel of peace.

EPHESIANS 6:14–15 (NIV)

Living in Peace

Of all the promises I've made you, the promise that all I have is yours is strengthening and encouraging to your faith. I've made you the promise to give you peace and joy in the midst of doubt and uncertainly. Cling to it in your trying circumstances and know that I AM God.

The peace the world gives you is the kind that is based on positive circumstances. But I give you a supernatural peace that gives you contentment and security when there is no outward reason for joy. I don't want you to allow yourself to be fearful, agitated or disturbed. There's no reason for you to be unsettled. Christ's sacrifice for you was to give you peace, healing you and making you whole for all eternity.

Don't allow your circumstances to determine the state of your peace; rest in the true peace that I give you. I AM the One who calms the raging storm. I AM the One who heals every wound. My will for you is to rest in My truth and for you to live in peace with Me, yourself and others. With more of My peace, you can enjoy your life as you're supposed to—without worry and fear. I AM with you and I AM all you need.

> "All that belongs to the Father is Mine;
> this is why I said, 'The Spirit will tell
> you whatever He receives from Me.'"
>
> JOHN 16:15 (NLT)

The Big Picture

It's easy to focus solely on the negative aspects of life. Don't forget the blessings, the positive aspects of your life. Don't give in to the temptation to filter them out. There is always something good in every circumstance, especially when you trust in Me to work *all* things together for good.

You've got to focus your thoughts on Me. When you do that, your entire perspective will change. I see the big picture, and I'll help you to see it too. Continually resist the temptation to focus on the negative aspects of life and allow Me to strengthen your faith by taking you through the valley. Then you'll experience My presence, power and peace.

If you're constantly allowing your mind to wander to the negative, it will be hard to have any hope at all. So when your mind is lost and wandering and worry fills your soul, seek My promises and stay focused on Me. If you choose to trust in My truth, believing in My promises to you, you will be able to find peace and joy even in the worst challenges … and you'll never run out of hope. I AM your hope, the One Who hung the moon and the stars, the One Who holds your life in the palm of His loving hand.

As he thinks within himself, so he is.

PROVERBS 23:7 (NASB)

Undisturbed Composure

Life can cause your emotions to ebb and flow if they are not guided by My Word. Without warning, you can find yourself in deep despair—fearful and out of control. It's up to you to take every thought and emotion captive to the truth of My Word.

Emotions can run wild and out of control like an undisciplined child, and they need to be controlled. It's about living purposefully, being aware of your thoughts and actions at all times. Your self-control will play the major role in keeping you in a state of undisturbed composure and contentment.

Your feelings can manipulate your mind and cause you to say and do things that are contrary to My will, so you will need to focus on My Word when your emotions begin to run wild. It will take practice in disciplining your mind to think the way I think. You will need to spend constant time in My Word, listening to My voice and being patient as I work within you.

Never forget that I do the impossible. There's no reason to fear or wonder over the outcome of your troubles; there is never a reason to allow your emotions to determine the outcome of your life if you're trusting that I AM fully in control.

All your [spiritual] children will be
disciples [of the LORD], and great will
be the well-being of your sons.

ISAIAH 54:13 (AMP)

Whatever the Circumstances

Your relationship with Me must supersede whatever you do or do not have. Your contentment cannot be based on your circumstances, but on your relationship with Me alone.

I know your emotions can get in the way of your peace. Your contentment won't come easily; it's something that is learned and acquired. It is through the challenges of faith that your relationship with Me will develop over time as you learn to trust Me more and rely less on yourself and your own understanding. The key is knowing that it's Christ who will give you the strength to endure and overcome every situation you encounter. But you'll need to pray for that strength and contentment and then rely on the Spirit to give you what you need when you need it.

It's when you're at peace with Me, when you're spending time in My presence and getting to know Me better, that I AM able to reveal more and more of Myself in order that you might have confidence about the future and stay content.

I am not saying this because I am in need, for I have learned to be content whatever the circumstances. I know what it is to be in need, and I know what it is to have plenty. I have learned the secret of being content in any and every situation, whether well fed or hungry, whether living in plenty or in want. I can do all this through Him who gives me strength.

PHILIPPIANS 4:11-13 (NIV)

God's Will

Wisdom Shouts Out

My desire is that you might have My wisdom to make the right choices, to walk in My will and My ways. Know that you are not going through daily life alone; the Spirit is with you to lead you into wisdom, if you will simply ask.

It is easy to be led by your heart instead of relying on My Word as the wisdom that should lead and guide you. Your flesh and feelings can get in the way of making the right decisions in your walk of faith. When you're struggling for direction, unsure of which way to go, wisdom is shouting out to you. The Spirit is always at work in you, driving out your emotions and filling you with the truth you need to take the proper steps of faith. The Spirit will speak to your heart and give you comfort and peace as to which way to go, even though the direction may not seem like the right way.

You'll learn to continually and more readily trust Me when your hindsight shows you that My wisdom always leads you victoriously into My will. I want your choices in life; to be ones that lead to a life of joy, peace and happiness, so don't wrestle with the decisions in your life, simply come to Me. Trust the Holy Spirit to lead you to make the wise choices and be patient as I work within your situations to bring about your future and hope.

Wisdom shouts in the streets.

PROVERBS 1:20 (NLT)

Paying Attention

Things are not always what they appear to be. The troubles you are experiencing are not what they seem on the surface. I work behind the scenes of your life, so when you need direction and you're looking for My will for your life, pay close attention.

Spiritual understanding takes time and practice. You're so easily caught up in the natural world that the supernatural seems distant at best. But if you dedicate time to communing with Me and getting to know My Word, you'll more readily hear My voice. And as you grow in your understanding of Me and the promises I've made you, you will also grow in your ability to discern My will for your life. Never make decisions based upon your own understanding, emotions or circumstances.

Discernment is a gift that the Spirit enables you to use in ways that will powerfully lead you into My blessings for your life. As you live each moment, faced with countless decisions, pray to Me and ask Me to help you more clearly understand and discern My will. It's through My Word that My voice will speak to you and give you the direction you need to walk steadily in My will.

Let those who are wise understand these things.
Let those with discernment listen carefully.
The paths of the LORD are true and right, and
righteous people live by walking in them.
But in those paths sinners stumble and fall.

HOSEA 14:9 (NLT)

Trust and Confidence

Y ou should never put your trust and confidence in your-self or others; your faith must be in Me. When you trust and rely on yourself, there is no supernatural power to work in your life. You'll wear yourself out mentally and emotion-ally trying to do what only I can.

You need to fully rely on Me to take care of you. When troubles come, you often enter into a self-defeating struggle to provide answers that only I can. Your frustrations come from trying to live life according to your will instead of Mine. I need you to rely on Me, to trust that I can do the impossible and to wait expectantly for Me to do so. If you're trusting in yourself or others, the impossible will never happen. Only I work miracles.

I want you to more readily sacrifice all of your burdens to Me. I want you to seek My wisdom and guidance immedi-ately in every situation. When you're taking on the role of God in your life, I cannot do the work I need to do. Ask Me for what you need and trust that I will answer your prayers in My way and in My timing. My delays are not My denials, so don't give in to doubt when My answers don't come as quickly as you'd hoped. Simply put your trust in Me and be confident in that hope.

We rely on what Christ Jesus has done for us.
We put no confidence in human effort.

PHILIPPIANS 3:3 (NLT)

Undivided and Fully Decided

I have made clear, through My Word, My overall will for all humanity. And within the details of Scripture are the specific directions and instructions as to how you are to handle each and every situation in life. I don't want you divided within yourself, struggling as to which way to turn. You are to be fully decided that My way is the way that is everlasting.

It's easy to get sidetracked in daily life, with so many forces pulling you in every direction, but your faith must remain firm. I want you living in peace so that I might unleash My power and blessings in your life. Don't worry about how others think you should live; I AM the One who is leading and directing you. Any other way but My way will be the wrong way.

It's My Word that instructs, encourages and urges you into My will. Don't allow the worries of the world to cloud your vision. Stay focused on Me when you're torn in different directions and pulled by opposing opinions. Trust in the truth I've given you. Dive deep into all that I've told you, all that I've promised you. Keep your mind firm in your faith by casting out all fear. Lift up your voice to Me, call upon Me when you're in need, and I will lead, guide and direct you into My glory.

All the believers were one in heart and mind.

ACTS 4:32 (NIV)

Whatever Happens

I know life can take your emotions down unthinkable paths, driving them into unbearable places. Whatever your circumstances, you are going to need to remain in Me, relying on My Spirit to navigate you through the turmoil.

If My Spirit is within you, there is no room for being easily offended, bitter or resentful. My will for you in every situation you face in life is that you would choose how to respond instead of reacting based on emotion.

If you respond in the way that I would, then your troubles will be easier to deal with and your burdens will become lighter. It may not seem that important to manage your emotions, but it's vital to the state of your faith. Trusting in Me creates an inner and outer peace that is a testimony to others as you go through unthinkable circumstances. Your heart and mind must remain stable during times of difficulty in order to give Me honor. It is living proof that I AM in you and you are in Me.

When you allow yourself to lose control, you end up making unwise decisions that create even larger problems than the ones you're currently facing. Though it's hard to keep your feelings under control in difficult circumstances, you can do so in My strength. Come to Me in your weariness and don't let your circumstances defeat you. Allow Me to conquer them.

Whatever happens, conduct yourselves
in a manner worthy of the gospel of Christ.

PHILIPPIANS 1:27 (NIV)

Within Your Heart

You might think you know what will make you happy, which direction your life is to take, but though you can make your plans, I determine your steps. Come to Me continually for guidance and direction. Only I know how to fulfill your hopes and desires in ways that are in alignment with My will.

Your faith in Me has placed a new heart within you. Your joy and happiness will not come from the material world, but solely from the spiritual blessings that I will give you. First and foremost, it's obeying My Word that will bring you greater happiness than you can imagine. Being at peace with Me is what enables you to walk in My will and receive the fullness of My glory. When I AM flowing within you, you will experience a deep contentment.

It's when you rebel against what I've commanded you or turn away from the way that I've led you, that you will experience discontent within your soul. Don't be fooled by the temporary pleasures of life. They will lead your heart astray and you will lose out on the many blessings I have in store for you. There is nothing that can offer you the long-lasting happiness that I offer you when you are obedient to My Word. So keep it deep within your heart, always desiring to do My will.

I desire to do Your will, my God;
Your law is within my heart.

PSALM 40:8 (NIV)

Do What You Can

Y ou can't do it all. But although you may not be able to change the world, you can change a life. I know the problems you see around you are staggering. Don't be overwhelmed by them. Remember that I do the impossible. You should pray for miracles and then confidently wait for them.

I have given you life so that you might be My hands and feet on earth. I have asked you to partner with Me in filling the world with My love. Listen carefully for My voice as you live your daily life. I will bring about opportunities for you to be a blessing to others. I have a perfect plan to use your life in ways that you cannot imagine.

I will continually plant a desire in your heart to help others in specific ways, and although you may not have the resources to help, I do. Pray continually for Me to help you to make a difference in the world and I will show you clearly what to do. You can trust Me to help with all that I'm calling you to do. And through it you will get glimpses of My glory that go far beyond your wildest dreams.

"I can guarantee this truth: Whatever you did for one of My brothers or sisters, no matter how unimportant they seemed, you did for Me."

MATTHEW 25:40 (GW)

Discouragement

Walking Away from Trouble

Your disappointment can come from many different directions. It could come from a series of bad choices you've made, or maybe you're feeling as though nothing you do in life really matters. Whatever the cause, you need to let go of the past and embrace the future with hope.

Your wrongs can be made right. If you've been moving in the wrong direction, you can move in the right one. I will help you, if you'll let Me. You need to walk out of trouble by walking toward Me. It will take time, but I AM the great Redeemer, the One who makes all things new. There is nothing I can't do, so it's vital that you trust Me so that I can help you. Without Me you can do nothing.

Don't be distracted by feelings of discouragement and doubt. Stand firm in your faith, believing against all odds that help is on the way and you can have hope. Don't look back at all that has fallen to pieces, but keep your eyes on Me, the One who is building your future on a firm foundation.

If what you're going through is overwhelming, too much for you to endure, you're in the perfect place for a miracle. Keep seeking My face, listen carefully to My voice and let Me lead you to righteousness.

Look straight ahead, and fix your
eyes on what lies before you.

PROVERBS 4:25 (NLT)

Get Up

All too often you get caught up in negativity, focusing on all the things that are wrong in life and finding yourself overwhelmingly discouraged. There are times when you will not be able to change your situation and it is clear that I AM walking with you and not just solving your problems.

You may not be able to solve your problems, but you can move forward in hope, trusting Me through them. Don't sit by and allow your miracle to pass you by. Realize that faith requires action. Don't worry about what is happening around you, who is doing what or who is being blessed when you're not. Your time will come. While you wait upon My miracles in your life, I don't want you sitting idly by. I want you to live in confident faith, fulfilling My purposes in your life and believing that My help is on the way.

Take time to reflect on all that I've done for you. Recall the blessings you're aware of in your life and even those that you are not cognizant of. Trust Me, there are more than you can count. I'm holding on to you, even at times when you let go of Me.

How long will you lie there, you sluggard?
When will you get up from your sleep?

PROVERBS 6:9 (NIV)

When You Don't Understand

You might be carrying a burden you don't understand, or you might be experiencing depression over something you're not aware of. Whatever the case, come to Me and let Me give you insight into your heart.

Know that I fully search your heart. I can bring the darkness into light and help you to understand the reasons for your discouragement and despair. Sometimes you may understand it all clearly and are fully aware that the decisions you've made have led you into a state of being helpless and lost. At other times you may not have a clue as to why you're feeling the way you are, but I can help you to see more clearly, to dig deep into your soul and reveal the underlying truth.

I need you to sit quietly in My presence, releasing your spirit to Me so that I can go to work in and through you. I can lift you out of your depression and free you from your despair if you'll come to Me and allow Me to reveal the truth within your heart. Always be ready to confess your heart to Me, regardless of the consequences, and be certain that I can heal you in every way.

When I refused to confess my sin,
my body wasted away,
and I groaned all day long.

PSALM 32:3 (NLT)

Don't Be Fooled

In order to experience My very best for your life, you need to walk in My will, being led not by your emotions, but by My Spirit. Your feelings can fool you, but the truth will set you free.

My Word should be your deciding guide on all issues in your life. My Word will keep you on the straight and narrow path. You will not always feel like being obedient, especially when you don't understand My ways. You need to trust Me even when you don't understand the direction in which I'm taking you and your feelings don't agree with your faith.

Your emotions don't know what lies ahead in your future—only I do. They cannot direct you onto paths of righteousness, but My Spirit does. I want what is best for you. Sometimes that includes pain and sorrow for a season; so don't fear when troubles come your way. Many of your trials are merely a setup for My miracles.

I want you to continually find peace and confidence in knowing that I AM with you to give you a future and a hope. Don't allow your emotions to fool you. If you do, they will cause you to go down paths that lead to despair and disappointment. Live in My joy and find peace in My sovereignty and love.

Do not be misled.

JAMES 1:16 (AMP)

Wholly Trusting

Don't give in to your fears; this leads to overwhelming discouragement. When you're faced with troubles, you need to carefully watch your thoughts and pay attention to which direction they are taking you. When you feel discouraged and depressed, you need to keep your mind set on the things that I've asked you to: whatever is true, whatever is noble, whatever is right, whatever is pure, whatever is lovely, whatever is admirable … anything that is excellent or praiseworthy. These are the things I want you to think about.

Oftentimes your emotions get in the way of what you know to be the truth. Be sure to walk by faith, even in despair. I want you to wholly trust Me and to truly believe that you can do whatever I'm asking you to do through Me. I want you to be certain of My power and presence in your life—never doubting, even in darkness, that I can bring light to the darkest gloom.

Never will I leave you or forsake you. I'm always a ready help in times of trouble. As long as you're leaning on and depending on Me, you can completely trust that I will provide you with all you need. Don't allow the overwhelming circumstances of your life to threaten your faith. There is nothing I can't do. All you need to do is to wholly trust in Me.

What I always feared has happened
to me. What I dreaded has come true.

JOB 3:25 (NLT)

When There's No Way

It will often seem as though there is no way, but when you trust in Me, there is always a way. Don't give up until I make a way. Don't stop praying and hoping.

The way that I will make may not always be easy—it may not always be an immediate escape—but it is a guaranteed path to joy, peace and happiness. Know that I hear every one of your prayers. Some of them I can answer right away, but most must be carefully orchestrated into My will for your life. You tend to give up easily, believing I've heard your prayer and since the answer is not forthcoming in the time frame you desire, My answer must be a "no".

Keep praying until you're sure of My answer. Use My promises as your strength and your stronghold. They are given to you to give you peace as you trust in Me. It is up to you to draw near to Me and to seek Me with all of your heart. Don't stop hoping, believing and stepping out in faith. I will make a way.

> Some men came carrying a paralyzed
> man on a mat and tried to take him into
> the house to lay him before Jesus. When
> they could not find a way to do this
> because of the crowd, they went up on
> the roof and lowered him on his
> mat through the tiles into the middle
> of the crowd, right in front of Jesus.
>
> LUKE 5:18-19 (NIV)

Don't Look Back

As much as you worry about tomorrow, you also worry about yesterday. Your anxiety doesn't have a chance to escape as it stays imprisoned within your lack of faith. All too often you're just going to have to let it go, whatever it is, and move on. Don't allow your feelings and emotions to cause your faith to fail.

You will make mistakes and you will find yourself discouraged. But I don't want you to continue to wallow in self-pity, continually living in a state of regret about the past. The past will keep you in bondage and you'll be unable to walk forward in faith. Realize that I offer forgiveness for the past, faith for the future, and peace for the present moment.

I want you to keep your eyes on Me, drawing near to Me at all times and in all ways. Don't look back. I'm in the process of making all things new, so trust that I AM and rest in My grace. Don't allow your faith to walk by sight. Walk by trusting in My Word; move forward by believing what you know to be true and allowing your soul to experience the peace it longs for. There's no past in your future.

Jesus told him, "Anyone who puts a hand
to the plow and then looks back is
not fit for the Kingdom of God."

LUKE 9:62 (NLT)

Holy Spirit

In Everything You Do

The anointing of the Holy Spirit that I've given to you is the most powerful and precious gift in your life. It is what brings you into My presence and beckons My power. The anointing is present in your abilities and in your strength; it gives you life and fills your mind with peace.

In everything you've been called to do, you have anointing. You should have peace and be filled with strength knowing that I AM with you in everything you do. Do not allow your worries and the strife of life to block My anointing. Whether open or hidden, the worries within your heart can disrupt My anointing and leave you feeling empty.

I want you to be at peace, always having a calm spirit, being quick to forgive and slow to anger. Be patient, be kind, and work diligently at the purposes I've planned for your life. When you're feeling insignificant and helpless in accomplishing all that must be done in life, sit quietly and feel My Spirit fall upon you. In the Spirit, you will enjoy the simple things in life. In everything you do, you are to live in peace and harmony, trusting in Me to be all you need.

"Not by might nor by power, but by My Spirit," says the LORD Almighty.

ZECHARIAH 4:6 (NIV)

Burning with the Spirit

Each and every day is to be treasured, because each and every day is a day that I have made. I want you to rejoice and be glad in it, even though at times you won't feel like it.

Most days you will need to make a decision to rejoice, and then the feelings will follow. Don't wait to see how you feel—arise each day with a determination to be filled with joy. If you stay focused on spiritual things, you'll keep your feelings from dictating the course of your life. Your mind will be ready to receive My wisdom, enabling you to make right decisions for your life.

I work in extraordinary ways on ordinary days, so don't discount My ability to work miracles in surprising ways. Every day will not be filled to the full with feelings of happiness; there is a time for joy and a time for sorrow. In the darkness, light will come.

Don't allow your present circumstances or your feelings to define your future. I can move suddenly and powerfully. Be confident in faith, knowing that everything you do and experience in life is sacred if done in My Spirit. Believe that I AM with you at all times—if you truly believe that, you will experience a life that is burning with the Spirit.

Work hard and do not be lazy.
Serve the Lord with a heart full of devotion.

ROMANS 12:11 (GNT)

Spirit-Filled Emotions

There is always hope that you, and others, can change. It is the Holy Spirit at work that moves and transforms the heart … even the hardest heart. If you trust in My Word and pray the words you find there back to Me, I will give you a new spirit.

Christ has redeemed every part of your life, and that includes your feelings and emotions. You don't have to be enslaved by them. Your feelings can drive you into a state of negativity that can poison your faith and your life. I've given you a heart filled with emotions so that you can experience the fullness of My joy. But you'll need to focus on and embrace those emotions that encourage your faith and fuel your positive mindset.

My desire is that you would enjoy the life I've given you, so don't allow anything to take from you what I have given to you as a blessing. Dig deep into My Word and allow My Spirit to control your feelings and emotions instead of allowing them to control you. Allow the new spirit I've given you to embrace the purposes for your life, knowing that whatever I've called you to do, I will help you accomplish. Do not allow discouragement and despair to overrule the feelings of joy and tenacity I've placed within you.

"I will give them an undivided heart
and put a new spirit in them; I will
remove from them their heart of
stone and give them a heart of flesh."

EZEKIEL 11:19 (NIV)

Never Draw Back

You will have to continually choose to walk by faith, because the world is full of troubles that will fill you with fear. But you don't have to allow fear to rule your life. I've given you a spirit that is filled with My hope and strength.

Fear does not come from Me; it is the enemy's tool to keep you from living a life of joy and peace that I intend for you to live. Fear will cause you to draw back and even turn away from Me. But I've commanded you to never draw back in fear. When you do so, you keep Me from moving powerfully in your life. You must continually step out in faith, even in the face of fear.

If you will press through your fears, in My strength and My Spirit, you will reap the reward of My great blessings in your life. But they are only receivable by faith. Your faith declares that you believe in Me and the promises I've given you. Faith moves you forward, while fear keeps you bound in yesterday's chains. You must be firm in your resolve to continually step forward in faith, even through your fears, and never draw back. Then you'll see My power greater than ever before.

The Spirit God gave us does not make us timid,
but gives us power, love and self-discipline.

2 TIMOTHY 1:7 (NIV)

The Small Things

Amazing blessings come from even the smallest things that you do for others. My Spirit works powerfully within you, beyond anything you can imagine. I will bring about opportunities for you to live out your faith in front of others, and in turn your life will be enriched more and more.

There are so many needs in the world, and you can make a difference. I never expect you to take this journey alone; I never ask you to do more than I enable you to do. But the more I give you, the more I will ask you to give. Your love and kindness is an extension of who I AM through My Spirit, and all you do and say in My name will draw others to Me.

You have the ability to bring joy, peace and happiness into the lives of others with My help. So each and every day, keep your heart and mind open to the people around you. Look for opportunities to be a blessing to others, and I will make sure that I bless you. Blessing others won't always be easy, but in Me you can do all things. Be willing to be used by Me and watch how the little things you do and say become big blessings.

You will be enriched in every way so that you can always be generous. And when we take your gifts to those who need them, they will thank God.

2 CORINTHIANS 9:11 (NLT)

Authentic Faith

It does no good to profess your faith and then live a life that is contrary to your confession. The lost are looking for something real to believe in, and you have the great responsibility of living out a life that bears witness to My name.

More than anything, those who don't know Me need the truth. No one likes living in uncertainty or under an illusion that keeps them from experiencing the fullness of life. The best way you can witness to others is to be real about your own life. No one believes that a Christian's life is perfect and without problems, so don't pretend that all is well when it's not. Don't try to hide your feelings or pretend that your life is care-free.

People will be drawn to Me if you are authentic in your faith and honest about your troubles. Allow the Spirit to lead and guide you about what to do and say as you live out My purposes for your life. Speak in truth, live in faith, and allow the Holy Spirit to work miraculously through you in every way, each and every day.

With Christ as my witness, I speak with utter truthfulness. My conscience and the Holy Spirit confirm it.

ROMANS 9:1 (NLT)

In Pursuit of Holiness

The process of faith does not end in your coming to Christ as Savior—it is then that I begin to sanctify you. You must draw near to Me and have an open heart so that I can go to work. You must strive for holiness.

The process of becoming holy requires a constant effort. You must be focused and determined to live a life that is worthy of Me. My goal for you is that you would live in holiness so that you might reap the greatest of My blessings in your life. There will of course be temptations and difficulties that you have to get through. Anything and everything will try to keep you from Me, so you must remain focused on Me so that you do not lose sight of the goal.

Rely on My grace to help you through when you lose strength to move forward in your faith. You will not always be able to avoid sin, but when you come to Me in confession, I will help you to overcome. Don't feel like you are to live a holy life on your own; you will continually need Me to help you, and I AM always with you. Make sure that your holiness is anchored in My grace and you'll find yourself living purposefully, joyfully and peacefully.

Make every effort to live in peace with everyone and to be holy; without holiness no one will see the Lord.

HEBREWS 12:14 (NIV)

Waiting

Turning Points

There will always be times in life when you are faced with opposing paths and you're uncertain about which direction to take. My wisdom can lead you clearly along the path that leads to My glory in your life.

Don't be overwhelmed by the turning points in your life. Although they are often accompanied by uncertainty, there is never a reason to fear if you're relying on My direction. Always come to Me first and seek My wisdom through My Word. Don't reactively turn to your own limited wisdom or the opinions and advice of others.

You will often have to wait upon My voice, but you can find strength and comfort in My Word, and My Spirit will give you peace as you wait for My help. Don't fear what lies ahead, be with Me right now in this moment and be absorbed by My grace. I will enable you to walk upon the waters. I will call you out upon them, which means you will have to face your fears as you step out in faith. Keep your eyes on Me and don't allow anything or anyone to prevent you from standing firm in your faith and trusting completely in Me.

Does not wisdom call out? Does not understanding raise its voice? Wisdom takes its stand on high ground, by the wayside where the roads meet, near the gates to the city. At the entrance wisdom sings its song,

PROVERBS 8:1–3 (GW)

Waiting When It's Hard

I have not forgotten you. Though I may not answer at the moment you'd like Me to or in the way you anticipate, I always have your best interests in mind. Yet I know as you walk in great uncertainty, unsure of what the future holds, it is hard when I AM slow to answer.

I want you to be honest with Me regarding your doubts. I want you to open your heart to Me: the good, the bad and the ugly. You can trust Me and rely on My grace. I know that you feel I'm hiding My face from you, leaving you to your sorrows and heartache day after day. I know it feels as though evil is winning over good. I know you fear that I will never answer you. But you must continue to trust in, lean on and be confident of My mercy and loving-kindness.

There is no need for you to be shaken. Be in high spirits, knowing that I will bless you continually and bountifully. No matter how long it takes, know that I will help you, I will answer you and I will encourage you. You can trust Me with your deepest feelings; I can handle them all. Tell Me how you feel, and then decide not to be afraid, that you will trust and praise Me more and more.

O LORD, how long will You forget me?

PSALM 13:1 (NLT)

A Constant Longing

The time you spend with Me brings about a transformation of your inner spirit that radiates My glory. It's your longing for Me that creates the desire for you to please Me and glorify Me. The more you long for Me, the more you will become like Me. It's My ultimate goal in your sanctification.

My Spirit will work within you, creating a yearning in your soul for Me and a desire to earnestly seek Me. Your devotion to Me requires an attitude of reverence and awe. As you draw near to Me, you will have a deep desire to honor Me and love Me with all of your heart, mind and soul. In your waiting times in life, when My hand is not moving and you're uncertain about what to do, simply be consumed by My love and mercy.

Know that I work behind the scenes of your life and I AM always at work; I never sleep nor slumber. You can rest because I have everything under control. Though your circumstances may lead you to long for temporary pleasures, you must resist the temptation to long for anything but Me. I will be all you need, and I will be the One who will bring about the blessings you so desperately desire. Come to Me and I will answer you.

As the deer pants for streams of water,
so my soul pants for You, my God.

PSALM 42:1 (NIV)

Never Beyond the Reach of Grace

Don't aim to please Me in order to earn My love or approval; do it out of gratitude for all I've done and am yet to do. You may not always know what I require of you, but you must be patient, diligently seeking My Word and quietly listening for My voice.

Your desire in your life of faith should be to please Me in every way possible. You will fall short, but if you ask for My help so that I might continue to sanctify you, I will transform your life.

I AM your heavenly Father, disciplining you out of love for your good, not judging you. The blessings in your life are not based on your behavior and successes. You will always have impure motives and imperfect ways, but that does not hamper My grace.

In your humanness, it is often difficult to realize your depravity. That's why you must come to Me, spend time in My presence and wait upon Me to speak to your heart and reveal your sins. There will be good days and bad days, there will be times when I will answer you quickly and times when you must wait. But know that through it all, no matter what happens, you are never beyond the reach of My grace.

Carefully determine what pleases the Lord.

EPHESIANS 5:10 (NLT)

Day to Day

Life is all about your day-to-day relationship with Me. You stand in a grace that brings you into My presence and allows you to confidently and joyfully look forward to sharing My glory.

As you walk in faith, being transformed through My Word, you'll realize more and more the sins that need to be forgiven through My love, mercy and grace. Change doesn't happen within your soul suddenly. It is a step-by-step process—one in which you will need to patiently wait as I work in and through you.

I want you to witness My presence and power. Each and every circumstance in your life is an opportunity to bear witness to My grace. There's no need to cover up your faults and failures, no reason to be anything but real.

I have given you My grace to enable you to freely live your life in truth, drawing others to Me and leading them to a place of salvation through grace as well. Don't miss out on the day-to-day opportunities to be a blessing to others as you rely on My promises, assured that I will powerfully and endlessly bless you.

Because of our faith, Christ has brought us into this place of undeserved privilege where we now stand, and we confidently and joyfully look forward to sharing God's glory.

ROMANS 5:2 (NLT)

Just Wait and Trust

You have an important part in faith. Yes, I will work in and through you, but you must pursue holiness. No matter how long it takes, you must continue to commit yourself completely to Me and trust Me to help you.

In your pursuit of holiness, you must make the effort: training and disciplining yourself in My Word and in My ways. You must rely completely on the Holy Spirit to work within you, strengthening you with the strength of Christ. Faith is not always easy and you won't always understand why you do what you do. You'll want to do right but find yourself doing wrong. So you must utterly depend on the Spirit to help you.

Be patient in your pursuit of holiness, realizing that it will take time to transform your thoughts and actions. But don't let the process overwhelm you. Just keep digging deep into My Word, keep seeking Me with all of your heart. Don't give up when you fall short of My glory. I will help you get back on the path that is straight and narrow. I will give you peace even as you struggle to take another step of faith. Just wait upon My help and watch what I will do with your impossibilities.

Commit everything you do to the LORD.
Trust Him, and He will help you.

PSALM 37:5 (NLT)

At the Right Time

When you have to wait for something, you realize how much patience you have. When your circumstances keep you from progress and you're desperate to move on, you see just how much you need My Spirit to help you.

If you wait upon Me, you will more powerfully see My wisdom, My sovereign will, and the miracles I work step by step. You must learn to have trust in Me without borders. The waiting is teaching you to be completely dependent upon Me. And, while you wait, you are to rest. Rest and wait patiently—that is what I've commanded you. Resting in Me, My will, and the promise of My faithfulness will enable you to have patience.

I will give you peace that passes all understanding as you wait upon Me, allowing Me to quiet your fears and encourage your hopes. When you're anxious for something, make your requests known to Me and trust that I hear you and will answer you. You can find your strength and joy in Me as you wait. Know that if you're waiting on Me, every blessing will be yours. Be determined that your soul will only wait upon Me.

*"At the right time, I, the L*ORD*, will make it happen."*

ISAIAH 60:22 (NLT)

Sickness & Health

Healing the Hurt

Your physical health won't always be what causes you the most pain and misery. Often it is matters of the heart that cause the deepest suffering. People may say and do things that pierce your heart and crush your soul, but healing is in My hands.

I know that you have wounds of the heart that continually hurt. Sometimes others will work with you to heal those hurts, but at other times you will never find a remedy to the situation that has caused you pain. It's at those times that you must come to Me and allow Me to heal you. Dig deep into My Word and find the comfort you need to help you through it. Through the Psalms I give you comfort and healing. I AM with you to care for you in every way.

My peace will sustain you through the healing process of letting go and enable you to heal from the inside out. Allow Me to handle what is weighing you down and causing you hurt. Only I can transform your pain into joy. I can work miracles within you so that you can move on from the hurt. Trust in My Word that I will heal you. Speak words of faith and focus on the things that are lovely and worthy of praise. Then you'll begin to heal.

Careless words stab like a sword,
but the words of wise people bring healing.

PROVERBS 12:18 (GW)

Count on It

You need to count on My healing in your life. In whatever way you need to be healed, I will heal you. Knowing My promises to you is not the same as believing them, however. Choose to believe, even though in your pain and suffering you may not feel like it.

I will heal you so that you can be an encouragement to those who have lost their faith or wandered from Me. You will be an instrument of My grace, bringing those who have never known Me to My throne. I heal you, I give you comfort and strength so that you can be hope to the oppressed.

At times, when you are too weak to be My hands and feet, you can pray. You can lift others up, even in your own suffering. Sometimes all someone needs is My love. Often there is nothing you can do to heal their hurts, and I realize it often seems like there is nothing I can do to heal yours. But I can and I will heal you physically and spiritually. However, if I choose not to, or delay your healing in any way, know that I AM doing so with a purpose. Your deep suffering may enable Me to use your life more miraculously in the future. Don't doubt what I can do.

You know that God anointed Jesus of Nazareth
with the Holy Spirit and with power. Then Jesus
went around doing good and healing all who were
oppressed by the devil, for God was with Him.

ACTS 10:38 (NLT)

In His Hands

I know you question why I allow pain and suffering. You doubt My love and question My ways. Yet even through your failing faith you can choose to keep believing all that I've promised you.

Don't assume you can help yourself; you need Me. I AM the one who restores and redeems. I AM the God who heals you. Recognize that I AM in the midst of you. Praise Me for all I've done and am yet to do. How much closer can I be than dwelling within you? I have not lost My power to save, nor ever will. You can trust Me to handle all that concerns you, especially when the only answer is a miracle.

Amid all the brokenness, I AM still enthroned. If you are sitting in darkness, going through pain and suffering, with a spirit that is crushed and unable to have hope, keep coming to My throne of grace so that you might see My glory. My Spirit will lift yours out of the pit of despair and you'll find My all-sufficient grace in abundance. My peace will calm your mind and soothe your heart. My mercy and deliverance is ready for you. I alone can heal your brokenness and your failing health—I AM all you need, and you're in My hands.

The human spirit can endure in sickness,
but a crushed spirit who can bear?

PROVERBS 18:14 (NIV)

Wholly Healed

In your suffering you may find it difficult to bless Me with all your soul, to praise Me in the midst of all you have to endure. But My Spirit within you will be your strength, even in weakness.

Focus on what I have blessed you with, though there are still things you long for and pray for. Be assured that I hear you and will answer you. If you have breath at this moment, I have gifted you with life. Find joy in Me alone when all else seems to be failing you. Your health may fail, but I AM yours forever. I can bring healing to your spirit that ultimately will heal your body and soul.

Don't allow the thoughts of doubt and disbelief to cloud your vision of My greatness. You need to believe in My promises and trust that I can do all things. Remember that I move suddenly, powerfully and miraculously. When you need divine healing, I hold the power to give it. Spend time in My presence as you wait for Me to work your miracle. Believe in the hope that I fill you with. I can heal every kind of sickness and disease. Hope is not gone. I will wholly heal you.

Praise the LORD, my soul, and forget not all
His benefits—who forgives all your sins
and heals all your diseases.

PSALM 103:2-3 (NIV)

Prayer in Faith

In your sickness, remember to pray in faith, believing that My Word is true. Your faith may not be as strong as you would like it to be, but even a small amount of faith moves mountains. Faith can heal you.

Through your faith you are given hope. My promises can comfort you as you wait upon My mighty hand to heal you. My Word will bring healing to your Spirit as you endure. And remember that I AM with you, to save you. Keep your focused eyes on Me in your pain. You will have times of doubt, especially in physical suffering, but I'm asking you to trust Me anyway and to remember all those whom I have healed before you.

I will sustain you. I AM not too weak to save. Rest in My presence, and there you will find all the grace you need to soothe your soul. Be diligent in seeking Me with every breath you take. Pray earnestly for your healing and the healing of others who suffer with you. Your faith opens heaven's doors. Your ability to trust in Me even through your unthinkable suffering makes you strong, even when you are weak. Trust that I will heal you and raise you up.

The prayer offered in faith will make the sick person well; the Lord will raise them up.

JAMES 5:15 (NIV)

Restored and Healed

Just as broken bones become stronger, in your suffering, you become stronger. Through your brokenness I can heal you and make you even better than before—not just in physical ways, but more powerfully in spiritual ways.

In your broken places, the places where you've suffered pain you never thought you would and where you have fallen and failed … I will work in and through those circumstances. I use all things for good. Allow Me to heal you. Open your heart to Me and allow Me to cleanse you and pour out My mercy upon you. Stay faithful even when you don't feel like it. Keep trusting Me even when it seems unreasonable.

My strength will be made perfect in your weakness. My will is to heal you, so put your hope in Me and trust that I know what is best. Put your hope in My Word and its truth. Never give up seeking My divine healing. I AM able to restore you in every way. I have healed countless lives and performed unimaginable miracles. I can do the same in your life. If I could do it in the lives of others, if My Word tells you how I've healed so many in the past, trust in My power now. I AM the same yesterday, today and tomorrow.

> "I'll restore your health and heal
> your wounds," declares the Lord.
>
> JEREMIAH 30:17 (GW)

Hopeless Places

In My faithfulness I heal the brokenhearted and bind their wounds. I will heal *your* heart and bind *your* wounds—don't believe that My promises are for others and not for you. I know your sorrows and your griefs. I know what's crushing you and what is causing you to feel helpless or tempted to go astray. I AM here to help you in every way.

You'll find that I AM faithful to use your wounds to display My glory. I can be glorified in your broken places, and that will ultimately bring blessings to your heart and soul. Allow My Spirit to open your heart before Me so that I can give you My healing touch. I want you to let nothing come between My healing and your receiving it.

Let go of your past hurt, both physical and spiritual. Allow Me to make all things new, to give you a new heart. My Spirit can set you free. Let Me comfort you in all your disappointments, pain, loss, grief and fears. Keep focused on Me—My gentleness, kindness, love and power. Rest in My Word. Be blessed with confident hope that I will wipe your tears. Patiently wait and know that I will heal you and give you joy to overcome your pain.

He will wipe every tear from their eyes.
There will be no more death or mourning
or crying or pain, for the old order of
things has passed away.

REVELATION 21:4 (NIV)

What Lies Ahead

Trust Me with your past and your future. I AM sovereign, and I want you to have hope based on your faith in My promises to you. My mercies are new every morning, so let go of the past and have a vision through My faithfulness for your future.

Don't allow your failures and shortcomings to distract you from all that I have planned for you. Don't allow mental obstacles of doubt and disbelief to keep you from My greatest blessings in your life. Your past can become your prison and keep you from all the possibilities that I have in store for you. Know that your future depends on whether or not you trust Me with it.

Don't allow discouragement, regrets, grief, frustrations and failed expectations to keep you from My perfect will for your life. Be fully aware of the past, then let go of it and allow Me to redeem and restore you. Set your eyes on the prize of living your life for Me and allowing Me to work miracles in and through your life. Then press forward in My grace and trust Me for what lies ahead.

No, dear brothers and sisters, I have not achieved it, but I focus on this one thing: Forgetting the past and looking forward to what lies ahead, I press on to reach the end of the race and receive the heavenly prize for which God, through Christ Jesus, is calling us.

PHILIPPIANS 3:13-14 (NLT)

Topical Index

Notes